Teaching Empathy:

Animal-Assisted Therapy Programs for Children and Families Exposed to Violence

by
Lynn Loar, Ph.D., LCSW and Libby Colman, Ph.D.

Foreword by Barbara W. Boat, Ph.D.

A LATHAM FOUNDATION
PUBLICATION

I N THE PAST DECADE, I HAVE HAD THE PRIVILEGE OF WORKING WITH MANY CARING AND DEDICATED HUMAN SERVICE AND ANIMAL WELFARE PROFESSIONALS. From different perspectives, they all want to make the world a better and safer place. Through overspecialization, though, important things sometimes get overlooked. A humane educator may not understand why presentations about responsible care of pets elicit tales of abuse from children, much less how to handle this sensitive information. A therapist may intend only to provide clients with an opportunity to enjoy the company of a dog and learn safe and gentle touching, and be caught off guard when the dog introduces the subject of nudity into therapy sessions with sexually abused children. This book is an attempt to show both human service and animal welfare professionals how to design humane education and animal-assisted therapy programs that are safe for human and animal participants and that introduce change responsibly and enjoyably.

This book developed from a chapter the authors wrote for Pamela Raphael's book, *Teaching Compassion: A Guide for Humane Educators, Teachers, and Parents,* published by the Latham Foundation in 1999. It is a pleasure to acknowledge and thank the Latham Foundation for its generosity in publishing materials, hosting conferences, and especially in making available the talents and assistance of Judy Johns for this and other projects. Despite the challenges of these projects and the quirky people involved, Ms. Johns has never gotten to the end of her rope with us. The authors would like to express their gratitude for Ms. Johns' very long rope.

Jane Tamagna edited this book, as well as several others published by the Latham Foundation, all with dazzling clarity and none with remuneration. Ms. Tamagna embodies the components of effective intervention this book extols: mastery through incisive editing; empathy and literacy through gentleness to the authors' egos while allowing their meaning to emerge more clearly through her improvements to their text; future orientation and social conscience through her chronic and now predictive refusal of compensation for her priceless labors.

Many people have given generously of their time and talents to the Strategic Humane Interventions Program (SHIP), the animal-assisted therapy program which this book describes, and to help this book take form.

Karen Pryor and Barbara Boat, my friends and colleagues at the Pryor Foundation, always provide insight and good humor and make learning a pleasure. Karen Pryor's book, *Don't Shoot the Dog!,* is the foundation on which this book is based. Her introductory guides on clicker training led to the development of the materials for children that are published in this volume. Barbara Boat's inventories to structure conversations with people about their experiences with animals elicit information crucial to safe participation in animal-assisted therapy programs and are included here with her permission.

Randall Lockwood, vice president of research and educational outreach, the Humane Society of the United States (HSUS), who pioneered the field of animal cruelty and human violence, generously allowed the instruments he designed to be reproduced here.

Steve Eckert, executive director of North Peninsula Family Alternatives, San Mateo County, CA, and former clinical director of the Community-Based Sex Offender Treatment Program at San Quentin State Prison, designed the offender risk assessment and intake materials that are reproduced in this book.

Marcia Mayeda and her wonderful dogs Carlisle, Montana and Henry co-facilitated the pilot project that later became SHIP. Her insight and gifted way with the first participants created a vision that was a privilege to build on.

Michael Levy and Ann Mizoguchi of the California Governor's Office of Criminal Justice Planning (OCJP) have generously supported SHIP's philosophy and implementation.

Ten years ago, Carol Rathmann, the shelter manager of the Humane Society of Sonoma County and director of SHIP, took an idea for a small intervention and turned it into a wonderful program available to at-risk children in Sonoma County. She has also mastered the behind-the-scenes skills necessary to run programs safely and responsibly. Through her efforts, SHIP has been made available to children and families in both San Francisco and Sonoma counties.

Elaine Pomeroy McKellar, the clinical director of SHIP, is the best social worker I know. She is indefatigably optimistic, finding strengths to build on and reasons to be hopeful even in the most difficult situations and the most taxing times. She is gentle and caring in ways that inspire everybody to ask more of themselves and to give more to others.

Donna Duford and Sue Sternberg know dogs, their temperaments and behaviors. They make it safer for people and dogs through their work. Donna Duford wrote the guide to assess dogs' behaviors presented in this book. Sue Sternberg's book *Great Dog Adoptions: A Guide for Shelters,* also published by the Latham Foundation, provided groundwork and guidance.

Hilary Louie and Evelyn Pang worked hard and well in their free time for close to a year to write *Teaching with a Clicker: How to Train People and Animals with a Clicker and Treats* and *Teaching with a Clicker: How to Teach Your Dog Good Manners and Tricks* and to translate them into Chinese. Priscilla Galvez and her mother, Maria Garcia, joined by Lina Tam-Li, devoted much of their summer vacation to the Spanish translation of the texts. Anh Tang drew the delightful illustrations that appear throughout the book. These children's names are used with permission and pride because of the excellence of their work. All other names and identifying details have been changed to protect the confidentiality of the participants.

Dinora Castro and Jackie Kan are bilingual colleagues who volunteered time to facilitate the translation of the children's writing projects into Spanish and Chinese, respectively. Karin Schlanger and Octavio Garcia proofread the Spanish text. Carl Friedman, Susan Phillips, Mary Tebault and Karen Wood proofread the final draft of the monograph, sparing the readers many typographical errors and the authors much embarrassment.

Lynn Loar

T HE YEAR WAS 2000. The Colorado wind was whipping our coats as we walked to dinner following a meeting on working with children who abuse animals. I was straining to hear what Lynn Loar was saying (she is rather short, you know) because I did not want to miss a word. Lynn was talking about her new and amazing intervention called SHIP: Strategic Humane Interventions Program. I was immediately smitten with the project. SHIP worked with caregivers and children from high-risk backgrounds. SHIP solved the problem of cultural, racial, educational and language barriers simply by using dogs and clickers and treats as the main intervention tools. SHIP taught skills in observing carefully the behaviors of other beings, marking behaviors that were desired with a click and rewarding those behaviors with a treat. Children and their caregivers from destitute and traumatized backgrounds could learn these skills. They could teach shelter dogs behaviors that would enhance the dogs' adoptability. They could interact with each other, using these same skills, to become more empathic, tolerant, observant, generous and effective. And all of this could occur while having FUN! What a win-win for everyone involved! At that moment I became Lynn's disciple and later developed a SHIP program in Cincinnati, Ohio.

Now you can share in Lynn's and her colleague Libby Colman's knowledge and expertise. *Teaching Empathy: Animal-Assisted Therapy Programs for Children and Families Exposed to Violence* is a repository of practical skills and interventions. You can select from a rich menu of ideas, assessment tools, worksheets and resources to design humane education and animal-assisted therapy programs that are safe for both the human and animal participants.

One powerful message of this book is that children live in families, not with their therapists or humane educators. You will be encouraged, and provided with resources, to involve parents and caregivers whenever possible. As we partner with parents and caregivers, we acknowledge that it is their positive attention and generosity to their children that is primary in promoting growth.

The shared impacts of abuse and neglect on children and animals are skillfully and eloquently inter-woven. The humane educator and animal-assisted therapist are on the same team as human service professionals and have similar responsibilities to children, animals and society. Thus, information about mandated reporting, managing disclosures and reporting pet abuse is relevant for all readers. You will not take an animal into a classroom again and be ignorant of the possible impact of your words and the animal's behaviors on certain children. In reading this book, you will learn more than you wanted to know and more than you wanted to take responsibility for. However, all of this knowledge is essential to safeguard the welfare of both humans and animals and to promote the best that the fields of humane education and animal-assisted therapies have to offer.

Barbara W. Boat, Ph.D.

Associate Professor, Department of Psychiatry
Executive Director, The Childhood Trust
Cincinnati Children's Hospital Medical Center

Table of Contents

O VER THE PAST 10 YEARS, ANIMAL-ASSISTED THERAPY AND HUMANE EDUCATION PROGRAMS HAVE GROWN IN NUMBER, QUALITY, AND SUCCESS. These programs bring animals into classrooms, therapy sessions, after-school programs, and homeless shelters to support a therapeutic or educational goal. One program focuses on wildlife rescue, teaching adjudicated inner-city youth how to care for and rehabilitate injured animals. Another program teaches sexually abused adolescent girls how to care for horses and other farm animals. Yet another program brings abandoned animals into homeless shelters where families work together to train dogs so they are more adoptable. These and similar programs help children and their families increase sensitivity, self-control, and the ability to develop attachments to animals as well as people.

This book is intended to support the development of animal-assisted therapy programs, whether they serve therapeutic or educational ends. If you work as a teacher, an animal-assisted therapist, or a humane educator, you are probably familiar with these programs and may have thought about creating a program of your own. If so, this book can help. It is intended to provide you with the information, examples, and tools you need to create a safe and successful program. To support your efforts, this book answers three basic questions:

- What is the link between children and animals that underlies humane education and animal-assisted therapy programs?

- What do I have to think about and do to create a successful program?

- What proven tools and resources exist that I can draw on?

The programs you create from this information will serve diverse needs and may look very different. Fundamentally, however, all successful humane education and animal-assisted therapy programs share certain basic characteristics of content and structure. They are carefully planned with a curriculum that creates safe environments and positive learning experiences in which vulnerable children and families can develop skills sustainable beyond the humane education or animal-assisted therapy experience.

Whether you are thinking of a program involving dogs, horses, or wildlife rehabilitation...whether you are focusing your program on self-control, attachment, literacy, or skills that build confidence...whether you are just starting or are reviewing an existing program, this book offers a guide to the characteristics of sound humane education and animal-assisted therapy programs and provides resources to help you build and sustain your program.

1

The Connection between children and animals in good times and bad:

Why humane education and animal-assisted therapy programs work

Chapter One

Understanding the connection between children and animals

Overview

CHILDREN HAVE AN INHERENT FASCINATION WITH AND AFFECTION FOR ANIMALS. Both children and animals hold positions of vulnerability in families, and both children and animals can benefit from the kindness and suffer from the abuse and neglect of a family. For this reason, therapeutic and educational programs that responsibly include therapy animals benefit from the affection and bond children feel for animals.

At the same time, this bond can involve violence and neglect. Both children and animals can be the observers or targets of abuse and neglect. Both children and animals can be used as pawns in violent activities, and, eventually, both children and animals can become aggressors toward one another or toward others. For this reason, animals in a therapeutic or educational program with children and families can generate reactions of fear and anger.

Understanding the relationship between children and animals, especially in abusive or neglectful circumstances, can help us understand the power of humane education and animal-assisted therapy programs and the importance of thoughtful planning and careful program construction.

Children and Their Connection to Animals

CHILDREN ARE FASCINATED BY ANIMALS. Infants pay rapt attention to the puppets and live animals on popular videos from *Bugs Bunny* to *Baby Mozart*. Two-month olds coo at a stuffed bear, and 2-year olds toddle around the house with a patient dog or cat draped in their arms. Folk tales of cultures throughout the world and across time feature animals wise and foolish who teach children the ways of life. From the simplest bunny rabbit to the big bad wolf, from friendly Dino to scary Tyrannosaurus Rex, children's yearnings, joys, and fears are enacted through animals in books, puppet shows, theater, television, movies, videotapes, and computer games.

Perhaps children are drawn to animals because of their emotional candor. Like young children, animals express their emotions directly and are not misled by words. They are earnest and attentive, and respond honestly and consistently to the approaches of others. Children identify with animals. Both tend to be smaller and lower to the ground than adults, and both share the largesse and bear the brunt of benign and harmful human behavior.

Children seem to understand intuitively that there is a connection between the way the world treats animals and the way it treats children. Some animals are cherished pets; others are beasts of burden or future food for the table; some are objects of contempt and abuse. Similarly, some children are cuddled and adored; some serve a family function as a farm hand or errand runner; still others are beaten or ignored. Children, like domestic animals, depend on the adults of the family to take care of them. They cannot be economically independent in the adult world. Without a benevolent caregiver, they would not survive. With a negligent, cruel or sadistic caregiver, they cannot thrive.

The lives of young children, like those of domestic animals, are circumscribed by the families with whom they live. Like any weak or dependent household member, children and animals may become victims of neglect or abuse. Both often are at risk in the same ways and for the same reasons: they are trapped in a relationship with a more powerful and potentially dangerous person in a private place – the home. No one outside the home knows when a severely depressed parent fails to get out of bed for days and the children and pets go without food. No one knows when a parent comes home after being humiliated at work and takes out frustration and rage on the weaker members of the household. Neglect and abuse occur because they can, because there is no one around to see it or stop it.

In the United States, approximately 75 percent of families with children also have pets. Healthy and troubled families own pets at the same rate, but the similarity ends there. Healthy families adopt a pet or two and make a lasting commitment to each animal for the pet's life. The message to the children in these homes is that life is precious and living creatures should be cherished. Troubled families, in contrast, cannot create a stable enough environment in which pets grow to a ripe old age. Even if they are not abused, the pets may run away, get lost, be hit by cars, be injured, or suffer from malnutrition or disease. Children in these homes realize quickly that life is cheap and short. They learn that those who cannot fend for themselves are at great risk of harm or abandonment as they see pets get injured, die, or disappear.

These lessons become visible when neglected or abused children write about their pets as part of humane education and animal-assisted therapy programs. Children write compelling poetry and stories, often describing the death or disappearance of a pet and their own reaction to the loss. In one example, an elementary school student described the devastating impact of the loss of many pets in this poem:

> I had too many pets that died.
> I really don't want to write about it.
> I can't tell you about them either.
> I just don't want to.
> It makes me too sad.
> Don't ask me any more.
> I will cry into the ocean.

(Raphael, 1999, p. 25)

The pain that children feel over the loss of animals is considerable at first, but diminishes as losses accumulate. Children learn there is little point in caring about and attaching to such transient creatures because there is always another one who will come and go. And because children readily identify with animals, they generalize that experience to other living beings and relationships. Serial pet losses lead to social withdrawal, numbing of feelings, and a seeming indifference to the feelings of others.

Such lessons are also evident in the artwork of neglected and abused children. A child living in abusive circumstances drew her experiences with animals:

These are all the
Animals I had.
Some of them are dead.
Some of them are gone.

(drawing and poem from Raphael, 1999, p. 95)

The poetry and artwork of children in humane education and animal-assisted therapy programs often reveal neglect or abuse. These poems, pictures and stories show that the strong, natural ties between children and animals are altered by neglect and abuse. Children who experience neglect or abuse themselves or witness its impact on their pets learn lessons from these experiences. At the same time, they fail to learn other lessons commonly absorbed by children in healthy family relationships.

Because of children's connection to animals, humane education and animal-assisted therapy programs provide a tool to challenge these negative lessons and begin to replace them with healthier lessons about empathy, compassion, self-discipline, and patience. To create a successful humane education or animal-assisted therapy program, teachers and therapists must begin with an understanding of the reality, experience, and impact of neglect and abuse.

 ## Families Who Neglect Animals

MANY PARENTS BUY, ADOPT, OR OTHERWISE ACQUIRE A PET TO SHARE THE JOY OF ANIMAL COMPANION- SHIP WITH THEIR CHILDREN, TO TEACH RESPONSIBILITY AND RESPECT FOR LIFE. They think carefully before choosing a pet and make sure their home and lifestyle can accommodate the needs of a creature who cannot care for itself. Other parents simply begin feeding a stray animal who becomes a member of the family more casually. Nevertheless, they take adequate care of it and make a life-long commitment to it.

Still others see animals as undeserving of much care or attention. They may buy a Dalmatian puppy after seeing the movie about Dalmatians, or buy a bunny or chick for Easter without giving much thought to the needs of such a fragile young animal. It is simply a toy or decoration acquired on a momentary impulse and kept because it is cute and the adult wants to be loved. The adult may have given little thought to the care the pet will need over time or to the adult's ability to allocate time, skills and resources to provide adequately for the animal. Or, the adult may expect the child to assume full responsibility for the care of the animal, something children are not mature enough to do.

But animals are not mere decorations. They can be noisy, barking at passers-by or howling when lonely. They can be destructive, especially when young or left unattended for long periods of time. They need exercise and attention. They may eat food that is not theirs and chew up shoes that are left lying around. They may have housebreaking accidents and be unable to go an entire day without being let out to relieve themselves. They may not always come when called or obey commands that have not been systematically taught.

These are normal and predictable behaviors recognizable as such to a sophisticated pet owner who expects to train an animal to be a good member of the household. Less knowledgeable or experienced pet owners may have less realistic expectations and find these behaviors hard to tolerate. They may decide that the animal is bad or does things just to create more havoc for the caregiver. They blame the animal for misbehaving instead of taking responsibility for teaching the animal more desirable behaviors.

Children demand even more care and attention than animals. They are often noisy, messy, destructive, oppositional, incontinent, and otherwise annoying. They, like young pets, are energetic and need constant supervision. They toilet-train relatively late and frequently have bed-wetting accidents at night long after they are dry during the day. Defiance and disobedience are normal parts of the limit-testing that healthy children engage in, especially when they are toddlers or teenagers.

Some parents resent the demands and feel depleted by the need to care for others. In neglectful households, neither the pets' lesser needs nor the children's greater needs for physical and emotional care are met. The result is that the animals and the children live together in a filthy household, often denied clean water, adequate nutrition, attentive companionship, or medical attention. Sometimes it is even worse. The annoying pet or child may be locked away without food or water.

For example, when 4-year-old Jamie was removed by the juvenile court from his family because he had been left home alone for extended periods of time, he told his social worker about his puppy who whimpered and urinated in the kitchen. His father put duct tape over its muzzle, shoved it into a kennel, and left it on the back porch. Jamie did not know what happened to the puppy after that, but he never forgot what he had seen and learned from the experience.

Like Jamie, all children learn from their life experiences – whether healthy, neglectful, or abusive. Children who do not experience or observe healthy, supportive treatment learn instead through neglect and abuse.

What Children Learn (or Fail to Learn) from their Experiences of Neglect

NEGLECT IS TAUGHT ACCIDENTALLY, SIMPLY BECAUSE ITS OPPOSITE, ADEQUATE CARE, IS NOT PRESENT. Neglected children learn a pattern of helpless submission, resigning themselves to the only world they know. Neglect may not be sadistic or malicious, but it is nevertheless emotionally and physically devastating to children.

In attentive families, there is much hoopla when children take their first steps – flash bulbs, video cameras, phone calls to grandparents, emails to everyone in the address book. Such attention and encouragement are necessary to children's growth and development, especially because children are apt to fall more often than stand for the first few steps. Encouragement by parents gives children the fortitude and motivation to pick themselves up and try again.

In inattentive families, parents are overwhelmed or unavailable (not home, drunk, high, hung over, or passed out), so children's first steps go unnoticed. So do their cries when they fall on the second step. Or, worse still, these cries may disturb or anger the parent who dislikes noise and activity. Soon, the children realize that safety lies in being quiet and staying still. Learning, however, involves activity and exploration, which may create mess and noise and require encouragement when things go poorly.

Neglected children are not encouraged to try new things. They are not reinforced for babbling, for grabbing at things, for trying to roll over, for scooting across the floor. Instead of associating new activities with excitement and adventure, they learn that safety and a small measure of parental approval lie in passivity. They fall behind their more active and inquiring peers in the development of fine motor skills, the ability to concentrate and develop a long attention span, the appreciation of cause and effect, the art of problem solving, the capacity to tolerate frustration, and the ability to read social cues and develop interpersonal skills. Neglected children rarely learn hope or autonomy, much less initiative or mastery. At every stage of development, they tend to fall further behind other children of the same chronological age.

In spite of these deficits, neglected children grow up. Most of them will eventually learn to walk and to talk. They will go to school where teachers and other children expect things of them. This may be confusing and frightening to undersocialized and inexperienced children. They are likely to have trouble being successful.

But what if a neglected child has a friendly dog in the household? When that child takes his or her first step, the dog responds enthusiastically, reinforcing the stride and the effort behind it. When that child stumbles, the dog is there to lick his or her face and watch to see what will happen next. The child is not alone; another living being cares about what he or she is doing and reinforces attempts to explore the world and figure out how to do new things.

Despite parental neglect, these children learn they matter to another living creature. Both may be hungry and scared, but they are less likely to be lonely because they have each other. Even children from healthy homes have occasion to feel that they have been misunderstood or unfairly treated and often turn to a patient pet for solace.

A pet may represent earlier stages of development to school-age children. They may identify with both the animal's helplessness and freedom from responsibility. That is why many school-age children adore books and movies about animals in difficult situations. They identify with the creature's inability to help itself; they long to help it get to safety and freedom. Children who have some hope will feel compassion for the animal, will yearn to comfort it and strive to rescue it. This empathy encourages children to think about ways to help an animal in distress. Thus, they develop strategies to protect and soothe themselves as well.

To sustain these lessons of hope, compassion, and self-protection, children need stability and continuity. They need someone who will empathize with their feelings and explain how the world works. In a dysfunctional family, a child may wake up one morning to find a stranger in the house or, conversely, to find the beloved pet gone. The parents may never tell the child what happened. Such fateful – and often fatal – mystery creates fear and insecurity in children. In such families, few pets live to an old age. Many children can rattle off a long list of animals they had, adding, often with little feeling, which ones were run over, which ones they know were killed, which ones are believed to have died, which ones disappeared or were given away. A fifth grader in one of Pamela Raphael's humane education classes wrote about her experience, which is like that of many other children in uncertain circumstances:

> FooFoo got hit by a car.
> I cried.
> Cream, my dog,
> Born with a bad hip,
> Got put to sleep.
> I cried.
> The rat's teeth overlapped.
> She got put to sleep.
> My ferret died.
> All my animals die.
> 3 dogs, 7 cats, 10 fish, one bird.

(Raphael, 1999, p. 94)

The same children may also be able to tell devastating stories about all the humans they have lost. Ten-year-old Tasha can tell you about grandma who died of a heart attack, of Aunty June who died of AIDS, and little brother Andy who got hit by a car when, at eighteen months of age, he wandered into the street while unattended. Thirteen-year-old Velma, living with her aunt and a cousin in a shelter for homeless families, can tell you how much she misses her mother who died recently and her grandmother who died the year before.

Accidents and ill health are the natural companions of neglect. Children learn to expect suffering and loss. They try not to attach to people or animals because they want to avoid the pain of loss. They grow depressed and isolated. They may not only cut themselves off from their own painful feelings, but from their capacity to appreciate the feelings of others. They shield themselves from happiness, which is risky because it gets expectations up, and that leads to inevitable disappointment. They also block out suffering which is all too pervasive and demoralizing.

Children who have surrendered to neglect often feel helpless and numb. They may laugh at the plight of a suffering animal and even taunt it or throw things at it. Without special help, these children are on the way to becoming cruel and abusive adolescents and adults.

Families Who Abuse Animals

FOR SOME CHILDREN, NEGLECT IS COMPOUNDED BY ABUSE. The abuse may occur in many forms: physical or sexual, directed toward the child, or directed toward a pet. The child may be a victim, an observer, or a participant. In any case, an understanding of the nature of abuse against children and animals is critical for successful humane education and animal-assisted therapy programs.

Physical Abuse and the Family Pet

Joey was neglected by his mentally ill mother, then physically and sexually abused first by his grandfather and later by his mother's boyfriend. In the course of several years, he moved from family member to family member. Those who cared for him either abused him or failed to protect him. He had no consistent, benevolent caregiver. At age 12, he was living with his great aunt and a sister. By that time he had set fires in trash cans, tormented the family's small dogs and been explosively defiant with his great aunt and teachers. Left alone to take care of his little sister, he got rough with her. When their great aunt came home and heard the sister's complaints, she said, "this time you have gone too far; I can't take care of you any more." She called Child Protective Services (CPS) to request Joey's removal from her home. Joey begged her not to send him away; others, he claimed, had done worse things to him than he had done to his sister and they didn't get punished. Why was she rejecting him just because he was mean? Everybody else was mean!

Joey is an example of the tragic cycle created when the victim (Joey) goes on to become a perpetrator. He cannot understand why he is not allowed to be a bully; all of the other men in his family get away with it. In fact, his great aunt did tolerate it when he tormented the dogs; it was only when he turned on his sister that she had him taken away. From his point of view, why him? Why not his sister? When he had been abused, he had been removed; now that he is the abuser, he is again the one removed! He had been trying to change his role, not the pattern of abuse.

When children see adults responding to frustration with rage, they learn to do the same. They do not learn to express their feelings or talk things over. They only know how to rage or to submit. They may even be systematically taught to be aggressive and cruel.

For example, an animal protection agency investigated a report of animal abuse and discovered that a father was teaching his 18-month-old son, David, how to punish their eight-week-old pit bull puppy. The father made David watch while he beat the puppy with a chain. Then he gave the chain to his son and insisted that the child beat the dog with the chain also. He said pointedly to David, "Now you beat the dog with the chain or I'll beat you with it." When interviewed by an animal control officer, the father insisted his only aim was to "toughen both of them up." David had to shift from victim to perpetrator to be safe and to earn his father's approval. Empathy for the dog or reluctance to harm it would have jeopardized his safety at the hands of his father. Parental approval as well as safe passage lay in hurting the dog.

In a sense, the father was right: he was toughening the boy up, teaching him to be cruel rather than compassionate and defining masculinity as inflicting abuse on those smaller and weaker than oneself. His desire to toughen up both his son and the puppy stemmed from his own inability to tolerate vulnerability in the young of any species. He believed that real men had to learn to fight to survive, a belief passed down to him from his father. In his teens, he had submitted to a beating at the hands of his best friends as an initiation rite for membership in a gang. He was teaching his son to follow in his footsteps, to be a man, not to cry or cower "like a woman." Unfortunately, homophobia drives much of this hypermasculine aggression, putting all but the biggest and meanest men at risk of abuse and debasement.

Family violence like that experienced by David takes place in a larger context of social violence. An inner-city teenager named Barry was deeply depressed and hopeless after three youths close to him – a cousin, a good friend and a neighbor – died within four months of each other. Drive-by shootings and other forms of community violence take a toll on the neurological and emotional development of children. Violence perpetrated on neighborhood animals and violence in the media and on computer games add to the atmosphere of cruelty, hopelessness and despair that surrounds many children.

Societies vary greatly in their tolerance for physical violence and cruelty. Some cultures teach people to avoid harming even a fly. Others celebrate warriors and encourage the very young to fight. Some violent acts, like bullfights, are contained within restricted, ritualized settings. Others, like muggings, are perpetrated on strangers for personal gain. The impact of a violent act depends on its meaning to the affected individuals in their familial and social context.

For example, children growing up on farms learn that many of the animals they see around them will die. These children may even participate in their slaughter from an early age. They quickly learn about the cycle of life and death; they may be desensitized to the plight of farm animals but do not necessarily become violent or traumatized from these experiences.

Unfortunately, if children do learn to care about an animal, attachment can become a source of distress. When a parent beats the pet for being noisy, wetting the carpet or being disobedient, the child is impotent, unable to protect the beloved animal. The parent's message to the child is also clear: "Watch out – you're next!"

Some parents threaten to injure, kill, or get rid of the family pet as a way to control the other members of the family. These are not idle threats. Parents on occasion do harm, abandon, or even kill pets. Sometimes it is simple anger at the animal, but other times it is to intimidate or punish the children or other family members. A parent may say, "If you do not (clean your room; do your chores; come home right after school; teach your dog not to chew on the furniture), I will get rid of it." When parents do get rid of the pet, their children initially feel profound guilt, as though they had killed the pet themselves.

After this pattern has been repeated several times, though, the children feel less responsible, and feel less in general. They distance themselves from the care and compassion they felt earlier on.

Sexual Abuse and the Family Pet

The emotional distancing that results from neglect and physical abuse can grow into isolation through sexual abuse. Adults and older children having sex with minors typically isolate their child victim in order to maintain their access to the child and to keep the victim from telling an outsider what is going on. They often say things like, "I love you in a special way, but others would misunderstand," "If you tell, I'll get arrested and go to jail, and I pay the rent, so the family will become homeless," "Nobody will believe you," "Mommy will never hug you again," and "If you tell, I'll kill your pet."

Molested children are usually estranged from their non-offending parent(s) who have failed to protect them. They are also cut off from other people because of the need to keep the molestation secret. Their only carefree, physically affectionate and non-sexualized relationship may be with their pet. Thus, the pet provides a safe haven for these children and their needs for touch and affection. However, the pet also becomes a weapon the perpetrator can use to ensure a child's silence: the perpetrator may threaten to harm or kill the pet if the child tells anyone about the abuse. The child learns that seeking help will seal the violent fate of the beloved pet.

Children as Witnesses to Abuse

Children can be as profoundly affected by witnessing abuse inflicted on others as they can by being the target of abuse themselves. Similarly, children who witness domestic violence can be as traumatized as children who are beaten. Children who have witnessed animal abuse report feeling powerless and desolate because of their inability to protect the animal they love. They are so deeply disturbed by the events – whether they, an animal or a person close to them were the victim – that they may have psychological and psychosomatic symptoms including emotional withdrawal, dissociation, loss of memory, recurrent nightmares, acute anxiety, difficulty concentrating, and a compulsion to reenact the traumatic events. The disturbing events of the past intrude in their memories and may be so real that the children feel as if they were re-experiencing the upsetting experiences. This pattern of re-experiencing past traumatic events is often called Post Traumatic Stress Disorder (PTSD).

Many children literally cannot talk about their traumatizing experiences. Trauma changes the way the brain works, impairing its ability to connect the areas of the brain that process emotions with those that process language. Traumatized children cannot speak of or analyze their experience, nor can they stop it from intruding in dreams and even waking images. With words and reasoning unavailable as coping strategies, abused children grasp for other ways to come to terms with their frightening and overpowering experiences.

Abuse-reactive children may thus play out their traumas with others. When they do so, they choose those they can easily dominate and victimize. They may berate, bully or hit smaller children or animals. Some children who have been sexually molested then molest smaller or younger children or animals if they have no other opportunity to work out their overwhelming experience. They feel compelled to repeat what happened to them in a futile attempt to master their feelings of fear and powerlessness.

What Children Learn (or Fail to Learn) From their Experiences of Abuse

WHETHER CHILDREN EXPERIENCE OR WITNESS ABUSE, THEY LEARN FROM THE EXPERIENCE. Like neglected children, abused children learn patterns of behavior from their own treatment and from the treatment of the family pet.

As children grow, they seek to make sense of their lives and to understand how things work. A common way children figure out how families work is by playing house. They usually want to take the role of mother or father, the positions of power, and often repeat in play a recent troubling or problematic event. By taking on the larger, more powerful position, children experience in play the authority they lack in reality.

The next challenge children seek to decipher is school, an institution run by adults for the education of children. Again, children typically play school, desiring the role of teacher – or principal if they've been sent to the office often enough – to explore the power of the authority figure not available to them in reality.

Role playing people in authority is a good way to gain mastery over a new or frightening situation. Adults encourage this behavior when children face certain challenges: children about to have an operation will be given medical scrubs to wear and stethoscopes to toss around their necks; they'll be asked to repeat to the stuffed animal on their laps the physician's explanation about the upcoming procedure. By becoming the doctor in role play and reassuring the toy patient, children gain control of their fears and master information about what will happen. For the same reasons, children arriving at a foster home might be given a stuffed animal to hold while the foster parent explains the house rules and shows them around their new home. By repeating the information to the stuffed animal, the children become the hosts welcoming their friend into the home. They learn by teaching the key to success in the new setting.

Just as children tend to repeat adult quirks and weaknesses when playing house or school, they may also repeat negative behaviors, including abuse and violence they have seen at home and elsewhere. Unfortunately, this behavior requires a smaller or weaker partner, making younger children and small animals vulnerable to abuse at the hands of larger children who have been victims of or witnesses to violence. A child who had been bullied at school took it out on his pet cat:

(drawing from Raphael, 1999, p. 78)

Sexually abused children may also repeat their experiences with peers, siblings, younger children or animals. Children's sexual activity with animals, particularly the family pet, tends to go unnoticed or ignored by family members. Therapists rarely ask their clients specifically about sexual contact with animals, with the unfortunate result that people can remain in treatment for years without ever divulging these behaviors that are both reinforcing and felt to be shameful by many who engage in them. Such secrecy is also common among adult survivors of child sexual abuse who voluntarily enter treatment but never disclose to their therapist that they engage in sexualized behaviors with their pets. Burdened by behavior they consider humiliating and repugnant, they talk about the violations of the past but do not volunteer current practices that keep the wounds and self-loathing current.

Exposed to abuse often enough, traumatized children and adult survivors of abuse or neglect may no longer be able to feel their own feelings, or even to feel physical discomfort. And so they may burn themselves or cut themselves in an attempt to see if they can feel anything at all. They may engage in dangerous sex, use drugs, drive riskily or explore other thrill-seeking behaviors to see what – if anything – will trigger a rush. They may also hurt others to see if inflicting pain on another will make them feel something.

When interviewed about their exposure to animals, children may tell with great emotion the cruelty they were made to watch at home, even how they were forced to participate, and then how they repeated the behavior on their own. Often they add the tag line, "But I didn't care about that dog anyway." Obviously from the sincere pain in the child's earlier narrative, this statement is not true initially. But children cannot afford to remain open to such tender and therefore threatening feelings. Neither they nor their parent(s) can risk such vulnerability. So, to make the tag line true, these children repeat the behavior until they are desensitized, and eventually indifferent, to the pain of the victim and their attachment to the animal.

Children often know it is only a matter of time until a parent gets rid of or kills a new pet because they have been through it so many times before. Waiting for the other shoe to drop is stressful, often intolerable. It is worse if the last few pets were fatally injured but took a long time to die and no one in the family was allowed to help them. The pain of the hopeless situation, the animal's inevitable death, and the children's powerlessness to protect it gain momentum. To cope, children begin to close off the sensitive and empathic parts of their personalities.

Some children manage to love their pet despite the uncertainty of its future and welfare. Under these circumstances a child may decide to kill the beloved pet to preempt the parent and spare the animal the worse fate of a drawn-out death inflicted by a cruel adult. This child has two goals: both to alleviate the anxious waiting and also to give the animal a quick death at the hands of somebody who loved it. Euthanasia, certainly, but impossible for a child to come to terms with. Again one hears the tag line "I didn't care about that dog anyway" followed by the killing of enough animals to make the tag line true.

Unfortunately, along with the desensitization also comes a feeling of power, of holding the animal's life in one's hand and of taking that life. In a frightening way, such power can be exhilarating and arousing. The exhilaration makes daily life look bland and uninteresting by comparison. And the arousal is alluring, especially if children are experimenting with animals as they approach their pre-teen years when they are also beginning to develop curiosity about sexuality. In some cases the arousal becomes a sexual arousal, making the experience of abuse that much more exciting and reinforcing. In extreme cases, boys have videotaped themselves torturing or killing animals in order to offset later boredom by watching the tape. It is not uncommon for them to watch the tape with friends and to masturbate while viewing it. Thus, the infliction of pain becomes paired with sexual arousal and climax. Peer pressure and comradeship increase the likelihood of additional acts of cruelty.

Some troubled children wonder about taking their own life or the life of others. They may be rehearsing suicide or homicide when they torture or kill animals. The children who killed people in their schools, called by the media "schoolyard shooters," had prior histories of torturing and/or killing animals. These histories were well known to many of the children's peers and usually also to a number of adults in positions of responsibility. The consistent response of the children and adults was a combination of minimization ("boys will be boys") and avoidance. Consistent also was a failure to report behavior that was both cruel and criminal to law enforcement and animal control/humane authorities.

Children at risk of abuse or neglect, children who witness the abuse or neglect of other people or animals, and children who harm other living creatures themselves need timely and appropriate help. Whether you are a therapist, teacher, humane educator, parent, neighbor, or friend of a child at risk, you are that child's best chance of getting help. If you are a therapist, classroom teacher or humane educator, you may be looking for programs that can help. Because of the link between children and animals – both children's natural affection for animals and the vulnerable position of children and animals in families – humane education and animal-assisted therapy programs can be successful.

The first step in creating a successful humane education or animal-assisted therapy program is to develop a sound understanding of the connection between animals and children and of the experience and lessons from neglect and abuse. You've just taken this first step.

The second step in creating a successful program is based on the reality that, during these programs, children will share stories with you about abuse and neglect. Step two requires that you understand and accept not only this reality but also the requirements for reporting and methods of managing the confidences, both in the session and with the individual child. Before creating your program, it is important that you decide whether you want and are able to handle these confidences. If your answer is yes, you are ready to begin designing your program.

The third step in creating a successful program is to take the time to plan a thoughtful, highly organized structure that integrates the realities of neglect and abuse with sound program development.

And the last step in creating a successful program is to develop content that integrates these realities into lessons that teach essential skills leading to pro-social world views.

The following chapter helps prepare you to respond appropriately to indications of neglect and abuse that may come up in any humane education or animal-assisted therapy program.

Chapter Two

Preparing to handle indications of neglect and abuse

Overview

AS A HUMANE EDUCATOR, TEACHER, THERAPIST, OR CONCERNED ADULT, YOU HAVE SEEN THE IMPACT OF ABUSE AND NEGLECT ON CHILDREN AND ARE CONSIDERING A HUMANE EDUCATION OR ANIMAL-ASSISTED THERAPY PROGRAM AS A RESPONSE. Chapters 3, 4, 5, and 6 help you design effective programs by offering guidance about program structure and content.

But before you begin building your program, you must take a look at a reality common to all humane education and animal-assisted therapy programs whether they are therapeutic or educational, whether they involve children or families, whether they are centered around dogs, horses, wildlife, or other animals.

The reality is this: during programs about or involving animals, children reveal instances of neglect or abuse. Before you consider the design of your program, it is critical to understand and be prepared to deal with this reality. This chapter provides guidance in recognizing and responding to indications of neglect or abuse both through interactions during the program and through reporting that may take place outside the program.

Why children reveal neglect and abuse during humane education and animal-assisted therapy programs

ANY SENSITIVE ADULT WHO ENGAGES WITH A CHILD ON A MEANINGFUL LEVEL MAY HEAR MORE THAN HE OR SHE WANTS ABOUT WHAT GOES ON IN THAT CHILD'S HOME. Humane educators are especially likely to be told very specific stories as children react to their descriptions of responsible care for animals. Humane educators do not have to try to elicit this material; it emerges as a natural consequence of their classes and often reveals instances of abuse or neglect.

Think about the situation:

You bring an animal into the classroom. The children all have preconceived notions about animals, whether they are safe or dangerous, whether they are clean or dirty, whether they need to be hit to learn to obey. An inner-city child might be familiar with pit bulls tied in the back yard and starved until they rip apart anything that comes near. That child may be terrified at the idea of petting a dog or even holding on to the other end of the leash. A farm child may be familiar with a wide range of animals, but might also have learned that they are being raised for consumption, not to be objects of affection. Farm children may think of domesticated animals as livestock not worth investing with emotion. A child from a rural area may have had the chance to observe animals in their natural habitats, growing familiar with deer, raccoons, opossums, and a wide range of foraging creatures. They may also know that the older boys go to the dump to shoot the rats and rise early the first day of hunting season to bag a deer before they go to school. Children from any of these environments may have a special animal companion whom they confess secrets to and rely on for comfort. For one child, this relationship is nurtured and sustained by the family. For another, the beloved pet becomes a source of vulnerability, pain, and loss. Both children, responding to the animal in the classroom, are likely to share stories from their homes.

A fundamental message of humane education and animal-assisted therapy programs is that people are responsible for attending to the needs of others. Because children bring their prior experience into the classroom, many will already know that animals, like people, need food, water, and shelter, and require comfort when they are afraid and company when they are lonely. Other children, however, will not have thought much about the needs of either humans or animals. As you talk about the importance of a good diet, regular habits, attention and grooming, these children may be startled into a new perception of their own home life. They may realize for the first time that they receive less care than you have described as minimally necessary for a pet. Without careful handling, an unintended consequence of this well-meant but naïve presentation is the child concluding he or she gets worse care – and is worth less – than a dog.

When teachers talk about how humans can nurture other living creatures, they do not intentionally contrast good pet care with the inadequate care some children receive at home. Nonetheless, neglected children hear clearly the teacher's opinion that things should be different "even for a dog." The message is that all living things deserve love and attention. Here at last is an adult who, like most children, wants life to be fair and just and loving. It is a message of hope. No wonder children want to talk about upsetting things with such a person.

Thus, the inherent message of a humane education or animal-assisted therapy program is likely to prompt stories of neglect or abuse. At an even more basic level, the presence of the animal(s) also triggers disclosure, often about sexual abuse. Think about the natural state of animals who are brought into the classroom. They are naked; their genitals are exposed, and they have no inhibitions about scratching, touching, or licking their genitals in the presence of the children. A sexually abused child may find the exposed genitals disturbing and may perceive the grooming as sexually provocative, even threatening. Caught off guard by behaviors the sexually abused child sees as emotionally charged and aggressive, that child may start talking about other experiences of nudity, oral-genital contact or other sexual activity. The humane educator, classroom teacher or therapist must be prepared to deal with such revelations.

If you are not prepared for possible revelations of abuse or neglect to come up in the classroom, you may be unsure of effective ways to respond to them. Should you try to get help for a child or family caught up in a cycle of violence? Might you do more harm than good? Could the child be exaggerating or even making things up? The first thing to do, before a child confides in you, is to plan for the likelihood that a child's behavior or confidences will alert you to abuse or neglect. The second thing is to prepare to respond to these behaviors or confidences. Here are some guidelines to help you plan how you would handle situations ranging from a child's roughness with an animal in class to a child's disclosures or your suspicions of abuse or neglect.

When a child is rough with an animal in class

HUMANE EDUCATION AND ANIMAL-ASSISTED THERAPY PROGRAMS OFTEN BEGIN WITH CHILDREN LEARNING HOW TO APPROACH THE ANIMAL SAFELY. For some children, this may be a natural sequence that they have already learned from their own families. For others, it is startling because it is so different from all that they have experienced.

On rare occasions, this instruction may reveal behavior indicative of abuse or neglect. A troubled child may attempt to hurt the visiting animal or the classroom pet by handling the animal roughly or aggressively. Adults must take prompt action to ensure everyone's safety. Here is what you can do:

◆ Separate the child and animal immediately.

◆ Say "nobody gets hurt here; everybody is safe." With this statement, you are not blaming anyone, and you are assuring the children that there will be no violent retaliation for the behavior. Instead, you will protect them and teach them all how to stay safe.

◆ Give the offending child a brief time-out to regain self-control.

◆ Ask the child to describe what triggered the aggression. Ask what the child could have done instead of hurting the animal to get help or attention.

◆ Have the child articulate how the animal reacted. How did it behave? How did the child think it was feeling? See if the child can talk about how it feels to have hurt another living creature and why it is better to be gentle. Praise the child for appreciating the importance of safety and gentleness.

◆ Include the other children in your discussion of humane values and encourage them to suggest behavioral alternatives to aggression.

◆ Conclude with a highly supervised, brief contact between the animal and the child, perhaps allowing one gentle pat, and end on a positive note by praising the child for being gentle this time.

◆ Have the children draw a picture and write a story of the protective alternative (developed in the discussion of humane values) if time permits. If not, ask the teacher to have the children do that later in the day or as soon as possible. Drawing and writing are excellent ways to think through and commit to new behaviors (see Chapter 4, pp. 74-76, and Chapter 5, pp. 97-103).

◆ When appropriate, refer the child to mental health or social service programs.

Anticipate that you may experience a child's roughness toward animals during your program. This experience can be managed in ways that ensure a safe environment, communicate that adults can respond to aggression without violent retaliation, and transmit humane values.

When a child describes abuse or neglect

ROUGHNESS WITH ANIMALS MAY BE AN EARLY SIGNAL THAT A CHILD IS TROUBLED. As the humane education or animal-assisted therapy program progresses, the signals are likely to become more direct. In many cases, children will be prompted by something in the program to tell a story about their experience of abuse or neglect.

The first thing to remember when a child tells you a story about abuse or neglect is that you should not ignore what you have heard. If you continue teaching as though nothing happened, the children will feel that the story was not shocking and that you did not consider the behavior inappropriate. Your program needs to allow time to stop and deal with the story as a group.

Children disclose stories of child and animal abuse or neglect for a reason: they want the abuse or neglect to stop. They are asking for an intervention, or at least for someone outside their family to validate their own feeling that what happened was wrong. All of the children in your classroom need to know that abuse and neglect are not okay, and that there are things that can be done to protect victims of cruel treatment. How can you respond when a child tells a story about abuse or neglect?

◆ *Draw out the child about the experience to get as full a picture of what happened as you can.* Then, ask the child about his or her reaction, including thoughts, feelings, options, and concerns. Allow the child to tell the entire story. You will be able to formulate an appropriate response and intervention, if necessary, at the end of the story.

◆ *Engage the other children.* The children who heard the disclosure need to share their reactions, too. What has happened to one child could easily have happened to another. Help all the children understand what they have heard. Help them articulate how they felt about it and what can be done to help the victim of abuse or neglect and any child witnesses.

◆ *Ensure the child's safety and trust.* Remember, a child is taking a great risk when violating the family's rule of not telling the secret of abusive or negligent behavior. Once a child reveals a family problem, you must react promptly and appropriately so that the child can learn to trust adults to respond and follow through. Be sure that you ask the child if he or she is afraid of getting into trouble or of being harmed for telling the secret. It is essential that you not expose a child to danger; any action you take must ensure the safety of the child who revealed the abuse. Include any suspicions or fears you have of child abuse when you report a story of animal abuse. You may need to contact both child protective services and your municipal animal care and control agency to provide protection to all living beings at risk of harm (see below, pp. 21-23 for specifics on reporting abuse and neglect).

◆ *Validate that a child's values may differ from those of the abuser.* When children describe the abusive behavior of family members, they are indicating that their values are different from the abuser's. Let these children know that it is okay to have different values and behaviors than other family members. Elicit and validate the humane views of the situation, the true feelings that lie beneath the social attitudes. Make sure to advise these children that they should not confront violent parents with the opinion that their behavior is cruel. Such a confrontation would only increase the risk for the child. Help the children figure out what they might do instead both to ensure their safety and to find support for their humane values.

◆ *Teach children how to get help.* Any real-life story of abuse or neglect is an opportunity to teach the entire class about safety. Do the children know how to get help for an animal, for themselves, for siblings, or for an elderly or disabled relative in an emergency? Teach them the local reporting numbers, and remind them that 911 is always available for them in an emergency. Role play making a call to 911 with a gruff and impatient actor as the emergency responder. Children often know that they should call 911 for help but get rattled when they are interviewed tersely. To be able to get help when needed, they must know that they can deliver relevant information even when pressured and addressed sharply.

◆ *Reinforce humane and responsible assessment and values; compliment the children on their values and on their ability to discuss such a difficult topic.*

At this point, a child's behavior or comments may cause you to suspect abuse or neglect. A child who is aggressive with the animal or who tells stories of abuse or neglect may cause you to be concerned about the child's own safety. Handling the behavior or comments in the classroom is an essential step, but it does not deal with the abuse. Now you need to get help by reporting your concerns, building a team who can monitor the situation, and making sure that everyone follows up to help the child.

When you suspect a child is being abused or neglected

ALL TEACHERS, PUBLIC AND PRIVATE, ACADEMIC AND ENRICHMENT, INCLUDING HUMANE EDUCATORS, ARE REQUIRED UNDER STATE LAWS TO REPORT SUSPECTED CHILD ABUSE AND NEGLECT. All licensed health and mental health professionals, along with many other people who work with children, are mandated as well. In California and a few other states, state humane and animal control officers are also mandated reporters of suspected child abuse and neglect. Mandated reporters have absolute immunity from suit or prosecution. Failing to report is a misdemeanor, with possible consequences of a jail sentence and/or a fine. The reporting law is designed to encourage responsible adults working with children to make reports to the appropriate protective agency as soon as they become reasonably suspicious of abuse or neglect. Anybody concerned about the safety or welfare of a child may make a report to their local child protective agency; mandated reporters MUST report.

Many therapists, teachers and principals, even if they host humane education classes or animal-assisted therapy programs each year, are not aware of animal protection laws and of the resources provided by humane societies and municipal animal care and control agencies. The humane educator, on the other hand, should be very familiar with local procedures to report animal cruelty and neglect, able to obtain assistance for the animal in question, and know how to educate the school's faculty and other mandated reporters on reporting animal cruelty and neglect.

If you have reason to suspect an incident of child abuse or neglect, you must take three steps. First, make a report to Child Protective Services (CPS) in the child's county of residence. Second, create a team to support the child once the humane education or animal-assisted therapy program is over. And, third, make sure that everyone follows up to support the child.

STEP ONE: Report to Child Protective Services (CPS) right away.

How do you know where to report?

The reporting number will be listed in the emergency numbers at the front of the local phone book. Unfortunately, each county has a different phone number for its child protective agency, although 911 can and should be used in emergencies. Call CPS in the county where the child lives, regardless of where the abuse or neglect took place. For matters concerning the welfare of children, jurisdiction is based on the child's residency; in criminal matters, on the other hand, the county in which the crime occurred has jurisdiction.

How can you be sure your report is effective?

To make an effective report, focus on current harm to the child and the likelihood that the child will continue to be at risk. Emphasize matters affecting the child's safety and welfare. These may include the child's age and level of maturity; whether the child is afraid and has good or poor judgment about safety and danger; and whether the child has any special needs that limit his or her ability to manage. Add what you know about the parent's capabilities to recognize the problem and respond appropriately and protectively. Be objective and avoid judgmental language.

At this point you may have some concerns about reporting your suspicions. Reservations about reporting abuse and neglect are common. Here are some frequently voiced concerns.

◆ *What if I'm wrong? Won't the child be removed and put into foster care?*

Making a report lets the child protective agency know that a responsible adult is worried about the safety of a child for a specific reason. The report triggers an assessment by a social worker trained in evaluating allegations of abuse and neglect. What happens after a report is made depends on what the investigating social worker can substantiate. In fact, few children are removed from their homes and only in the most serious cases. Most of the children who are removed stay with relatives. Only a few children end up in foster care, and most foster homes (despite media coverage to the contrary) are pretty good.

◆ *Don't parents have a right to rear their children as they see fit?*

Parents have a great deal of discretion in child rearing, but this discretion stops short of willfully endangering, injuring or neglecting minors. Children are entitled to personal safety as well as food, shelter, clothing, basic medical care and supervision.

◆ *What if the parent finds out I made the report?*

Although every practical attempt is made to keep the identity of the reporter confidential, parents do sometimes guess correctly who made the report. If you are worried about retaliation or your safety, you must ask yourself how safe the child is in this person's care. Add your concerns about retaliation and safety to the information you report.

◆ *What if all I have is hearsay?*

You should report when you are reasonably suspicious. Child abuse and neglect most commonly occur at home in private when nobody is looking. Eyewitness information is rare. Remember also that a child may confide in you the woes of another child. If it sounds credible and serious, report it. The investigating social worker will assess and sort out the second- and third-hand information received.

◆ *I was told in confidence; won't telling make me lose this trust?*

Children who disclose family problems take a great risk and are probably violating implicit, if not explicit, parental dicta by disclosing the problems at home. The response the child receives will significantly influence his or her ability to trust the adult world in the future. Therefore, the recipient of the confidence must respond promptly and adequately. Here are two suggestions.

First, do not promise more than you yourself can deliver. That is, do not predict or guarantee what the social worker, police officer or animal control officer will or will not do; do not let the child think he or she can come home with you or that you will rescue the pet; do not predict the future or make promises you may not be able to keep. Most children are satisfied with a remark such as, "I am glad you trusted me enough to tell me about the problem at home. I care about you (and your pet) and want to do what I can to help you. I need to ask for help from somebody who knows more about these types of problems than I do. I am not sure what he or she will decide would be best, but I will continue to listen, to care, and to do what I can for you."

Second, model responsible adult behavior. Do not let the demand for secrecy control or constrain your behavior. The child may say something like this: "I'll tell you if you promise not to tell anybody else." In all likelihood, the child comes from a family that has difficulty setting limits, establishing and honoring boundaries, and delineating the roles and responsibilities of children and adults. Afford the child the opportunity to see a caring and capable adult take on a difficult chore in a timely and appropriate way. You may not be able to fix the family's problem, but you can give the child the experience of observing decent and responsible adult behavior. The unspoken message that not everyone is abusive or irresponsible will resonate loudly for the child. Reply with words like these: "Thank you for trusting me enough to consider telling me the problem. Most of what we talk about can stay between us, but not something that affects your safety. I cannot promise to keep a secret without knowing what it is. I can promise that I will tell you first if I have to get additional help and you can listen while I make the phone call asking for that help so you'll know exactly what I say."

◆ *What if CPS does not take seriously the information about cruelty to animals?*

Few child welfare workers get training in the link between cruelty to animals and human violence – even in states where state humane and animal control officers are mandated reporters of suspected child abuse and neglect. Thus, you should be prepared for some skepticism when you call and should be prepared to explain clearly and calmly the dangerousness of the behaviors toward a living being with needs similar to the child's (see Chapter 7, pp. 138-149, on family-based risk assessment) and how they put the child at risk. Use language to describe the common denominator: "The parent responded violently to noise, in this case the normal barking of the family dog, injuring the dog who is approximately the same size as the child. The child is also noisy and reports having also been hit for disturbing the parent in the past. The child is at risk of injury because the parent has responded abusively to noise in the recent past." Make sure also to report the animal abuse or neglect to your local department of animal care and control. Let them know of the presence of children in the home and the common risk. Tell them you filed a CPS report and request that they follow up with CPS when they have assessed risk to the animal.

Then there are two more steps you should take.

STEP TWO: *Build a team.*

Because the school has an ongoing relationship with the child and the humane educator generally visits only once or twice a year, the teacher and humane educator should collaborate on the report. Many schools have protocols for reporting that include involving the principal or another designated administrator. It is in the child's best interests that people in a position to observe the child regularly get involved in reporting so they can watch for recurrence and continue to request help for the child as needed.

STEP THREE: *Follow through.*

Things sometimes fall between the cracks, especially unpleasant things. The conscientious humane educator will insist that the initial report to Child Protective Services be made at the conclusion of the humane education class. Child abuse reporting laws require that reports of suspected child abuse and neglect be made immediately. Additionally, once the humane educator leaves the school, he or she has no way of knowing if the teacher and/or principal followed through. Especially if the teacher had already known of or suspected the problem that the child revealed during the visit by the humane educator, it is possible that the report might not be made without the humane educator's leadership.

Sometimes, people become concerned about a family's functioning, but their concerns do not meet the threshold for child abuse reporting. There are other community services available to offer assistance to a family in distress. Health departments employ public health nurses who make home visits and give parents advice on health and safety matters without charge. Parental stress hotlines, which children can also call, offer 24-hour assistance and referral to appropriate resources. Many non-profit social service agencies have outreach workers who can offer help. The humane educator can make these referrals him- or herself. It is important to know the resources in your community.

As you think about creating a humane education or an animal-assisted therapy program, prepare yourself to deal with difficult realities. You will provide information, a context, and an approach that children will respond to. Talking about safety, compassion, and animals with an attentive, understanding adult who does not ignore unpleasant stories gives children a place to unburden themselves. How you respond will influence the child's willingness to seek help in the future.

Because you are willing to address issues of neglect and abuse, you can make an impact on the life of a child and a family with a well designed humane education or animal-assisted therapy program. Successful programs share design characteristics. The next two chapters guide you through the work of deciding how to structure your program and how to focus your content.

Part Two

Creating programs that work

Creating programs that work

Overview

WHAT ARE HUMANE EDUCATION AND ANIMAL-ASSISTED THERAPY PROGRAMS? Successful humane education and animal-assisted therapy programs bring animals and people together to serve a defined therapeutic or educational goal. Beyond this basic definition, successful programs vary greatly in design and content.

Successful programs can rely on a variety of animals: dogs, cats, horses, wildlife, and other animals have all been used as part of effective programs.

Successful programs can be designed around a variety of contexts: rehabilitating injured wildlife, training shelter dogs, bringing animals into a classroom, or caring for farm animals.

Successful programs can serve a variety of clients: abused or neglected children and at-risk families are served by some programs; other programs focus on specific groups or needs such as incarcerated teens, sexually abused girls, teen parents, or young people with learning, emotional, physical or developmental disabilities.

Successful programs can be designed around a variety of specific problems: developing child care skills for pregnant teens, creating a safe and developmental environment for supervised visits between parents and children, teaching effective parenting skills to neglectful or abusive parents, or enhancing physical capabilities in children with developmental disabilities.

Given all this variety, what makes a humane education or an animal-assisted therapy program work?

All successful programs meet a few basic criteria: the structure ensures safety for all participants; the content promotes growth in essential therapeutic components, and the program is measured to determine whether the goals have been met.

You already understand the value of bringing people and animals together to meet defined therapeutic or educational goals, and you have accepted the responsibility of children's confidences. Now you are ready to begin thinking about the design of your program. The following chapters are intended to help you create a structure and content that will enable your program to meet the goals you set.

Chapter 3, Developing the Structure of Animal-Assisted Therapy Programs, establishes four criteria for creating structurally safe programs and provides guidelines you can use to create your program's structure.

Chapter 4, Developing the Content of Animal-Assisted Therapy Programs, defines five essential therapeutic components that should be part of any successful program. This chapter takes a step-by-step approach to explaining the skills involved and showing how they can be applied to a successful program.

Chapter 5, Changing Behavior and Outlook – The SHIP Model, pulls Chapters 3 and 4 together by describing a comprehensive example of a tested program.

And Chapter 6, Applying Animal-Assisted Therapy to Special Problems, provides examples of programs that have applied the structural and content guidelines to create programs meeting specific needs.

Chapter Three

Developing the structure of animal-assisted therapy programs

Overview

AS A PROGRAM DESIGNER, YOU MUST CREATE A CULTURE OF SAFETY FOR ALL LIVING BEINGS PARTICIPATING IN YOUR PROGRAM: THE CHILDREN, THEIR PARENTS, THE STAFF AND VOLUNTEERS, AND THE ANIMALS. Since most of your clients have not been safe at home with their own families, it is especially important that you make your program a model of safety and security. This begins with decisions you make about how to structure your program.

This chapter helps you answer four questions critical to structuring your program effectively.

■ How do I select a safe setting for the animals and people in the program?

■ How do I screen, hire, train, and motivate qualified and safe staff and volunteers?

■ How do I select a safe animal?

■ How do I select suitable participants?

Structuring a successful animal-assisted therapy program begins with your choice of setting.

How do I select a safe setting for the animals and people in the program?

CLIENTS WITH HISTORIES OF ABUSE, NEGLECT, OR EXPOSURE TO DOMESTIC OR COMMUNITY VIOLENCE ARE QUICK TO SENSE – AND ANTICIPATE – DANGER. Therefore, choosing a safe setting is crucial to your program's success. The setting must also be safe and suitable for the participating animals, easily and safely accessible for them as well as for the human participants.

You can consider a variety of settings for your program. As you think about where to hold your program, you will find that some settings are more suitable for the animals and others are more suitable for the people.

Animal shelters are used to host some humane education and animal-assisted therapy programs. A shelter guarantees the availability of animals in a setting that is safe and appropriate for them. It eliminates the need to transport the animals, thereby reducing their stress, minimizing the possibility of injury or escape, and saving staff time and cost. It also provides other protections: protection from chocolate and other toxic or dangerous edibles likely to be found at non-shelter sites and protection from taunting or unwanted attention by passersby or school or agency clients and staff. Shelters offer a safe and quiet place for the animals to retreat to when overwhelmed by the unfamiliar environment or the press of eager humans. As a setting that provides safety for the animal, shelters seem a logical choice.

But how well do shelters work for the people participating in the program? Animal shelters tend to be located in industrial parts of cities, and these areas are not always welcoming or familiar to prospective participants. Other settings are more suitable for the participants. Some humane education and animal-assisted therapy programs bring animals to schools, treatment programs, community organizations, and even locked facilities such as juvenile detention programs, county jails and state prisons. These settings are generally acceptable to the clients who already attend other programs there. The people, facility, and the neighborhood are familiar and participants know about transportation to and from the building. As settings that provide safety and appear suitable for the program participants, non-shelter venues seem a logical choice.

Unfortunately, the answer is not quite that easy. Any location designed for human clients may have concerns about accommodating animals. The available space may be too small, especially since large and hardy animals work best with at-risk clients. The school, social service agency or locked facility may have additional problems: limited space, clients with allergies who are not attending but are affected by the program, liability limits, and an unwillingness to deal with damage to carpets and other property from housebreaking accidents. There may also be other complicating factors relating to the novelty of the animals' visit. People in the area who are not part of the animal-assisted therapy program may be excited by the arrival of the animals and want to play with them. This can cause problems both for the facility and the program.

So, how do you choose a setting that ensures safety and meets the needs of both the animals and people participating in your program? Unfortunately, there is no one answer. As the designer of the program, you must work your way through the following ten questions; your answers will help you select the best setting for your program.

Here are the questions to think about when considering possible sites for a humane education or an animal-assisted therapy program:

1. Is the neighborhood safe?

2. Are the prospective clients already familiar with the neighborhood?

3. Is the building safe?

4. Are the prospective clients already familiar with the building?

5. How will participants travel to and from the site? Who is responsible for bringing them?

6. How will animals travel to and from the site?

7. Is the meeting room conducive to safe interaction and quiet learning?

8. How shielded are participants and animals from people passing by?

9. How safe are participants and animals from other clients?

10. How will non-participants be turned away when they want to see and interact with the animals?

Let's look at these questions one by one.

1. Is the neighborhood safe?

Many programs serving at-risk children and their families are neighborhood-based. Providing services for people in their own communities has many advantages including creating a safe haven in a dangerous neighborhood and providing safe adults nearby for at-risk children and their families to turn to in times of stress or danger.

Additionally, transportation to distant programs is often difficult and costly, as well as time consuming. Because overwhelmed families rarely travel far from home for resources, their ability to use services depends on the proximity of those services to their home, place of employment and school.

However, locating programs in schools, shelters, and social service agencies serving at-risk families in marginalized neighborhoods often means locating programs in dangerous areas. People need to feel – and be – safe in order to relax their guard enough to focus on the task at hand, learn new skills, and develop concern for others. Moreover, bringing animals into risky areas introduces other concerns about their safe passage and their possible defensive or aggressive responses to perceived threats.

2. Are the prospective clients already familiar with the neighborhood?

Familiarity is a form of safety, even if the familiar comes with its own risks. Asking people to leave their familiar surroundings to come to a strange area may introduce obstacles, often insurmountable ones. If you decide to locate your program in a setting new to the participants, structure ways to prepare them for the change. Consider having program staff meet the clients first in their own neighborhood to establish ties and introduce the program. Use photographs, or, better still, a videotape of the site to help people become familiar with the location of the program. Talk about transportation, landmarks along the way, and neighboring buildings to ease the uncertainty and make the challenge of going to a strange place in a strange neighborhood less daunting – especially if the clients like the program staff and want to see where they work. Eagerness to meet the animals should help sway the less venturesome.

3. Is the building safe?

Does the building provide safety for both the people and animals involved in the program? Think about who has access to the building. Is a receptionist, security guard or other person on duty keeping an eye on the front door? Do people loiter in or around the building? Do people have to sign in or pass through metal detectors to gain entry?

Buildings that do not monitor their doors may feel more welcoming to participants but may actually present greater risk. Bullies, gang members, and other problematic people may enter and disrupt activities. They may heckle people going into the building and attempt to persuade clients to skip the session they came to attend. Additionally, some clients may be under court protection; one or more of their relatives may be prohibited from seeing them or may be allowed only supervised contact. In adversarial divorce cases, there may be a risk of kidnapping or other custodial interference. If the family is residing in a battered women's shelter, there may be additional concerns about stalking, even attempting to learn the location of the safe house by following the family back from the community activity. The arrival of the animals may draw all sorts of problematic attention to the members of the group.

Buildings with door monitoring and metal detectors increase safety and protection for participants. On the other hand, they can also create an officious and intimidating feeling. The monitoring staff focuses on security; there are lines while people wait to be cleared to enter. Order must be maintained lest guards think a diversion is being created by one party so another can slip by or sneak in contraband. This emphasis on security tends to decrease relaxed exchanges among participants waiting for their group to begin.

Buildings also raise concerns about safety for the program's animals. Are there dangers facing animals coming to and going from the building? Does the building have a parking area that affords easy access to the building? Can loiterers and passersby be avoided? Is there broken glass on the sidewalk or roadway? Will the animals and the people bringing them have to go through building security? Might the animals be scared or overwhelmed by the number of people waiting in a congested lobby? The doors in locked facilities tend to have noisy air locks. These may scare both animals and children.

4. Are the prospective clients already familiar with the building?

If clients are attending the humane education or animal-assisted therapy program in a neighborhood and building they already frequent, they may be used to and willing to tolerate the various hindrances involved in arriving and gaining entry. A new building or neighborhood, however, may create significant obstacles. The unwelcoming feel of a new building, the inhospitable entryway, the possible curtness of guards, and the sense of being an outsider may combine to make the diffident client feel unwelcome, perhaps even humiliated. Whatever good the session could accomplish may be completely offset by the difficulties of getting to it.

If you choose a building new to the program's participants, think about how to structure ways to make the environment more inviting. A friendly and welcoming presence at the doorway, and a hospitable gesture such as an offer of a cup of tea or coffee to an adult and juice to a child, can go a long way to set the positive tone therapeutic programs depend on to make meaningful change.

5. How will participants travel to and from the site? Who is responsible for bringing them?

Overwhelmed families are rarely equipped to travel far from home for resources. They need services near their homes, schools and places of employment. How people travel to the meeting, how long the trip takes, and how difficult it is will affect clients' ability to attend and concentrate during the session. Public transportation is often unreliable and tiring, especially if several changes of buses or trains are involved. Mass transit vagaries often contribute to tardiness. Traffic and poorly maintained private cars may also compromise clients' abilities to arrive on time.

Some agencies provide transportation for their clients to attend a program at an animal shelter or other facility. While solving a multitude of problems, this introduces a few of its own. The staff person available and licensed to drive the agency's van may not be the best person to co-facilitate the group. If a staff member is sick or on vacation, the agency may not be able to spare anyone to drive resulting in a last minute cancellation of the session. The size and membership of the group may be influenced by the size of the van, the number of children in the group supervised by the driver, and other programmatic considerations unrelated to the needs of the humane education or animal-assisted therapy program.

6. How will animals travel to and from the site?

Logistically, it is easier to transport an animal or two to a school or agency all the clients already attend. If the program is using owned therapy dogs, they are usually good travelers and enjoy the car ride as well as the session with clients. Shelter animals may find travel stressful, though, for any number of reasons. They are new arrivals in a strange and perhaps frightening place. They may not be used to traveling – at least not in a cage in an animal control vehicle. They may be afraid of being taken somewhere and abandoned. If they need to be coerced into the car or van or are scared by the trip, they will not likely be eager participants in the session much less good learners of new behaviors.

7. Is the meeting room conducive to safe interaction and quiet learning?

Schools, non-profit organizations, and locked facilities are routinely overcrowded and short of space, staff, and resources. Space available for the humane education or animal-assisted therapy program may be limited and less than ideal. At a minimum, consider these factors:

Space:

◆ Is the space large enough to accommodate all the participants and give the animals a quiet corner apart from the multitude?

◆ If more than one animal comes, is the space large enough for the two animals to keep a comfortable distance between them?

Clutter:

♦ Is the space relatively uncluttered so that people and animals can move around freely?

♦ Are there distracting piles of supplies or toys?

♦ Are edible things stored there?

Quiet:

♦ Is the space quiet during the meeting time?

♦ Will there be traffic outside the door as people switch classes?

♦ Will bells ring signaling the end of one period or another?

Set up and clean up?

♦ Who will set the room up before the group and return it to its original condition after the group?

♦ Who will handle necessary clean up, including the inevitable housebreaking accidents?

8. How shielded are participants and animals from people passing by?

Doors, picture windows, and busy streets and hallways can distract people and animals, particularly those who are on guard because they have experienced or witnessed violence. The quieter the room the better, but too isolated a location, especially if the group meets after dark, can also frighten people. Frequently, only one room is available and it is a question of making do.

If you must use an isolated room, structure ways to increase safety and comfort. Reduce fears by having good lighting, even if you have to purchase a couple of floor lamps, and make sure a safe person is available to walk people down hallways to and from the sessions.

9. How safe are participants and animals from other clients?

Programs serving at-risk clients must plan to protect vulnerable clients from harm that could be inflicted by more aggressive clients. Risk of harm to the visiting animals must also be considered. Excitement or fear triggered by the novel presence of an animal might affect those with poor impulse control or fearful or aggressive behavior. Giving some clients the privilege of a session with animals may put them at risk at the hands of the excluded clients. Make sure you structure practical and responsible plans to deal with these issues, and make sure an extra staff person will be available to help should a dangerous situation occur.

10. How will non-participants be turned away when they want to see and interact with the animals?

Because of the presence of animals in humane education and animal-assisted therapy programs, uninvited people often want to join in. To maintain group cohesion and confidentiality and to get work done, you will have to gently turn away unenrolled enthusiasts. Not everybody handles rejection well, particularly those with poor impulse control and a great desire to play with a dog. Insensitively turning somebody away can create a number of problems: upsetting a vulnerable or explosive person, making the invited participants wary of the facilitator's ability to handle problems sensitively, and creating recruitment and retention problems for the program as the grape vine alerts prospective clients to avoid the insensitive facilitator.

Therefore, you must structure ways to dissuade outsiders humanely. If time and space permit, one possible solution is to let the agency's clientele visit with the animals for 10-15 minutes before the session starts. A lobby or yard, if available, would suffice – but not the meeting room. Moving an animal or two to a separate room is much easier than asking a potentially large number of people to leave a room they are already in. Transitions are difficult for children under the best of circumstances. It is hard for a child to say goodbye to a dog other children will continue playing with, particularly for a child who has already endured a number of losses.

Once you have considered and answered these questions, you can select the setting best suited for the goals and needs of your program, a setting that provides for the safety of the animals and people in your program.

The next step in creating a structurally sound program is to assemble and manage an effective staff and cadre of volunteers.

How do I screen, hire, train, and motivate qualified and safe staff and volunteers?

PROGRAMS PROVIDING SERVICES TO AT-RISK AND ABUSED OR NEGLECTED CLIENTS MUST BE ESPECIALLY CAREFUL TO SELECT STAFF AND VOLUNTEERS WITH GOOD JUDGMENT AND MATURE BOUNDARIES. That means they must recruit, screen and supervise carefully. Clients in these programs typically have had damaging experiences with adults who abused or neglected them. These clients may not have the social or emotional skills to protect themselves from inappropriate overtures from people in positions of authority. It is your responsibility as the program designer to make sure everyone who has contact with clients is able to relate appropriately to them.

Many people who are drawn to work with troubled children or rescued animals experienced abuse or neglect in their own childhoods. They have compelling motives to do this work, both to work through their own concerns and to "give something back." While community service is a vital part of therapy (see Chapter 4, pp. 76-78, and Chapter 5, pp. 103-104), people seeking to meet their own, and often urgent, needs may not have the necessary mastery and balance to subordinate their own concerns and focus objectively on the needs of their clients. This is not to say that people with troubled childhoods should not work or volunteer in treatment programs, humane education or animal-assisted therapy programs, but rather to stress the need to assess the impact of the candidate's past on current judgment and functioning. Such risk assessment should begin in the initial screening of prospective staff and volunteers, and continue as part of on-going supervision.

How do you assemble and supervise staff and volunteers who support the success of your program? Structure an approach to these five distinct aspects of staffing:

1. Screening,

2. Interviewing,

3. Training staff and volunteers,

4. Maintaining quality and motivation, and

5. Ensuring collaboration between social service and animal expert staff.

1. *Screening*

Deciding whom to bring into your program can be a time consuming and difficult task. Your program may require paid staff, volunteers, or both. In any case, screening is the first step of your staffing process. Screening serves two purposes. First, it ensures that the staff and volunteers you bring into your program will work safely with the clients. Second, it eliminates inappropriate people before you invest the time to interview.

Screening requires you to structure three pre-employment checks:

◆ Fingerprinting,

◆ Reporting statements, and

◆ Driving record checks.

Fingerprinting

Most states require that people working in responsible positions with children (teachers, day care providers, recreation staff, health care and mental health personnel as examples) pass a fingerprint check before beginning employment. Programs with high standards require that volunteers be fingerprinted as well. Fingerprints are submitted by the prospective employer to the State Department of Justice where they are compared with criminal and child abuse indices.

This screening bars people with known histories of abuse or neglect from having employment that involves responsibility for children and from gaining access to and responsibility for potential victims.

Reporting statements

Additionally, people working in responsible positions with children are required by state law to report reasonable suspicion of child abuse or neglect to the appropriate child protective agency. Because this is a legal requirement, or mandate, these people are called mandated reporters. At the beginning of their employment, their employers are required to have them sign a statement indicating awareness of and willingness to comply with the reporting laws. The employer must keep a signed statement in each employee's personnel file.

This screening attempts to ensure that signs of abuse or neglect will be reported promptly so that those in need of protection and assistance receive such services quickly.

Driving record checks

Programs that have staff or volunteers provide transportation for clients must also require a clearance from the Department of Motor Vehicles (DMV) and keep proof of automobile insurance on file. The program's liability insurance must address this aspect of the program as well. This screening increases the safety of participants while traveling to and from the program.

How can you use these three requirements to structure your screening? Although not all states require all program employees and volunteers to submit to these checks, you will strengthen your staffing and reduce your liability by requiring anyone interested in working with your program to go through the screening process.

How can this generalized approach help your program? First, this broad screening signals to all volunteers, staff, and participants that responsible behavior is expected of all affiliated with the program. Second, this policy can serve as a deterrent, discouraging those looking for opportunity to take advantage of easy victims from attempting to participate in your program. Third, broadening the screening requires little additional time and expense – usually the State Department of Justice will waive the fee to screen fingerprints for volunteers who will be alone with children – yet provides a considerable measure of protection and safety to those receiving services. And finally, such safeguards are likely to convince members of your board of directors, donors, and insurers of the commitment and integrity of your program.

On the other hand, this approach may raise concerns for you, particularly about requiring volunteers to undergo a rigorous screening process. To resolve these concerns, consider these options.

◆ *If you are concerned about a volunteer's ability to assess and therefore report risk,* consider requiring volunteers to report concerns to a staff member who will phone in the report, sign and submit required forms. The volunteer should still fill out an incident report but will not have to handle reporting requirements he or she may not be trained to manage.

◆ *If you are concerned that these requirements submit volunteers to legal and financial liability,* remember that mandated reporters have absolute immunity from suit. If the volunteer clearly documents a concern to a mandated reporter on your staff who makes the report promptly, your agency has met the statutory requirements to alert the appropriate child protective agency when reasonably suspicious of child abuse or neglect.

◆ *If you are concerned that volunteers will be offended by the paperwork and signing requirements,* structure positive ways to present this information to volunteers. When presented positively, the request for fingerprints and compliance with reporting laws can be seen as the program's commitment to provide safe and responsible services to potentially vulnerable clients. A positive explanation can also help volunteers understand the importance of their role in your program. Screened like paid staff, volunteers in your program will be treated with respect and responsibility comparable to permanent staff members and will be an integral part of a program with high standards. Your request will be persuasive if presented with sensitivity and tact. Consider the following language:

"We are committed to providing services of high quality to our clients and their families, and assuring them of a level of skill, responsibility and safety when they are with us. To that end, we ask that all staff and volunteers follow the procedures required by law of mandated reporters, namely to review a summary of the law describing the requirements for reporting suspected abuse and neglect, to sign a statement indicating awareness and willingness to comply with these reporting laws, either by reporting directly to the appropriate protective agency or requesting that a mandated staff member make the report, and to provide a set of fingerprints (which we send to the Department of Justice for clearance). We are eager to welcome you as a volunteer and trust that you share our commitment to assure our clients and their families that their safety and welfare are our highest priorities."

2. *Interviewing*

Screening is likely to eliminate some candidates. Some will not want to submit to the requirements; others will be screened out by the results. Those who are left are candidates for interviewing.

Volunteers as well as staff should be interviewed carefully before working with at-risk clients. Interviewing provides an opportunity to encourage the candidate's enthusiasm for the program, to assess the candidate's relevant skills and interests, and to screen out or direct away from contact with clients those people who would not be a good match for direct service programs with vulnerable populations. The interview should assess maturity, judgment, appropriateness, limits and boundaries of candidates, both volunteer and paid.

Interviews should be divided into two parts: informational and behavioral. The informational part of the interview comes first and is intended to collect basic factual information about the candidate. Describe your program to the candidate and discuss both its fundamental goals and specific ways of implementing them. Encourage the candidate to ask questions and point out roles and responsibilities he or she would enjoy taking on. If the candidate appears unsuitable at this point for any reason, do not continue with the interview.

If the candidate appears suitable after the informational section of the interview, move on to the behavioral section. In this part of the interview you will present questions intended to gain information about key behaviors, attitudes, or experiences critical to being an effective part of your program. These include questions about:

- Attitudes toward friendship and people in authority,

- Experiences with children, and

- Setting limits.

The answers to these questions provide a sense of how the candidate would be likely to behave in unstructured settings and how he or she might handle requests for favors or special attention (both appropriate and inappropriate) from clients. Here are a few questions that, when modified to fit the specifics of your program, might be useful in eliciting information about judgment and boundaries in a courteous and respectful manner.

Questions about attitudes toward friendship and people in authority

Questions like these will help you gauge the candidate's experience with and attitudes toward friends and authority figures.

"What in your past experience makes you particularly interested in a program like this one?"

"Clients in our program often relate to our staff members and volunteers as if they were friends. Please tell me about a situation in which you were perceived of as a friend."

Absent a recent death, divorce, or similarly ominous life event, the applicant should volunteer a recent and relatively casual and benign story involving a peer as an example of friendship. Intensity should be minimal, reflecting the level of conversation between the candidate and the interviewer. If the candidate has to go back 20 years to tell about a high school friendship, it may mean that he or she currently lives an isolated life and may bring too many needs for companionship to the position. If the candidate tells a story of a friendship with somebody much older or younger than him- or herself, perhaps he or she has difficulty establishing friendships with peers. A deeply emotional or dramatic story is inconsistent with the tenor of the conversation and likely with the expected role the candidate would assume in the program.

A candidate may recount an otherwise appropriate anecdote about a friendship with a child because he or she is applying for a position working with children. If that happens, go on to ask the next set of questions about experiences with children. Then ask for an anecdote about a friendship with a peer and one about attitudes toward authority figures. You might, for example, ask

"Some clients in our program think of staff and volunteers as people in authority. So, please give me an anecdote involving you and a person in authority."

The anecdote relating to a person in authority should reflect an understanding of the difficulties involved with and an ability to deal with authority with moderation and flexibility. The anecdote should focus on a relatively commonplace experience, perhaps with a parent, teacher, or boss and not suggest a particularly confrontational or combative interpersonal style.

Questions about experiences with children

A second area of questioning seeks to gain information about the candidate's experience with children, perhaps one similar to the clients served by the program. You might ask a question like

"Since you are interested in working with children, tell me about your experience with children."

Absent recent traumatic events in such a relationship, the anecdote should match the conversational tone of the interview in style and intensity. Needs to rescue or save, over-involvement, judgmental attitudes toward the child's parents, desires to have enormous influence in the child's life might be revealed – and are cause for reconsideration of the candidate's suitability for your program.

Questions about setting limits

Anyone who works in humane education or animal-assisted therapy programs must be or become skilled at setting limits. To understand a candidate's views about and experience with setting limits, you should explain that work with abused and neglected children can be draining and at times provocative or overwhelming. At such points, people tend to fall back on their own experiences. As you listen to the stories, ask how affection, limit setting, and discipline were handled in the candidate's family of origin. If the candidate is a parent, follow up with a question about how the candidate handles affection, limit setting, and discipline with his or her own children. Use questions like these:

◆ Where did you grow up?

◆ Tell me a few memories from your childhood.

◆ How was affection demonstrated in your family?

- How was discipline handled?

- How do you feel now about your family's way of handling affection and discipline?

- As a parent, how do you show affection to your child(ren)?

- As a parent, how do you discipline your child(ren)? (For those who do not yet have children,) How would you discipline your own children?

The purpose of this section of the interview is not to imply that people from abusive or negligent families of origin should be denied opportunities to work with at-risk children. Instead, the purpose is to suggest that people need to be aware of their likely first reactions and have a capacity to override them with better behavior. Let the candidate show both what he or she learned in childhood and how he or she has incorporated and modified those lessons as an adult. Descriptions of current behavior with his or her children that show inappropriate affection, poor boundaries, and overly harsh or lax discipline would be grounds to turn the candidate away.

Specific answers to any of these questions should not necessarily screen anybody in or out of a given program. Rather, use the anecdotes to gain a sense of the candidate's interpersonal style, ability to set and honor boundaries, and capacity to make responsible decisions when faced with potentially difficult, upsetting, and emotionally charged situations. Inappropriate answers, in either affect or content, should raise serious concerns that would lead to a more thorough assessment of the candidate's suitability for work with potentially vulnerable clients.

Not all areas of concern can be observed in a preliminary interview. Therefore, it is imperative, both for safety and for the quality of the program, that ongoing training and supervision be provided.

3. Training Staff and Volunteers

Once you have screened and interviewed candidates, you are able to select staff and volunteers who will create a safe environment for participants. To sustain this atmosphere, you must structure training designed to give volunteers and staff opportunities to continue to learn and grow, and to keep them from getting into situations they are not prepared to handle. Whether training is begun during the screening and interviewing phase or once you have completed hiring, new employees and volunteers need information and training on six basic issues:

- Mandated reporting of suspected child abuse or neglect,

- Boundary issues,

- Requests by clients for gifts, treats, or food,

- Transitions,

- Working with parents, and

- Setting realistic expectations.

The following sections provide suggestions of issues to cover as you design training in each of these areas.

Mandated reporting of suspected child abuse or neglect

Mandated reporting, covered during the initial screening, must be reviewed once work has started. Because some candidates will not be comfortable with reporting, effective training will review the reporting laws, provide specific examples of behaviors to report, and explore the volunteer or staff person's attitudes about reporting abuse and neglect. After basic training has been provided, assign supervisory staff to work with new employees and volunteers to make sure they neither overreact to family interactions nor ignore incidents that should be reported.

Boundary issues

Boundary issues are the most subtle and important aspect of the relationships between clients and staff or volunteers. New employees and volunteers must be trained to understand their role in the relationship, the problems that can be created when their role is not maintained, and the physical reserve required by their role.

What information is useful for new employees and volunteers as they conceptualize their role in the relationship with clients?

Humane education and animal-assisted therapy programs are not designed to create best friends, surrogate parents or rescuers for children. Instead, programs are designed to teach skills that will help families cope more effectively. Volunteers and staff are there to facilitate that process. They can be friendly – indeed, they must be – but their relationships are dictated by the requirements of the program. They are not the client's psychotherapist, social worker or benefactor. They must retain objectivity and clarity in the sessions. A trusting and meaningful relationship with the clients may develop, but it should be circumscribed by the roles they play in the session, with the volunteer or staff person providing support as the clients learn.

Even with this background, new employees and volunteers need to understand the problems created when this role is not maintained.

Staff members or volunteers who become too personally involved with clients may lose their ability to work appropriately in the program. Because the clients are likely to have a long history of intractable problems, a personally involved employee or volunteer in a single humane education or animal-assisted therapy program is not going to transform the client's life. Personal involvement violates appropriate boundaries, interfering with the objectivity and clarity required by the program and diffusing attention and effort from the program's and client's goals. Reviewing the program's goals and explaining the role an objective staff member or volunteer plays in supporting those goals can help new employees and volunteers recognize the importance of maintaining boundaries.

Training also helps inexperienced staff members and volunteers understand the special boundary issues important for abused and/or neglected children. This training helps explain why people cannot relate to these children in the same spontaneous manner that they do with their children, nieces, nephews or grandchildren. Instead, training should focus on the importance of behaving with respect and appropriate reserve toward all children involved in the program.

For example, touch may have a very different meaning to abused and/or neglected children than it has for others. Children who have been abused may fear that an arm around their shoulder might slide into an inappropriate caress, a raised hand might turn into a slap, or a hug might become a restraint. If the clients have been taught to report every physical contact they have with an adult, a boundary-crossing casual pat might end up with a full police investigation. If clients have been abused or neglected, they may have inappropriate boundaries, either becoming instantly affectionate with strangers or holding themselves at a distance, unable to tolerate any physical contact. In either case, training must help adults who work with clients respect their interpersonal style, model appropriate, affectionate but respectful relating, and sustain defined boundaries.

Requests by clients for gifts, treats, or food

Children and adults with poor boundaries may make requests that untrained staff or volunteers might find rude or covetous. As a result, training must help staff and volunteers understand their own assumptions about politeness and gratitude and recognize that clients may not share those assumptions. Training should also provide staff and volunteers with the skills to deflect inappropriate requests kindly. Prepare supervisory staff to help less experienced adults stay clear about their role and support them in saying no graciously to inappropriate requests.

Transitions

Children who have not had consistent parenting have trouble negotiating the boundaries between one activity and another just as they have trouble negotiating the boundaries between one person and another. They are particularly susceptible to tantrums while in transit between one place and another. They may become frantic when told that they have to stop doing something they enjoy or become withdrawn when told that it is time to start something new. Anticipating problems at transitions will keep volunteers and staff from becoming frustrated or impatient with clients who need their support, not their disapproval.

Teach inexperienced staff and volunteers the skills to help children manage transitions. This training should emphasize the importance of establishing a consistent routine for each session and sticking to it, announcing every activity clearly in advance, providing explicit expectations, making time for transitions, and clearly warning in advance the conclusion of each activity.

Working with parents

Staff and volunteers who are drawn to vulnerable children may forget that the parents of those children were vulnerable children themselves not too long ago. To work effectively with dysfunctional parents, staff and volunteers must learn to be proactive and supportive, not reactive or judgmental. Training can help staff and volunteers examine their own assumptions about the responsibilities of parents so they can work effectively with families in which the 12-year-old child is more mature than the 30-year-old parent or denigration is a routine style of relating. To understand and challenge their own assumptions, staff and volunteers need training in cultural sensitivity and in becoming aware of their own values so that they can respond appropriately in their supportive role in the program.

Any program that serves families with a history of violence must provide special training to keep staff and volunteers safe. Employees must develop strong conflict resolution skills and must learn to respond to provocative outbursts by adults with tactful, diffusing responses.

Setting realistic expectations

Finally, training can help you avoid the expensive and time-consuming problem of staff and volunteer turnover. If staff and volunteers are choosing to work with at-risk children and families because they want to be appreciated, they may find themselves disappointed, resentful, and burned-out within a few weeks. Screening should investigate their vulnerability to this issue; training should prepare them for the probability that their efforts will be taken for granted rather than appreciated by the clients, and support throughout the program should help them express any frustration or disappointment they have as the program goes on. This training will help you keep good employees and volunteers who might otherwise leave because of frustration and burnout.

4. *Maintaining Quality and Motivation*

Effective screening, hiring, and training are the foundation of high quality programs with motivated staff and volunteers. Screening and interviewing will redirect prospective staff and volunteers not ready to work with at-risk families and leave you with a pool of qualified candidates from which you will select your new recruits. Training prepares the new hires to provide safe, effective services for clients in your program.

Your next consideration is to maintain the quality of services and keep staff and volunteers motivated. The key to sustained quality and motivation is ongoing supervision. Ongoing supervision can best be structured around three core activities: session reviews, staff coaching, and group activities.

Build in time after each session to provide ample opportunity for staff and volunteers to review the session and discuss how it went. This means talking about whether or not the goals were achieved and how each person responded during the session. Did any of the clients have trouble with anything that was going on? Did staff and volunteers find themselves pleased or dismayed at the way the families responded? How can everyone fine-tune skills to facilitate the learning going on in the session? The more explicit the goals of a session, the more easily staff and volunteers can recognize whether progress has been made. These session reviews help staff and volunteers assess and improve the quality of their own work and stay focused on the program's goals. The reviews also allow supervisors to identify individuals who need additional training, support, or motivation.

A supervisor must keep careful track of how each person, paid or not, is feeling and behaving. Work with highly stressed families generates stress. Even very experienced therapists and social workers can find themselves burning out if they do not remember to process their responses to their work. Volunteers are especially vulnerable to burn out. They come with the highest expectations and often believe that they will make a profound difference very quickly. When the overwhelming forces at work in the lives of at-risk families become apparent, volunteers can become discouraged and feel like abandoning the project. At the other extreme, they can feel like exerting heroic efforts and saving the families on their own, either by seeing them after hours or giving them extravagant gifts and money or in some other way breaking the boundaries of their role.

Structured individual supervision and coaching are essential to sustaining the quality of your program and the motivation of your staff and volunteers. The session reviews offer one opportunity to hear and respond to feelings and behavior. In addition to the group de-briefings, structure other opportunities for each staff person and volunteer to discuss how he or she is feeling about the work. These meetings may not be weekly, but they should occur at least monthly, either in a support group or in an individual supervisory session. Finally, be sure to do a formal evaluation of each person annually. These evaluations should be conducted with volunteers as well as paid staff and should provide an opportunity to evaluate the program as well.

5. *Ensuring collaboration between social service and animal expert staff*

Every animal-assisted therapy program is designed differently but most rely on a variety of people trained in different disciplines. Animal control officers, animal trainers, therapists and educators are likely to view the same program from very different perspectives. An ideal program would have animal handlers and trainers who are as well trained in human behavior as they are in animal behavior. However, this is rarely the case. The animal control officer who brings dogs from the shelter to a class may have limited patience with hostile parents and impulsive children. The animal trainer may have little understanding of the special sensitivities of sexually molested children and may propose activities involving proximity with the animal that activate fear and discomfort.

One way to minimize problems that can surface from these different viewpoints is to develop and maintain a high degree of structure in your program. Plan all of the exercises in advance with defined goals, content, steps, and timing. Although you can always leave some room for last minute changes, this should only be a matter of choosing among pre-approved exercises, not introducing an entirely new trick or game. Because of the volatile nature of some of the families, do not allow for surprises in class.

Any program that integrates staff from separate disciplines is bound to have tensions between the assumptions of one group and the other. A second way to minimize these tensions is to make sure that every person who will have direct contact with clients has a sensitive understanding of the special issues typical of the particular client population and is prepared to deal with them in a way that is in keeping with the philosophy of your program.

Consider what you have already decided as you develop the structure of your program. You have selected a setting that encourages clients to attend and ensures a safe environment. You have screened, interviewed, trained, and provided for ongoing supervision of qualified, motivated staff and volunteers prepared to work respectfully with appropriate boundaries toward your program's goals. To complete the structure of your program, you need a way to select suitable participants, both animal and human.

How do I select a safe animal?

YOUR FIRST CHOICE IS A VERY FUNDAMENTAL ONE: WHICH TYPE OF ANIMAL SHOULD YOU USE TO ACHIEVE YOUR PROGRAM'S GOALS?

Most animal-assisted therapy programs focus on people's interactions with dogs. There are many reasons for this: dogs are personable animals, having been socialized for millennia. Many people keep dogs as family pets, so clients will likely have had some prior exposure to dogs. Dogs have been associated with therapy programs for decades, most notably service dogs for the blind and as hospital visitors, and more recently for many other therapeutic purposes as well. There are lots of dogs around, in homes and in shelters awaiting homes, so they are ready and usually eager candidates.

Some programs, however, focus their programs around other animals. Equine-assisted therapy programs have shown considerable promise. Children with orthopedic and developmental disabilities learn balance and torso control through riding; autistic children focus on something bigger and larger than themselves; timid and shy children develop confidence and self-efficacy atop a large and wondrous creature. However, horses are expensive to house and care for. The potential for injury also cannot be ignored. As a result, equine-assisted therapy programs are costly and comparatively rare.

Wild animals are the focus of programs that teach children to care for injured wildlife. These enriching programs require land, full time care for their resident animals and specialized veterinary care as well. The commitment of time and resources to the animals is year-round regardless of the number and frequency of participating children. To sustain these programs, considerable funding is required and additional effort must be made to establish and maintain working relationships with referring social service and probationary agencies as well as with wildlife and animal rescue groups.

Still other programs work with farm animals. Pigs and goats are used in some cases because they are good with snacks and easy to train with positive reinforcement. Making mud puddles for pigs and tolerating ubiquitous goat droppings increase tolerance for mess and acceptance of normal detritus.

School- and agency-based programs may not be able to take children to a humane farm for such exposure, though. Instead, the program designer may have to choose from small domestic animals other than dogs available at the animal shelter. Cats, for example, can be used in clicker training programs, and excellent materials are available (Pryor, 2001). But cats don't travel well and may be unable to focus in a strange room filled with especially curious and enthusiastic children. They also scratch and are more likely to trigger allergies than are dogs.

Selecting smaller animals, pocket pets and birds in particular, pose additional problems. First, children's and adults' likely prior experience with these animals is with their neglect in a cage in a classroom or at home. Moreover, at-risk and marginalized people feel caged-in enough without being confronted with an incarcerated bird or hamster to identify with and emphasize the point. Second, the desire to touch these small animals often overrides inchoate impulse control resulting in a bite or a scratch. Not seeing the animals' behavior as self-protective and motivated by fear, the clients perceive the animals as vicious and attacking. They may even respond by throwing the animal on the ground, either reflexively in response to being bitten or in retaliation.

At an absolute minimum, you must be able to guarantee the physical safety of every living being in the session. Caution being the better part of valor, it is wise to stick with large and sturdy animals until clients' self-restraint and understanding can be counted on even in the whiskered face of a nippy rodent. Availability, modest cost, practicality and canine enthusiasm for human interaction make dogs the most popular and appropriate choice for most humane education and animal-assisted therapy programs.

Whichever animal you choose will direct the structure you create for your program. Because most programs are structured around dogs, this section outlines those things you need to prepare for to safely and effectively integrate a dog into your program. Four issues are key:

1. Choosing between an owned therapy dog and a shelter dog,

2. Assessing suitability of shelter dogs for participation in humane education and animal-assisted therapy programs,

3. Minimizing risk, and

4. Anticipating and handling clients' responses to dogs.

1. Choosing between an owned therapy dog and a shelter dog

Two types of dogs can be used in your program: privately owned therapy dogs or shelter dogs. Although it may be tempting to opt automatically for the well cared for, well trained, therapy dog, both types of

dogs have much to offer. Your decision will dictate what you need to do to structure your program to achieve your goals in a safe, effective way.

Many visits to schools and intervention programs thrive through the dedication of a humane educator or volunteer who brings his or her own dog to the class or social service agency. There are many advantages to starting a program this way. First, the program is ready to begin as soon as the group and location are established. The leader of the group is highly motivated and eager to share a beloved dog with others. The dog will likely be docile, well trained and outgoing, tolerant of new situations and people, and a pleasure to be around. He or she will likely have completed a canine good citizen course and may carry his or her own insurance from the Delta Society which indemnifies dogs. (For more information about the Delta Society, call 1-800-869-6898 or access their website at www.deltasociety.org.)

There are, however, some disadvantages to using well cared-for, owned and cherished dogs. To start with, the dog likely has a better life, home and diet, more adequate health care and supervision and more enjoyable and positive companionship than the participants. This opens the possibility that a program facilitator may unwittingly make children feel they are worth less than a dog because the child's quality of life does not even live up to the standard enjoyed by the dog and established by the program as necessary for the responsible care of a dog. Additionally, many of the children will develop an attachment to the dog if the same dog comes each week for several weeks or months. When the program ends, those children will experience the loss of a living being they have come to care about, replicating the pattern of loss in their lives. Essential to empathic intervention with children whose short lives have been plagued by loss is protecting them from additional unnecessary losses.

Another difficulty with the owned and well behaved dog is that the children will not be able to learn the basics of dog training from a dog who readily and reliably sits when asked, comes when called, and waits politely for treats. Finally, a number of the children – those who did not form an attachment – may get bored if the same well-behaved dog comes week after week.

Other programs, such as the SHIP program (see Chapter 5, pp. 79-104), use shelter dogs primarily and focus on having clients train the dogs in the basics of good manners and behavior to increase their prospects for adoption. This emphasis on training gives clients opportunities to learn how to use positive reinforcement, communicate without yelling, elicit desired behaviors without coercion and break a task down into smaller and more manageable increments. It also appeals to their social conscience, giving the dogs the skills they need to be successful adoptees. Without drawing overt attention to the topic, facilitators are able to learn about and address the children's concerns regarding their own placements and future. The Texas SPCA and Project Pooch in Oregon bring shelter dogs to incarcerated youth for intense training. These well trained dogs are then placed in carefully chosen adoptive homes (Duel, 2000).

The programs using shelter dogs reach troubled families readily. The participants identify with the dogs' needs and uncertain future. They buy in to the goal of increasing adoptability through mastering impulsivity. Because of their eagerness to work with the dogs, they are open to instruction in the exclusive use of positive reinforcement to shape behaviors. They are reinforced by the dogs' progress and feel more efficacious as they master training skills, also taught exclusively through positive reinforcement. The emphasis on training and learning and the rotation of dogs as some get adopted reduce the risk of the therapy program's perpetuating the cycle of attachment and loss. Clients also generalize skills and build confidence through their successes with a number of dogs. Helping the dogs have better prospects for the future gives participants a safe way to consider their own futures more optimistically. Many programs encourage writing, artwork and volunteer activities as part of their enrichment or aftercare programs to solidify gains and weave them into the ongoing fabric of clients' lives.

Finally, the skills that each dog learns will contribute to its adoptability. Children in at-risk families are well aware of this. They identify with an animal who has been cast out, who is homeless and undervalued. They are moved by the knowledge that what they have taught the dog may actually help it find a home and family of its own. For many, this is the first time they themselves are aware of providing a social benefit to the outside world and they truly find that awareness reinforcing.

As with owned therapy dogs, shelter dogs present some disadvantages. Shelters may have a limited number of available dogs and occasionally no suitable dogs at all. Although appealing in the shelter, some dogs may not travel well, making them hard to work with at the program's site. In general, shelter dogs are likely to be less tolerant, flexible, and accommodating than owned dogs in a stable home. To overcome these problems, consider using shelter dogs primarily, but rely on an owned therapy dog as a back up, for a change of pace, or to show what advanced training looks like.

Exercise particular care for safety and risk management if you decide to use shelter dogs in your program and always have a safe alternative available to avoid disappointing a room full of budding dog training enthusiasts.

If you decide to use shelter dogs, you must have a structured protocol for selecting a suitable dog and for minimizing risk in your program. The following sections provide models for assessing suitability and minimizing risk when using shelter dogs in humane education and animal-assisted therapy programs.

Because owned therapy dogs do not present the same selection or risk issues, you may want to skip the next two sections if you have opted to use an owned therapy dog.

2. Assessing suitability of shelter dogs for participation in humane education and animal-assisted therapy programs

If you use shelter dogs in your program, you will need a structured approach to selecting suitable dogs. Donna Duford, a behaviorist with the San Francisco Department of Animal Care and Control, designed this suitability assessment for dogs participating in the SHIP program. The complete assessment is provided here; a shorter checklist is available in Chapter 7, pp. 120-124.

Suitability Assessment for SHIP Dogs

The selection of dogs for the SHIP Project should be done by someone with dog training experience and comprehensive knowledge of dog behavior. Experience with other forms of canine behavior and temperament evaluation is also helpful.

Safety is the primary concern when determining suitability of dogs for SHIP. Dogs should be friendly toward children and adults, have a high tolerance for sudden movement, noise and handling, and be comfortable in new environments. They must be very interested in treats without exhibiting guarding or competitive behavior around food or objects.

This series of tests does not a serve as a predictor of temperament. It is a tool for assessing suitability for a set of tasks required of SHIP dogs. There are many factors that affect behavior and behavior is constantly in flux. When testing and training SHIP dogs, be prepared for anything. Err on the side of caution and use common sense.

The following are guidelines only. This project is new and constantly evolving. These guidelines were created based on the population of adoptable dogs at the San Francisco Department of Animal Care and Control. These dogs have already passed a temperament assessment for adoptability. If you are working with an untested population, your evaluation should be much more comprehensive, and you should have a minimum of two people for safety. For in-depth treatment of and an easy-to-follow format for temperament testing shelter dogs, read *Great Dog Adoptions: A Guide for Shelters* by Sue Sternberg, published by The Latham Foundation in 2002.

General: Act like an average non-dog-savvy person. If you handle the dogs with the confidence of a handler, trainer, groomer, or veterinary professional, you may mask behaviors the dog may exhibit with the general public.

Equipment:

- ◆ Martingale collar
- ◆ 6' leash
- ◆ Fake hand
- ◆ Treats
- ◆ Clicker

History: Start with dogs with a known history of living with and liking children. If none is available, try to observe dogs as children walk through the kennel. Dogs who readily approach the front of the run with an open wag probably like children. Conduct the rest of the tests on these dogs first. If none of them pans out, or if you have no information about the dogs relating to children, move on to Affiliation, Round One with all dogs.

Affiliation, Round One: Walk through the shelter. Stop at each kennel and face the dog, using benign facial expression and body language. If the dog readily approaches you, he or she is a good First Round Pick. If he or she does not, talk to him or her in a friendly tone of voice. If he or she approaches, put him or her on your First Round Pick list as well. Dogs who do not approach may still be good candidates. Their behavior may be kennel-specific. If you see more obviously friendly dogs, test them first, and save the quiet dogs for back up.

Interest in Food: Have a second person do this test, if you can. If not, you can do it yourself, though it may influence the next test. Offer each of your First Round Picks a treat. Choose dogs who readily eat over dogs who are tentative.

For each dog who passes the preceding tests, continue with each individually.

Affiliation, Round Two: This part of the assessment should be done in a room new to the dog and relatively free from distractions. Testing outdoors is not ideal, but if you have no other option, you will need to allow more time for the dog to settle and tune in to you.

If you can, have a helper bring the dog to you, on a leash. If you must get the dog yourself, do so with as little interaction and handling as possible, then go to your test area. Sit or stand silently, holding the leash, and observe the dog. Ideal candidates orient and initiate interaction immediately, good candidates within 30 seconds, acceptable ones in under a minute.

Watch for these positive behaviors:

- Friendly approach with soft eye contact,

- Open or circular tail wag,

- Leaning, nudging, licking.

After the dog starts to interact with you, talk to and pet him or her. Observe the dog's reaction. Positive behaviors include:

- Prolonged physical contact,

- Increased tail wagging,

- Soft eye contact,

- Licking,

- Leaning.

Any dog who does not exhibit any of these behaviors is not suitable for SHIP.

If you are in a distracting environment, allow the dog more time. Interact with the dog in a friendly manner before proceeding to the next test by petting and talking to him or her for 30 to 60 seconds.

Tolerance for Handling: Do the following tests, in order. Stop any time you feel uncomfortable. If at any time you feel uncomfortable, the dog is not suitable for SHIP.

◆ Pet the top of the dog's head and down the back.

◆ Pet down the dog's back and tail, pulling the tail firmly and evenly (no yanking).

◆ Firmly grab the dog's back.

◆ Firmly grab a handful of skin on the dog's flank.

◆ Lift the dog's lips as if to look at the teeth. If the dog pulls away, let go. Repeat five times.

◆ Poke the dog – with the pressure of a child – on the head and on various parts of the body.

Ideal candidates will have no reaction, or only look in your direction. On the lip portion, if the dog pulls away each time, but does not escalate the behavior, this is fine.

Good candidates may flinch, startle or get slightly excited, but recover quickly and seek your attention – as in the Affiliation tests – within a few seconds.

Tolerance for Movement and Noise: Do kid-like things.

◆ Run,

◆ Squeal,

◆ Yell,

◆ Point in the dog's face,

◆ Wave your arms in the air,

◆ Wave your hands in front of the dog's face,

◆ Click the clicker once, pause, then click a few times.

Ideal candidates will seem unfazed, remaining sociable with you. Good candidates may get slightly excited or apprehensive, but without barking, chasing or mouthing, and should settle and connect with you when you stop.

Resource Guarding: Feed the dog a few treats sequentially from your hand. Drop a dozen treats on the floor, then try to move them with a fake hand. Try to push the dog's face away from the treats. Ideal candidates will stop eating to look at you softly or continue eating in a relaxed manner. Good candidates may eat slightly faster, but not race you to the food. Dogs who race you, resist your pushes, get stiff, growl, snarl, snap, or bite are not suitable.

Stress in New Environments: During the testing, notice the dog's reaction to the environment. Ideal candidates appear confident. Good candidates may be cautious at first, but begin to relax and act more confidently quickly.

Stress in Vehicles: If the dogs are to be transported, take them for a brief ride to make sure they are not overly stressed by car travel.

Dog-to-Dog Behavior: If you will be using more than one dog and they will be in the same space while training or waiting turns, test them for friendliness with each other. Depending on your comfort level and how much experience you have with dog-to-dog introductions, you may introduce them on opposite sides of a fence, on leash, or off leash in a safe area. Ideal candidates are friendly, but not preoccupied with each other.

Other Considerations

- _Exuberance:_ Exuberant dogs are fine in general, and they are great for demonstrating the power of positive reinforcement and incremental training for learners lacking impulse control and attention span. Exuberant dogs who can focus on treats are great. Avoid exuberant dogs who cannot settle. Keep your client population in mind. If all of your clients are afraid of dogs, you may want a dog with a little less oomph.

- _Barking:_ Avoid overly vocal dogs. Incessant barking can be scary for some people, and can inhibit training. Dogs who bark occasionally and/or only at specific triggers like other dogs running by the kennel, may be fine in the training setting.

- _Wounds and Scars:_ If possible, avoid dogs with obvious wounds or scars, or with cropped ears or tails. This can be disturbing.

- _Mouthiness:_ Dogs who are mouthy in play or out of frustration are not suitable for SHIP.

Food Grabbing: If possible, avoid dogs who grab the treats hard. If this is not possible, instruct the clients to feed the dog with an open hand or by dropping the treat on the floor.

Be Prepared to Shift Strategies: Even the most carefully tested dogs may exhibit unexpected behaviors in new settings. For example, a dog who is calm in the test setting may become stressed or agitated in a new place with a group of strangers. Dogs who take food gently during the test may get grabbier in a more stimulating environment. Be aware of and prepared to respond to changes in the dog's behavior during the training session, and change your training plan accordingly to make the session positive for dogs and people alike.

3. Minimizing risk when using shelter dogs in humane education and animal-assisted therapy programs

Even if you have carefully assessed the shelter dogs and found one suitable for your program, it is important to structure policies and practices that minimize risk. Edith Markoff designed this risk management protocol for the SHIP program in Cincinnati. You can adopt this protocol or use it as a model to structure your own approach to minimizing risk.

— Risk Management for Dogs in the SHIP Program —
On-Site Management

Dogs will be on lead and under the supervision of an animal evaluator at all times. Animal evaluators will be watching and will intervene to make sure that the animals are not treated inappropriately or reacting inappropriately.

When dogs arrive at the training site, they will be evaluated for signs of stress resulting from having been transported. Dogs unable to recover quickly from the stress of the vehicle ride will not be brought into the training session.

Dogs will be continuously monitored for signs of stress throughout the training sessions. Dogs showing significant stress levels will be removed from the training area. Signs of significant stress include, but are not limited to: refusal to take food, excessive licking, excessive barking, excessive yawning, ears flattened back, tail tucked or very stiff, raised hackles.

Group sizes will be small; each group will be supervised by a professional involved in the intervention.

The focus of the training will be on teaching the dogs behaviors such as sitting, lying down and targeting. Treats will be dropped on the floor rather than fed to the dogs. There will be no boisterous interaction with the dogs.

Interactions with the dogs will take place for only about 30 minutes during each one-hour session, decreasing the possibility that the dogs will become stressed.

4. Anticipating and handling clients' responses to dogs

You've decided to work with shelter dogs, and you have structured ways to select suitable dogs and minimize risk. Or maybe you have decided to work with an owned therapy dog. In either case, you are almost ready to move forward. One last step remains before you begin to define the content of your program.

The reality of humane education and animal-assisted therapy programs is that, no matter which type of dog you select, at least some of your clients will be afraid. Most clients will have had bad experiences with dogs – pit bulls guarding homes or drug labs in dangerous neighborhoods, aggressive dogs jumping and biting, or maltreated dogs lunging against chains in back yards. In many instances, these scary dogs were large and black, creating a general sense of vulnerability in the presence of large, black dogs.

In addition, clients will have experienced abuse, neglect, or violence and may have seen these behaviors inflicted on their own pets as well. Because of these abusive experiences and their own fear, clients may react to the program's dogs in ways that appear unpredictable.

In many cases, the facilitators do not understand these responses. They may, in fact, provoke some negative behaviors by the activities they present, the way they handle the dog, or the way they respond to client's behaviors.

An effective, safe program needs facilitators who can anticipate and respond appropriately to clients' experiences with and responses to dogs. With structured approaches, staff and volunteers can help clients move past their fear and develop new, more positive behaviors both with the dogs and with others.

This section provides guidance to help anticipate and respond to clients' experiences with dogs. You will find guidance covering six common issues:

◆ Overcoming fear, especially of large, black dogs,

◆ Dealing with clients' reactions to animals' exposed genitalia and fears of mutilation,

◆ Preventing predator/prey dynamics,

◆ Responding to housebreaking accidents,

◆ Responding to fears of abandonment, and

◆ Responding to questions about euthanasia.

Overcoming fear, especially of large, black dogs

Because clients come to your program with fears of dogs, particularly large, black dogs, structuring your program to respond to these fears is critical. Although it may seem logical to use small dogs with a group afraid of large dogs, large dogs are preferable in treatment programs for a number of reasons. First, clients are less likely to rush at and crowd large dogs. Large dogs are not as apt as small dogs to feel overwhelmed, or to become defensive, bark, nip, or lunge. Second, overcoming the fear of large dogs creates a first milestone of progress. Clients can be taught to read the dogs' body language, recognize their comfort zone, and learn to approach slowly and respectfully. Large dogs given room by clients create a safe learning environment. This lesson also helps people remain calm when passing a large dog on the street or in a park.

Susan Phillips, then the social worker for a housing project in San Francisco's Tenderloin, the city's most dangerous and crime-ridden neighborhood, said large visiting dogs from the city shelter "gave many of the inner-city children living here their first chance to interact with animals and learn about touching and being touched in a friendly manner. Through this program, the children learned about the habits and natural habitats, the likes *and* dislikes of other creatures, and, most importantly, they learned respect for life. Because of this program, we were able to introduce the concepts of personal boundaries, good touch and bad touch, to very young children in a manner that made sense to them" (Loar, 1996, p. 7).

Her colleague, John Chan, added, "the children have learned that the animals are not objects, but have their own nature and sensitivities. In the beginning many lunged at the animals, forcefully petting them, generating fear in the animals. And when the animals were afraid, so were the children. Now they have learned that animals have their private space which must be approached respectfully, and that touching must be sensitive to the animals' feelings. They have become more aware of the things they can do to frighten and hurt these animals. In turn, these same lessons can be transferred to themselves and how they would like to be touched. That is so important in this Tenderloin environment" (Loar, 1996, p. 7).

People fear black dogs disproportionately. This is true for people of all races and ethnicities. In fact, it is not just a matter of dogs. The color black has been associated with danger and evil across time and culture. It is reflected in myths and legends, in religious symbolism, psychological dualism and dread of the dark side, and in popular culture. The darker, or blacker, a dog, the more likely the dog is to evoke fear in people, even if he or she is a gentle and affectionate creature.

SHIP's training team discussed the participating families' reactions and related them to the bigger issue of racism and how the color black had been viewed by people of all races and ethnicities. The team decided to share this with a class the next time it happened. A 75 pound black hound mix was introduced to a SHIP class that had been meeting for more than a month in a San Francisco shelter for homeless families. Participants in this group had learned basic training skills and were quite capable of reading canine body language. They were also past initial fears of meeting new dogs, and had developed trust and rapport with the facilitators. The shelter dog arrived wagging his tail enthusiastically, with his ears relaxed and flapping.

Children screamed and hid behind their parents who were themselves backing away as far as the room's limited space would allow. All asked anxiously if the dog would bite. In the preceding weeks, the adults had not exhibited much fear or ever asked about biting with any of the ten other dogs who had come.

The facilitator calmly reminded the group that all the dogs were temperament tested before being selected for the program. The participants, unreassured and even more anxious, asked again if the dog would bite. The facilitator sat with the dog close beside her until the participants felt less threatened. Then she asked why this dog seemed so frightening. One adult commented on his size. A child said that he looked mean. The leader validated their concerns. "He is big and maybe he looks a bit scary, but what do you notice about his body language?" Participants began to relax and observe his relaxed ears and wagging tail.

The facilitator then shared her observation that people tended to be afraid of black dogs, especially big ones. It was a rare opportunity for a Caucasian facilitator to discuss racial prejudice and attitudes based on blackness with a group of African American, Hispanic and mixed-race clients. She asked the group if this might be connected to racism in society, using them as the experts in the discussion but also bringing in examples from myths and popular culture. The group was quick to see the comparison and – after a spirited discussion – all were ready to start working with the dog and continued to ask about the dog's well being in the remaining weeks of the class.

Anticipating the fear of large, black dogs allows you to structure decisions about which dogs to bring into the session, which milestones to work toward, and how to handle clients' responses appropriately. It may also provide powerful teachable moments to bridge racial gaps and broaden multi-cultural awareness.

Dealing with clients' reactions to animals' exposed genitalia and fears of mutilation

Another consideration, one of particular concern for victims of sexual abuse, exploitation or rape, is the animals' exposed genitals which are visible and which the animals may lick during the session. People used to being around dogs and other animals take for granted that the animals are naked and their genitals visible. They therefore may fail to realize how provocative and even threatening victims of sexual abuse may find animal nudity, grooming and other normal behaviors like dogs rolling on their backs to stretch or have their stomachs rubbed. The inexperienced group facilitator may not realize the fears and flashbacks that might be triggered by having the group teach the dog to roll over.

Neutered dogs elicit comments, especially from boys who identify anxiously with the altered animal. Their questions range from concerns about pain, "How much did it hurt?" to those about masculinity, "Doesn't neutering hurt their pride?" "What about his manhood?" and responsible parenting, "Do you have to do it? What about all the unwanted puppies...?"

Other evidence of mutilation, including scars, missing parts of ears and other evidence of fighting, and cropping of ears or tails may also trigger anxious reactions. People with post traumatic stress disorder (see above, p. 13) are particularly prone to personalize and feel endangered by such evidence of mutilation. Gang initiations may involve human scarification or injuring, maiming or killing an animal – or even a person – with the result that gang members, aspiring gang members, and family and neighbors of gang members may also react with fear and horror when confronted with physical damage evocative of gang rites.

Responses to an animal's exposed genitalia, neutered state, and physical scars are predictable in humane education and animal-assisted therapy programs. Staff and volunteers must be prepared to handle these responses to create a safe environment for all.

Preventing predator/prey dynamics

Another concern is that animals may evoke a predator/prey response in youthful and adult clients who have become abuse-reactive or offending (see Chapter 1, pp. 14-16). If a small animal is used in the program, the animal, naked, smaller than the human, and submissive to the human, may evoke the predator/prey dynamic that the client found arousing in the past with human and/or animal victims.

Naïve clinicians sometimes think bringing a friendly and gentle dog into a session with a youthful offender will provide an opportunity to teach gentle, affectionate touching without considering whether the dog might be of similar size to the child victim, might trigger feelings of power over another potential victim, might trigger sexual arousal between its nudity and responsiveness to touch, and might cause a retaliatory response if it tries to withdraw from the client.

Nancy Craig, VMD, a veterinarian in Pacifica, CA, requested social services for a mother and her 7-year-old child, the child having injured a rabbit. She described the situation as follows:

"The client arrived, a woman with her young son in tow, the rabbit in a cardboard box.... I asked what had happened. The woman explained that her son had gotten angry at the rabbit the night before – the rabbit had scratched him – and he had thrown the rabbit to the ground. Three times....

"Then, the mother requested that I euthanize the rabbit in the exam room, in front of her son, so he would witness the result of his anger. The son...seemed oblivious to the import of this request. I, on the other hand, was now totally unnerved, certain that I needed not only time but help for both the mother and the son.

"I bought time. I suggested to the mother that she leave the rabbit to be examined by a colleague, due to arrive later that morning, who had more expertise in rabbit medicine. Although I expected intransigence, the woman easily – gratefully? – acquiesced to the delay" (Craig and Loar, 1998).

Dr. Craig promptly referred mother and son to a social worker who learned that the family was pet sitting and had no prior experience with animals, that the mother had shooed the curious child away from the rabbit a few times for being too rough with it and for misinterpreting the rabbit's attempts to protect itself. The boy had not immediately told his mother that he had hurt the rabbit. Instead, she noticed it was not moving when she went to feed it in the evening, which led her to confront her son. And he initially lied about having hurt it. When the mother arrived at Dr. Craig's office the next morning, she was furious as well as scared by the boy's aggression and seeming callousness to the animal's suffering.

Further inquiry by the social worker into the child's other experiences with life and death led the mother to confide that the child's father had committed suicide when the child was two years old. They had received counseling at the time but none in the past five years. The mother was amenable to further treatment that would culminate in a visit to the local humane society jointly facilitated by the therapist and humane society's behaviorist to focus on safe and gentle handling of animals (Craig and Loar, 1998).

Safe interactions between volatile clients and animals have structure and focus. Teaching a client to use positive reinforcement to elicit appropriate behaviors in the animal will keep the interaction on track and allow the client to feel masterful and efficacious in more constructive and less arousing ways. Chapter 5 is devoted to the implementation of these principles.

Responding to housebreaking accidents

It is not uncommon even for well-housebroken dogs to have accidents during sessions. They may not have been walked just before the meeting, especially if the group meets in a dangerous neighborhood; they may have an upset stomach or diarrhea from the stress of the trip, the number of new people in the room and the novelty of the setting; they may have gulped a lot of water along with the treats they were earning during the session.

Just as common as the accident itself is a thunderous overreaction by the human participants. Drawing on their own histories of humiliation for wetting the bed in childhood, the clients – adults as well as children – become anxious, distressed at what might happen next, and lash out at the hapless dog with harsh and demeaning language. Watching the person responsible for the dog quietly clean the mess up and calmly return to the activity shows an alternative to the abusive response familiar to the clients. Indeed, spontaneously taking the accident in stride, tidying up and moving on, compellingly models appropriate behavior. It may be one of the most therapeutic moments for the clients, clearly showing better ways of behaving without criticizing or finding fault with anybody.

Responding to fears of abandonment

Plagued by longing for physically or emotionally absent parents, troubled children readily identify with the plight of animals in shelters awaiting adoption or newly placed in foster or permanent homes. They ask numerous and detailed questions of people caring for these animals, such as "Why isn't he with his mother?" "Why didn't his original (human) family keep him?" "What will happen to her if you can't find a home for her?" "What if you decide you don't want her any more?"

Children too afraid to voice these concerns about their own predicaments will interrogate the people in charge of the animals with rigor, urgency and thoroughness. Their questions should be answered realistically and with a small measure of optimism. A short while later in more confidential settings, the children's therapists should participate in these discussions. The children need the opportunity to address their concerns about what the future holds for them.

Responding to questions about euthanasia

Most people realize that animal shelters euthanize animals. And children are no exception. They may worry that animals they have worked with and enjoyed will fail to be adopted and face euthanasia – and this does happen in some cases. But many are talking more about themselves and their desensitization to death. This is especially likely to be true if they talk glibly about friends, neighbors or relatives who have died, particularly if they have died as a result of family or community violence. Many troubled youth truly do not expect to grow up, and this is as realistic as it is pessimistic for inner-city adolescents. Called terminal thinking (Garbarino, 1999; Butterfield, 1995), this sense that the future is limited and unpromising thwarts therapeutic efforts. Why struggle and work hard for a non-existent future? Facilitators must plan ahead so they will be ready with constructive responses to seemingly cavalier and/or despairing comments about euthanasia specifically and death more generally. Chapters 4 and 5 (pp. 73-74 and 95-96) present ways to encourage clients to believe in the possibility of a more promising future and to take practical steps in that direction.

You have a setting; you have trained staff and volunteers, and you have chosen a dog. Now it is time to select suitable participants.

How do I select suitable participants?

THE RIGHT PROGRAM WITH THE WRONG PARTICIPANTS WILL FAIL JUST AS A POORLY DESIGNED PROGRAM WITH SUITABLE PARTICIPANTS WILL FAIL. Participants must be those who can benefit from the goals your program seeks to achieve and who can participate without putting others in the group at risk. Selecting suitable participants is a five step process:

1. Creating your framework,

2. Deciding whom to invite,

3. Deciding the size of the group,

4. Screening for safety, and

5. Making it easy for people to participate.

1. Creating your framework

Before you can select your participants, you must make some basic decisions for your program: which problem to tackle, whom to partner with, and what administrative and financial arrangements you need to complete before getting started. This section provides guidance on these issues.

Selecting the problem to tackle

A common beginner's mistake is trying to take on the world. Start with a small and manageable problem so you can make a difference while learning from your initial and inevitable mistakes.

Do you work in an animal shelter that has a barn with a couple of permanent and docile residents who would be amenable to grooming and clicker training by children? Great – then you must find an educational or therapeutic program nearby that supports the idea and can screen, select, supervise AND transport these few children for an agreed-on number of weeks.

Are you an educator or therapist who thinks your students or clients would blossom with the opportunity to work with animals? Then, you must locate a humane educator, animal behaviorist, clicker trainer or other "animal person" who also has an interest in relating to your clients.

At the outset, set small programmatic goals (getting people to show up at the beginning and leave at the end; everybody behaving safely around people and animals; having and cleaning up after a snack) and make big compromises in the interests of the program's long-term viability. For example, you might begin with three or four mildly learning disabled 10-year-old children who would love and benefit from learning to clicker train a dog for paying attention and developing impulse control around food instead of a class of a dozen or more autistic teenagers whose behavior around animals is unpredictable.

Nothing feels worse than hosting a party and having nobody come. Instead of starting with an elaborate program, begin by selecting a handful of clients most likely to benefit from the service you can offer and to attend the sessions. Stay with small and manageable problems until you have built expertise and a stable multidisciplinary team of human and animal service providers.

This team will be the foundation of your program, no matter which problem you choose to address and which goals you set. Successful animal-assisted therapy programs are staffed by two types of professionals: the ones who know how to work with the animals and the ones who know how to work with the people. If you are the animal professional, you will need to find a human services counterpart. And if you are the human services professional, you will need to find an animal professional counterpart. The success of your program depends on finding an effective partner and forging a good working collaboration. Each of you must keep a protective eye out for your charges and be ready to intervene as necessary. The team must show mutual respect and a willingness to learn from and defer to each other.

This is not as easy as it sounds. Animal professionals often elect to work with animals because they do not want to work primarily with people. You need not check the animal behaviorist's tolerance for handling as extensively as you would the animal's, but you must gauge personableness and suitability for work with trying humans, both children and adults. And human services professionals may come to the program with no experience, interest, or aptitude in working with animals. They too must be gauged for suitability to work with animals.

Whether you are the animal or human services professional, you will need to attend to numerous administrative and financial logistics before you begin your program. You will need your director's approval, proof of adequate insurance from both agencies' carriers, consents from parents and guardians for clients to participate and be videotaped and photographed, and perhaps even permission from the juvenile court. You will need to draft a memorandum of understanding clearly outlining who in which agency will do what, for how long, and how expenses will be covered. You will also need to do cross-disciplinary training for staff and volunteers of both agencies so everybody buys in to the basic concept of the program and appreciates the constraints and safety concerns of their professional counterparts. Samples of program announcements, consent forms, volunteer agreements and court permission are provided in Appendix 1.

If all of this seems overwhelming, consider the advice offered at the beginning of this section. Start small. Consider partnering with a well established and stable agency even if the population or problem it addresses is not your first choice. Given the financial and staffing uncertainties that plague many non-profit agencies, partnering will give you an opportunity to learn the ropes with a safety net.

2. *Deciding whom to invite*

Most programs serve one of two groups. They either work with children or they work with families. Both groups can benefit from humane education and animal-assisted therapy programs, and both present programmatic challenges. Deciding whether to serve children or families will influence the way in which you structure your program.

Serving children

The majority of humane education and animal-assisted therapy programs (other than those that take animals to hospitals and nursing homes) work with children. This is easy because children are captive audiences in schools, recreational programs, after-school and summer camp programs. Services also can be scheduled during the day rather than having to rely on evening and weekend hours when parents would be able to attend also. Age-appropriate lessons in pet care and responsible treatment are common components of these programs.

There are risks to offering appealing humane programs to children in the absence of their parents. Without the input of their parents, children can decide they are less valued by their families than the animals they meet in the program. Alternatively, they may regale parents with enthusiastic stories of wonderful experiences with animals and people. Deprived and needy parents often resent the enriching opportunities given to their children but not to them when they were young. This resentment can damage rapport between parents and their children, and even become dangerous if the child challenges the parents' values or actions, calling them inhumane, a word learned in the resented program. Unless the entire family grows in humane values and skills, children may actually be at greater risk of harm at home as a result of growth in the animal-assisted therapy program.

Serving families

Children live in families, not with their therapist or humane educator. The most meaningful and influential relationships children have are with their parents. A wonderful hour a week with kind people and enjoyable animals is simply not enough to offset the contradictory experience of daily harshness at home. Effective change is respectful of the parents' deficits and prior history of deprivation; it enriches parents and creates an atmosphere of sufficient abundance that even needy parents have enough to share with their children. Generosity from the parent, not from the therapist, is the hallmark of family-based treatment. It allows the child to grow as a person and as a family member without increasing risk at home or putting the child at odds with family or community values.

Getting families to come is an arduous and draining task, though. Sessions need to be scheduled when parents are available, times usually inconvenient for the staff who would prefer to be at home nurturing their own families in the evening or on a Saturday afternoon. Parents will require more cultivating than children, for whom the presence of the animals is usually sufficient to evoke their enthusiasm.

Many people find it hard to show respect for parents who have been harsh or abusive with their children. They prefer to work with children exclusively, and avoid the larger complications of the children's attachment even to abusive or negligent parents. However, these are the people closest and most important to the child in question. Lasting change comes from increasing the potential for the child to thrive within his or her family.

3. Deciding the size of the group

People learn best by doing rather than watching, so groups need to be small enough that everybody can participate most of the time. If the parents are as needy as their children, they must also get at least as many turns as their children do. Thus, a group of six to eight people (two, three, or four families depending on the number of people in each family), two dogs, a human services and an animal professional would be large enough to mix and match the subgroups. This would provide for enough people even with erratic attendance while still maintaining a responsible staff/client ratio and small human/dog ratio.

4. Screening for safety

Just as you screen the animals for behaviors that might emerge in a session, so you must also assess your clientele in order to choose appropriate activities and anticipate behavioral problems that may come up. Safety of the people and animals depends on thorough assessment, appropriate precautions and the ability to act quickly and effectively if things begin to heat up.

Chapter 7: Assessing Risk provides a number of assessments you can use to assess your clientele. Boat's inventory of animal-related experiences and Lockwood's animal thematic apperception test cards help you assess people's attitudes toward and treatment of animals. Loar's family risk assessment can be used to gauge risk to all living beings in the home, and Eckert's and Lockwood's dangerousness indices assess more troubled treatment candidates. All these tools will help you determine the suitability of participants for your program as well as highlighting problems likely to emerge as your participants work with the animal, the facilitators, and other participants.

Before you can decide which assessments to use, you must understand what you are assessing and know what to look for. The behaviors you will see in your program are likely to be symptomatic of those in the home; what you see in the program may simply be the tip of the iceberg. How do you know what to look for? This section provides an overview of risky behaviors and their impact on others.

Understanding and recognizing attitudes, risk, and dangerousness

All dependent living creatures have basic physical and affiliative needs. Caregivers must provide patience and protective responses so that these needs can be expressed. If a caregiver has limited skills or resources and is overwhelmed, any dependent being may be at risk for harm. Several indicators may suggest endangering behaviors. These include attitudes, behavioral cues, emotional context, condition of the home, and treatment of animals.

To understand the level of risk posed by an over-extended caregiver with limited skills, assessments must elicit attitudes and behaviors that could indicate danger. These can be identified through the following questions: What are the caregiver's capabilities? What demands does the parent/caregiver experience? Are attitudes indicating risk present? These can include disposability ("it's only a dog"), minimization ("she'll be all right, I had it much worse when I was a kid"), rationalization ("he won't learn any other way"), and justification ("she wet her pants because she is lazy"). Assessments must also take care not to minimize or ignore the cruelty or neglect of an animal by a pet owner. Such neglect would not only allow the continued and unchecked maltreatment of that animal and of any additional animals the person may acquire but also put humans at risk who exhibit comparable behaviors and make similar demands on the caregiver.

Identifying these behaviors is important because the behaviors are unlikely to affect only one person or animal – they can compromise the safety of any potential victim. If one victim is removed from the home, other targets may surface, thereby increasing the risk for other potential victims in the family or neighborhood. Since victims can rotate, abuse can be a combination of bad luck, bad timing, proximity, and availability, as well as individual characteristics that determine the hierarchy and likelihood of victimization.

Behavioral cues also serve as indicators of endangering behaviors and risk. Behavioral cues of the abusive or negligent caregiver are similar whether the one at risk is an animal, a child, an elder, or a person with a disability. These indicators include: a history of abuse or neglect in the caregiver's own childhood; the use of harsh discipline or rigid or inappropriate rules; a lack of knowledge about developmentally appropriate norms and the need for flexibility as well as boundaries; judgmental interpretation and cruel treatment of problematic behaviors; abuse of alcohol or drugs; overuse or inappropriate use of medication or physical restraints to control or punish; and restricting access to the outside or to other people.

The emotional context in abusive families often includes harshness; blaming and belittling; being cold and rejecting; failing to support, encourage or express positive values; being inconsistent and unpredict- able; being uninterested in or trivializing the problems; and failing to recognize the victim as a separate being with worthy wants, needs, and interests. In essence, the parent or caregiver fails to regard the other as separate, and fails to respond to his or her plight or vulnerability with compassion and empathy.

The condition of the home may also flag negligence or abuse. Negligent homes tend to be filthy, chaotic, unsanitary and unsafe. They may not contain nutritious food for any resident, regardless of age or species. The family is apt to be isolated from relatives and neighbors, and cut off from the environ- ment. Curtains maybe draped over the windows during the day and household members may rarely venture outside.

Animals may be the barometer of risk and endangering behavior, an indicator that a family needs help. An animal's requirements are more straightforward than the subtleties of bonding between parent and child; if the animal's needs are not being met, other household members may also have unmet needs. The plight of the animal may be more readily observed by neighbors, both because the animal goes outside unclothed so that starvation and injuries are visible and because it may howl and disrupt the quiet of the neighborhood when harmed or neglected. Moreover, people are more willing to report the maltreatment or neglect of an animal than of a child. With children, people tend to want to avoid interfering in someone else's family and may wonder what the child did to provoke the parent. Indeed, the role of the animal in troubled families may be to elicit intervention.

Endangering behaviors are often triggered by the behavior of others. This is not to say that victims cause abuse, but that when violent, neglectful, or abusive people interact with others, things may happen to trigger the abusive behavior. Someone with little tolerance for noise may be set off by a baby's cry, while someone with rigid views about neatness may be set off by a household item out of place. Understanding endangering behaviors and their impact requires a risk assessment of the interaction between the behaviors and the triggers.

Unfortunately, most parents spank their children as part of routine discipline, especially when their children are toddlers and pre-schoolers (Straus, 1994). What makes the "terrible twos" so terrible and so apt to elicit abusive behaviors is the confluence of a number of trying and seemingly contradictory factors:

◆ the child may be highly mobile, relentlessly energetic, and need constant supervision;

◆ the child may be noisy, crying or whining frequently, or banging things while playing;

◆ the child may be demanding, resistant, defiant or disobedient;

◆ the child may damage or break things, or make a mess;

◆ power struggles may develop over eating and other matters of self-regulation, and

◆ the child is not yet toilet trained.

This combination of energy (the child's mobility, demands, and resistance) and vulnerability (still in diapers and/or needing constant supervision) too often pushes parents beyond their limits. Throughout childhood, this mixture of active, oppositional, and/or messy behaviors puts children at risk of maltreatment by their parents and other providers of care.

Animal abuse tends to be triggered by many of the same behaviors as child abuse. A cute puppy is also a busy and energetic puppy needing supervision and activity. Animals bark and howl, especially when ignored or left alone too much. They can be destructive: chewing, digging, and jumping on furniture or people. They eat food left on tables or counters and may turn away from their own rations. Housebreaking problems are common triggers of abuse.

Elder abuse and abuse of people with disabilities stem from some of the same provocations. Limited activity may lead to boredom, frustration, complaining and other irritating behaviors, and these may create emotional and physical stress for caregivers. Incontinence is often the last straw that brings on abuse. It is also the most common reason people institutionalize their aging relatives.

Comparable behaviors can place children, elders, dependent adults, and animals at risk: the need for care and supervision; the level of activity involved in their care; noise (crying, whining, barking, complaining); resistant, oppositional, defiant or irascible behavior; eating forbidden food, refusing to eat or being a "picky" eater; damaging, breaking, or chewing treasured objects; and toileting accidents. Although these are normal, if trying, behaviors, problems arise from the limitations of the parents or caregivers in meeting these demands and the stressful circumstances of their lives. Intervention needs to address the potential for neglect or abuse resulting from the limitations of the person in charge and environmental stressors.

What should you look for if you suspect physical abuse? The physical, behavioral and emotional indicators of physical abuse also tend to be the same for people and animals: inadequately explained injuries, withdrawn or aggressive behavior; self-destructive behavior such as head-banging or creating sores; hypervigilance, extreme fear, or anxiety; toileting accidents; wariness of physical contact; anti-social behavior; drastic behavioral change in the presence of the caregiver, and running away. Across ages and species, the emotional reactions are also consistent: fear, obsequiousness or cowering; depression; failure to grow or heal; hyperactivity; apathy, aggressive or bizarre behavior; unprovoked yelling, howling or crying; and self-defeating actions.

Neglect, the failure to provide minimally adequate food, shelter, clothing (for humans), medical care, and supervision, poses a serious risk for all dependent living creatures. Unable to ensure their own safety, hygiene, or dietary needs, they suffer and are frightened when those they depend on fail them. Attempts to meet their own needs can create dangerous situations such as digging or climbing out of a fenced yard and getting run over by a passing car; eating poisonous substances when hungry or unsupervised; falling and injuring oneself in an attempt to find food, activity, companionship or to get to a bathroom.

The behavioral indicators evidenced by neglected animals, children, the disabled, and the elderly also have much in common: being dirty or hungry; lacking appropriate food, shelter, bedding and (for humans) clothes; being tired or despondent; having chronic untreated medical problems; showing fearfulness or learned helplessness; engaging in sucking, rocking, head banging and other regressive and self-destructive behaviors; begging for or stealing food.

You may see endangering behavior in your program. You may see attitudes, behavioral cues, emotional contexts, triggering behavior, or other indicators of physical abuse or neglect. The Boat, Lockwood, Loar, and Eckert instruments in Chapter 7 provide you with risk assessment tools useful as you select participants suitable for your program.

Above all else, make a home visit. A picture is worth a thousand words!

5. Making it easy for people to participate

Once you have selected suitable participants, make it easy for them to take part in your program.

Ask people to commit to a reasonable number (not many) of sessions; factor in school and other holidays, and build in reinforcers like graduations, certificates of completion and accomplishment, and field trips. People will join more readily and accomplish more if they agree to and flawlessly attend a six-session series topped off with a graduation and celebration, take a month or two off and then return for an advanced six-session series, than if they had committed to but attended erratically a semester-long class. Chapter 8 and Appendix 1 provide sample certificates and other reinforcers.

The intent of this chapter has been to help you create the structure for an effective animal-assisted therapy program by answering four questions:

- How do I select a safe setting for the animals and people in the program?

- How do I screen, hire, train, and motivate qualified and safe staff and volunteers?

- How do I select a safe animal?

- How do I select suitable participants?

At this point, you have made many decisions about your program. You have chosen a safe setting, you have recruited effective staff and volunteers, you have chosen the type of animal helpful to your program and know how to pick a safe one, and you have used risk assessments to select suitable participants.

If you have not completed these tasks yet, you know the questions to ask and decisions you must make as you design your animal-assisted therapy program.

Setting up the structure of your program takes a lot of time and effort, more, perhaps, than you had bargained for. But the stakes are high. Unstructured or poorly structured programs run the risk of inadvertently making things worse for a population already at risk.

The time you spend structuring your program will provide real returns to you, your staff and partners, and your clients.

Chapter Four

Developing the content of animal-assisted therapy programs

Overview

YOU HAVE MADE MANY DECISIONS ABOUT YOUR PROGRAM, DECISIONS THAT DETERMINE WHERE TO HOLD YOUR PROGRAM, HOW TO STAFF YOUR PROGRAM, WHICH ANIMALS TO USE, AND WHICH GROUP TO SERVE. Now you are at the heart of your program: the content. What objectives should you set? What activities should you create? What principles should you incorporate throughout the program?

These questions can be answered by using a conceptual framework of five core skills: mastery, empathy, future orientation, literacy, and balanced and restorative justice. Each of these components contributes to an underlying pro-social world view, which is necessary to help potentially abusive or neglectful people change their maladaptive patterns. This chapter defines this conceptual framework and its relationship to animal-assisted therapy programs. The next chapter presents SHIP, a successful program designed around these five components, to demonstrate how one program used this framework to design content.

Most of the clients in the animal-assisted therapy programs described in this book were at risk of turning to anti-social or violent behaviors. Many also felt isolated and cut off from nurturance and human connectedness. Overwhelmed by seemingly intractable and endless problems, they lacked the zest and energy to grow in new and enriching ways. They may not have been able to envision a happier future beyond the reach of their problems. Children in such depleted families may have experienced growth retardation and developmental delays because so much of their family's limited energy was directed to the challenges of immediate survival, and none was left to encourage normal growth and exploration. These families are often isolated from other people and from creative activities; they lack hope and opportunities for a better future.

Many children from dysfunctional families lag behind their more fortunate peers in understanding how the world works, how to engage peers, and how to elicit the help and support of adults. They are poor at solving problems, tolerating frustration, and deferring gratification. They lack expressive language and social skills with peers and adults. Daniel Goleman refers to these skills as the components of emotional intelligence; he demonstrates that these skills are at least as important as intellect (as measured by IQ) in determining success as an adult (Goleman, 1995). Without outside intervention, children lacking the skills of emotional intelligence fail at school and work, in moral and spiritual development, in relationships, and as contributing members of society. They are also more likely than others to rely on violence as a means to their desired ends. They waste their potential and make the world a more dangerous place for others (Garbarino, 1999).

Fortunately, emotional intelligence can be taught (Goleman, 1995) and animal-assisted therapy programs offer an ideal vehicle. These programs take place in a relaxed setting, a boon to children with cognitive, emotional or behavioral problems that interfere with classroom learning. The learning emerges from interactions with the animals and from following the advice of the animal experts, not from listening to a teacher at the front of a classroom. In this informal setting, clients develop collaborative relationships with each other while focusing on the animals. Meanwhile, they are having a good time. They want to go on working with the animals, so they control themselves in order to continue attending the program. Over time, the program can weave larger humane issues into the work, broadening the social conscience of clients and often providing vocational and avocational opportunities as well. Animal-assisted therapy programs that focus on the tenets of emotional intelligence offer opportunities for long-term success to children otherwise at risk of academic and interpersonal failure by creating repeated and consistent opportunities for them to acquire pro-social behaviors and attitudes in an enjoyable and non-didactic activity.

To achieve this goal, programs should focus on five core skills:

- Mastery,

- Empathy,

- Future orientation,

- Literacy, and

- Balanced and restorative justice.

Mastery

MASTERY CAN BE DEFINED AS FEELING AND BEHAVING COMPETENTLY. When we achieve mastery over a situation, we feel in control and behave capably, at least in a specific area. Teaching mastery over clearly defined, concrete skills in animal-assisted therapy programs can help clients begin to recognize their own ability to master a skill, their behavior, or an interaction. Mastery requires three components: gaining control, preventing relapse, and creating a positive self-image.

■ Gaining Control

An effective intervention can instill a sense of mastery over an area clients have hitherto experienced as unmanageable. Outside the realm of animal-assisted therapy programs, people learn to gain control and achieve mastery over all sorts of problems at many times in their lives. They learn to quit smoking, ride elevators, and overcome other fears. How do they do this? They gain control and move toward mastery by breaking the tasks down into very small steps and mastering them incrementally. They go at a pace slow enough for fears to remain manageable and impulses controllable. With repetition, they become more able to take scary situations in stride, to gain control over their reactivity and to apply effective coping strategies. As their experience and confidence grow, they generalize their new skills and learn to rely on them in various settings, eventually even when tired, under stress or caught off guard.

These elements – breaking tasks into small steps, incremental learning, appropriate pacing, repetition, and generalization – must be integrated into animal-assisted therapy programs to help clients gain self-control and mastery of a new skill.

Animal-assisted therapy programs should identify specific areas of mastery such as overcoming fear of the animals, teaching another sentient being to do something through positive reinforcement rather than threat or coercion, experiencing playful and cooperative activities with family members or peers, or developing skills to care for the basic needs of animals. Whatever the specific goals of a particular program, the clients can experience them in clearly structured activities each week. These activities should be broken into specific tasks, allow for incremental learning, and be appropriately paced. The activities must be structured to incorporate repetition and allow for generalization outside the program. Many programs are linked to after-care activities in animal shelters and community service so program graduates can apply their new skills to real-life situations and make ties to people and organizations in their community.

■ Preventing Relapse

A program that teaches participants to master a skill while at the sessions may be helpful for a short time and within the context of the program. Unless progress is reinforced through active steps to prevent relapse, however, the program is not likely to have a lasting impact.

How do people sustain mastery and prevent relapse? People learn how they inadvertently set themselves up for failure. They plan consciously and in detail how to make better choices. They develop back-up strategies in case they find themselves in a risky situation. People wishing to quit smoking, for example, might keep a chart for a week indicating the exact time they smoked each cigarette, where they were, what they were doing and feeling just then and immediately before. Even though people in the throes of an addiction feel subject to overpowering urges, they are not equally vulnerable at all times and in all situations. Putting the week's behavior on a chart allows a pattern to emerge. People see situations that suggest smoking, feelings that trigger the desire to smoke, friends or colleagues they smoke with, and the times of day when they are at greatest and least risk. They also realize how long the urges last and how much time elapses between urges. With this information, they can make a chart of their lapse cycle, listing particular triggers and alternative behaviors or coping strategies for each.

Some situations are easy to anticipate and make safer. People who routinely have a cigarette and a cup of coffee at their desk at 10:00 a.m. can notice this pattern from their charts and might find that switching to tea and a short walk with a friendly non-smoker at 9:55 a.m. defuses that trigger. Urges that last only a few minutes can often be managed by scheduling an incompatible and enjoyable activity. Urges that are more intense and last longer, especially if they are unexpected and catch already vulnerable people off guard, require a greater repertoire of skills as well as the motivation and ability to work hard when feeling vulnerable. To avoid the danger of falling back on dysfunctional patterns of the past, people must identify the pattern, develop new skills, practice and rehearse their new skills in a variety of provocative situations so that the newly acquired skills become second nature.

How can you incorporate mastery and relapse prevention into animal-assisted therapy programs? These programs often teach people the skills to care for, as well as about, animals. People learn to feed, bathe, clean, and tolerate annoying behaviors because they are motivated to work with animals. They also learn self-control because impulsivity frightens the animals.

The hope of these programs is not that these skills will be mastered only for the purposes of the sessions. Rather, the hope is that the clients will take these skills home with them and be kinder, more patient, and more capable with the people and animals they live with. To realize this hope, animal-assisted therapy programs must deliberately incorporate techniques to sustain mastery through relapse prevention. To help you do this, later chapters provide tools that you can incorporate into your program to prevent relapse. Chapter 5 provides a curriculum for introducing these skills in ways that stick and transfer to other settings. Chapter 8 provides a relapse prevention chart that can be modified for your program or by participants to plot their own patterns of relapse and list specific coping strategies at each step along the way. Chapter 8, pp. 168-169, also includes charts for warning signs suggestive of impending relapse and a relapse/recovery grid created by Terence Gorski, a leading researcher and writer in the drug and alcohol treatment field where relapse prevention was pioneered.

■ Creating a Positive Self-Image

Incorporating mastery into your program provides the context in which participants can gain control over a skill and sustain mastery by preventing relapse. When participants acquire and develop a skill through hard work, they also gain a sense of personal worth. They have accomplished something difficult; through their own efforts they now can contribute something valuable to society.

Mastery creates a positive self-image, a sense of efficacy that cannot be taken away when other people, even members of one's family, act selfishly or destructively. A child living with alcoholic parents may learn painfully that birthdays may be forgotten, or that birthday parties may trigger episodes of domestic violence or child abuse. However, the child taking music lessons or participating in an animal-assisted therapy program will still be able to play the clarinet or teach a dog to come when called despite the family's dysfunction. This child has developed an admirable hobby, interest or skill through the expenditure of considerable personal effort, a capability not compromised or lost even when parents fight, use alcohol or drugs, or become homeless.

An 8-year-old boy and his mother moved into a San Francisco homeless shelter. A staff member took him across the street to check out the after-school recreation program for homeless children in the neighborhood. He met the staff, explored the play area, and learned that the program was designed especially for children in his predicament – and that a number of homeless children just like him came every day after school. Nevertheless, when he arrived the next day and met the other children, he put his hands on his hips, struck a defiant pose and stated, "Just because I'm homeless doesn't mean I'm not a person, too." If joining a program he had already visited, one devoted to children just like him, evoked such shame and defensiveness, how much stigma and rage must this child feel entering less benign rooms? How likely is he to provoke aggressive responses in less sheltered settings? What price will this sense of stigma exact from this child over time?

Teaching a child mastery of a difficult skill allows him or her to enter a room head held high, ready to handle introductions with a statement of personal worth, "My name is Johnnie and I can read music and play the clarinet," or "My name is Suzie and I can teach a dog to come when called and shake hands with me." The development of a worthwhile skill and the mastery of the components of emotional intelligence provide the coping strategies needed to choose constructive behaviors and relationships instead of violence and victimizing relationships. This is the value of mastery and the reason your program should teach emotional intelligence, mastery and relapse prevention.

 ## Empathy

ACQUISITION OF SKILL IS A NECESSARY BUT NOT SUFFICIENT ACCOMPLISHMENT FOR EFFECTIVE THERAPEUTIC OUTCOME. People must care enough about the impact their behavior has on others to use their newly acquired skills outside the program's sessions. Therefore, programs must reduce emotional isolation and facilitate empathy and attachment, the humane context for the use of new skills. In other words, your program must teach empathy.

People who have been profoundly neglected in early childhood may never have learned the rudimentary skill needed for empathy, the ability to read the emotions in the faces of others. They could not trust that anyone would be there to respond to their most basic needs, and they rarely had loving or attentive faces to study. Now, years later, even as adults, they may not recognize facial expressions or body language indicating how another person is feeling.

Animals can become excellent teachers for such people. They express their feelings through explicit and predictable body language: wagging tail, bared teeth, alert ears. Observers can be taught to recognize what animals are feeling and encouraged to generalize this learning to an enhanced understanding of what members of other species are feeling.

People who have been abused or neglected have learned a key lesson about other people: they can hurt you. When the abuse or neglect occurred within a family, the lesson is even graver: people who love you hurt you. Unfortunately, many parents say to their child during a spanking, "I'm only doing this because I love you." Thus, the child learns that hitting is a gesture of love. Carrying this lesson forward, children now older and beginning to date will also interpret dating violence as gestures of love.

Some people decide that abuse is simply the price that must be paid for the benefits that come with relationships, namely affiliation and affection. Others decide that the price is too high, that people are too dangerous, and that safety lies in emotional, if not physical, isolation. Still others, feeling greatly imperiled, see the world as so dangerous that they must strike first lest they be harmed. They believe they are protecting themselves from injury. Some may also be so numb from their past hurts that they no longer care about the pain they inflict on others. It is not that such people do not know right from wrong when they hurt others, but that their targets have little or no value to them. Social or religious doctrines like the value systems espoused by gangs and some religious cults can reinforce this idea and even turn violence into virtue.

In *Lost Boys,* James Garbarino talks about the circle of caring, the group of people one truly cares about. He learned from interviews with teenage boys who had committed murder and other serious crimes that they cared about few, if any, people other than themselves. Thus, they considered taking the lives of people they did not value, people outside their circle of caring, of minimal consequence – rather like swatting a fly or stepping on an ant. Garbarino asked a teenager awaiting trial for killing a police officer, "What was the worst thing you ever did? What was the worst thing that ever happened to you?" The boy replied that "he couldn't think of anything really bad that he had ever done. After a brief pause, he added, 'Of course, the worst thing that ever happened to me is the present situation.' A minute later, he added that there were illegal things he had done that some people might consider bad from *their* point of view" (Garbarino, 1999, p. 53, italics his).

Garbarino's treatment goals with these alienated youth included increasing their empathy by expanding the boys' circle of caring so that they would grow to regard more people as worthy of consideration. "Depersonalization and desensitization open the door to unlimited possibilities for violence. When we depersonalize others, we fail to see their individuality, their humanity, and treat them in an impersonal way. If empathy is the enemy of violence, depersonalization is its ally. The more we are able to create psychological distance between us and others, the more likely we are to commit acts of violence and aggression against them…. By depersonalizing them, good, caring people can support barbaric treatment of others; they put them outside their own circle, into the category of 'the other'" (Garbarino, 1999, p. 114).

To achieve their treatment goals, the boys and others like them need to learn three skills: how to care, how to recognize the feelings of others, and how to build ties to others.

■ Learning to care

Numb and aggressive people allow few feelings to penetrate their outer shell of hostility or indifference. Years in the making, this protective strategy may have protected its practitioners from knowing their own emotions. They may not be aware of what they are feeling in the moment, and are therefore unable to gauge their arousal. They are unable to assess their feelings and factor them into decisions about relationships and behaviors. To replace this protective strategy with one based on empathy, people must get to know their own emotions and to tolerate experiencing them in the moment.

Openness to animals is a good starting place for people well defended against human emotions. Learning to read an animal's emotions is worthwhile in and of itself, allowing one to recognize safe and dangerous dogs while out for a walk, for example. More importantly, this knowledge allows people to participate in the positive exchange of emotions with another living being in ways that do not trigger their defensive arsenal. Animal-assisted therapy programs are particularly well-suited to developing empathy, even in those considered "hard to reach" by traditional therapeutic measures. People are eager to work with animals and care more readily. Many of those who are walled off from tender feelings for humans will let themselves feel warmth and affection for animals. They will be willing to tolerate frustration and develop patience and coping skills for the animal's sake. They will develop empathy through their relationship with the animal. This awareness of their own feelings is a necessary first step to recognizing the feelings of others.

■ Recognizing the feelings of others

Animal-assisted therapy programs that help participants gain in empathy by learning to care can help those same participants take the next step, recognizing the feelings of others. This second step requires the participants to increase their self-control and ability to view situations with objectivity.

Self-control

To focus on somebody else's feelings, people need to maintain self-control, to keep themselves on an even keel, and to step out of the picture they are studying. They must be patient and maintain focus in order to concentrate on something outside themselves. Paying attention to another requires subordinating one's own drives, tolerating frustration, and deferring personal needs, key elements of emotional intelligence (Goleman, 1995, p. 43).

Self-control becomes a desirable goal to people who want contact with animals. One 9-year-old boy, always in trouble for shouting, screamed with pleasure when a humane educator took a kitten from a carrier. The terrified kitten leapt back, cowering and trembling. The child was shocked that he had scared the kitten, its behavior making a far greater impression on the child than years of negative reactions and explanations by parents, teachers and peers. Now, others simply say in a soft voice, "What if a kitten were visiting?" and the child, mindful of the kitten he had scared, quiets himself down.

Objectivity

People can only learn to read the emotions of others, the fundamental skill for empathy, when they can separate their interpretations from the cues given by others. They must develop the ability to recognize facial expressions, body language, and social indicators. Neglected children may have very limited prior experience to bring to this challenge, their depressed or uninterested parents having rarely exposed them to smiles, loving looks, or hugs. Children exposed to violence may have considerable experience reading the negative emotional cues of others, but not the positive ones.

Humane educators and animal-assisted therapists know that even people who misread human affect learn to identify emotions accurately by observing them in animals. Animals demonstrate their emotions more directly than most people do, and people are more willing to set aside notions of disrespect and offense in observations of animals than of other people. Animals have different concerns and demonstrate enthusiasm and wariness differently than people do. Thus, participants in animal-assisted therapy programs can learn to see signs of acceptance and fear in the animals they work with more readily and without the baggage of hurts they carry from human rejection and intimidation.

By learning how dogs indicate they do not pose a threat to others, and how they negotiate relationships with other dogs using an elaborate assortment of calming signals (Rugaas, 1997), people can spot dogs' gestures of conciliation. Knowing and using the dogs' ways of showing that no threat is intended – which are different from primates' ways (McConnell, 2002) – people learn to use body language intelligible to a different species. Interspecific empathy is reinforced immediately by the dog's response. Objectively, tail wagging is a positive sign. So is the enthusiastic body language of a dog about to be given a tennis ball or treat. From there, people can begin to recognize positive emotions in other animals, including human ones. They can become bilingual and bicultural as they compare canine and primate indicators of safety and conciliation.

In one family, parents were referred by the juvenile court for therapy after having physically abused their 8-year-old son. They told the therapist their child was difficult and unpleasant. They maintained that the child had never given them any pleasure, and they could not remember a single enjoyable moment even during their son's infancy when he smiled, played with his toes or did anything else endearing. The therapist concluded that the parents needed to learn how to read positive emotions in children and sent them – without their own child so they could be objective – to a nearby ice cream shop to observe children getting ice cream.

The parents reported their observations the following week, with unprecedented good humor and accuracy, describing the decisive child who knew immediately which of 31 flavors to choose, the scammer who feigned indecision in order to sample many possibilities, and the overwhelmed child who asked for vanilla to end the anxiety of so many options. They added observations about the accompanying parents, those who let the children take their time and make their own choices, and those who became impatient or controlling and turned the treat into a bad experience. They asked the therapist if they might take their son for an ice cream to see how he would react. Having never done this before, they could not anticipate his behavior but were eager to observe and self-controlled enough to observe accurately and let him enjoy himself (Loar, 1998).

The intervention increased the parents' ability to see the situation with objectivity, moving them closer to an empathic interaction with their son.

■ Building ties to others

Self control, the ability to read others' emotions, and to respond appropriately and empathically are the fundamental skills for positive experiences in relationships. However, lasting change depends on using empathic skills to broaden the circle of caring, to form meaningful and sustaining ties with others, especially those with humane values and behaviors.

Garbarino observed, "violent boys often seem to feel they cannot afford empathy.... A lost boy's own vulnerability leads him to develop strategies to depersonalize other people, so that he can remain strong.... Because we know that empathy is the enemy of aggression and that depersonalization is its ally, all efforts at moral rehabilitation of violent and troubled boys hinge upon cultivating empathy and fighting against their tendency to depersonalize others" (Garbarino, 1999, p. 230f.).

People can learn to read the communicative signals of animals without initially feeling exposed and vulnerable. Thus, they can approach the task calmly and focus on the animals' movements and body language. By studying behavioral subtleties of dogs interacting with each other and with members of other species, people can appreciate how they may unintentionally come across as menacing, by walking straight up to a dog and making eye contact for example (Rugaas, 1997; McConnell, 2002), and as reassuring by being less direct in approach and regard. The human learner focuses on the individual animal's cues and modifies his or her own behavior in response. This respect for the comfort and boundaries of another living being, based on observation and awareness of one's own movements, combined with the conscious choice to behave so as to put the other at ease constitute empathy.

Future Orientation

PEOPLE DEMAND MORE OF THEMSELVES, CONQUER PROBLEMS, DEFER GRATIFICATION, AND PUT THE NEEDS OF OTHERS AHEAD OF THEIR OWN ONLY WHEN THEY BELIEVE THAT THE EFFORT THEY MAKE TODAY WILL CONTRIBUTE TO A BETTER TOMORROW. This optimistic world view is referred to as future orientation. Absent this view – the belief in a better future – there is no compelling reason to exercise self-control.

Living for the moment, for immediate pleasure or thrill, makes sense in a world filled with violence and limited horizons. How can teachers, therapists and humane educators give abused, neglected, depressed, homeless or otherwise disadvantaged people sufficient hope for a better future so that they will be willing to do the hard and painful work of mastery and empathy today? How can animal-assisted therapy programs promote an optimistic view of the future? They must present a challenge that realistically can be solved while maintaining the awareness that economic hardship, community violence and other large problems will remain.

Horticulture and animal-assisted therapy programs are ideally suited to teach this concept. Caring for plants and animals are ways for people to buy into the future because plants and animals grow quickly. People can see the fruits of their labors, seeds turning into plants with flowers and vegetables, baby animals getting bigger and stronger, and abandoned animals turning into well mannered candidates for adoption. The client who works to socialize and train a shelter dog and sees the dog's prospects for adoption improve has a sound basis for becoming optimistic about the dog's future which has improved because of the client's work. This is a first step. Once clients have experienced optimism about another's future, they can risk becoming optimistic about their own future. This optimism – future orientation – has an even greater chance of taking root in the program participant who has mastered operant conditioning (clicker training) and, as a result, has a realistic opportunity to continue contributing through volunteer and compensated effort (see Chapter 5, pp. 85-89 for a detailed discussion of clicker training).

Garbarino describes the life-changing significance of a humane intervention with a future orientation:

"When I think of helping violent boys find their way, I often think of one particular troubled youth who grew up in Jamestown, New York, in the early years of this [20th] century. The boy had to deal with the emotional predicament of living in a household dominated by an alcoholic and abusive father. To escape his horrible family life, the boy wandered the hills and found solace in nature, particularly in birds. This fascination with birds sustained him, but by the time he reached high school he was a lonely, troubled boy. A teacher in his school formed a Junior Audubon Club so that the boy would have at least one positive setting at school in which his interest in birds could be nourished. This act of acceptance was decisive. It provided a positive link for the boy to peers and adults. As a result of this experience, the boy did not get lost. He went on to become an internationally acclaimed expert on birds and wrote a best-selling guide. His name was Roger Torrey Peterson. When I met him near the end of his long life, we talked about his personal history, and he told me this story as a testament to the potential power of a caring teacher, to the power of hope" (Garbarino, pp. 91f.).

The skills of emotional intelligence are interrelated. Children who master skills and thereby improve their self-image can risk developing the empathy required to develop ties with others. Improved relationships, mastery of useful skills, and reasonable chances for contributing to society provide the fertile soil necessary for future orientation to take root.

Literacy

LITERACY IS A POWERFUL TOOL THAT CAN BE USED IN HUMANE EDUCATION, ANIMAL-ASSISTED AND OTHER THERAPY PROGRAMS TO PROMOTE AND REINFORCE GAINS.

Children from neglectful or violent homes or communities often fall behind their peers at school, sometimes due to learning disabilities, but often as a result of their fear and preoccupation with the stress of their lives. They have trouble concentrating in conventional classrooms because they cannot focus on the teacher who is talking in front of the class. It is easier for these children to focus and concentrate when learning is immediate and personal.

Children who are so preoccupied with problems can benefit from learning to write, because writing gives them a way to transform their private – and often frightening or shameful – experiences into a meaningful story that can be shared with others. Writing is a powerful tool to gain mastery over troublesome experiences and feelings. It involves motor skills, language, cognition, affect and imagination, and brings all of these attributes to bear in a single task, forcing systems to integrate and produce an intelligible outcome.

At its most basic, writing involves gross and fine motor skills as the writer sits at a desk or table and moves a pen or pencil across a sheet of paper causing recognizable symbols to appear. This is the beginning of gaining control over what was invisible and beyond one's grasp, making the invisible take shape on paper.

Choosing which words to use instead of other near-synonyms lets the author appreciate gradations and modulations. Writing in sentences gives the amorphous and terrifying past structure. Syntax shows that the experience is not totally beyond control or regulation.

Dividing the experience into paragraphs, the writer sequences what had been an overwhelming flood of events. Using a higher degree of abstraction, the writer creates introductory and concluding paragraphs, showing that the frightening episode is finite, with both a beginning and an ending. Children tend to write "the end" in big letters at the end of their essays, making clear the bad experience is over and not going to hurt the author again.

What people can carry around in a journal or diary, they need not carry around in their bodies as psychosomatic symptoms or in their psyches as phobias. Writing affords mastery over experience, making the invisible visible and externalizing the problem (White and Epston, 1990), and reducing its undesired and insidious influence over the present and future.

Participants in animal-assisted therapy programs should be encouraged to write about what they do and their reflections on it. For many, talking or writing about the instability of their own lives is too ominous, but writing about the plight of a homeless or endangered animal gives them ways to voice their concerns at a safe distance. Competent assessment of the animal's predicament and the ability to convey that through writing, combined with an expectation that readers will respond empathically, give the authors ways to express hope for the future.

Here are some poems by 4th and 5th graders demonstrating their command of mastery, empathy, future orientation, literacy and a social conscience:

My cat was found in a ditch.
She was skinny as a twig.
She cried and cried.
Now she is plump like a pillow.
Her fur is bright and shiny.
She has warm laps to sit on.

Katie, Grade Five (Raphael, 1999, p. 39)

I found my cat in the woods.
She smelled like dirt.
Her eyes looked like stones.
Her fur looked like dry leaves.
I took her home.
Now her fur glistens like night.
Her purr sounds as deep as a river.

Hannah, Grade Six (Raphael, 1999, p. 39)

I am the cat who has no home.
Who is all alone.
Who has no food.
Who is freezing cold.
Who needs water.
Who needs love.

John, Grade Four (Raphael, 1999, p. 39)

Compassion is when
You help a starving cat.
You put birdseed out for the birds.
You feed your animal when she's hungry.
You don't smoke in the house.
That's all compassion.

Lyle, Grade Five (Raphael, 1999, p. 38)

One day I was walking down a trail and I heard gunshots. I thought nothing of it. I walked farther down the trail and heard the weeping of a creature in pain.

I walked towards the weeping and I was stunned to see a deer lying still. I moved closer to its body and saw that it was barely breathing. I saw blood on the side of its fur. I thought about how no one really cares about this deer lying bloody and in pain in the woods. But I thought it was a big deal because deer aren't much different from people.

As I was thinking this, I looked down at the deer and saw that it wasn't breathing anymore. He wouldn't be scared any more.

Shalynn, Grade Five (Raphael, 1999, p. 74)

Literacy provides a way for children in humane education and animal-assisted therapy programs to gain control over situations, express empathy, and develop mastery over various forms of writing. Because literacy allows children both to develop and demonstrate their growing mastery, empathy, optimism and social conscience, opportunities for written expression should be built into the design of humane education and animal-assisted therapy programs.

Balanced and Restorative Justice

IN ADDITION TO DEVELOPING MASTERY, EMPATHY, THE ABILITY TO EXPRESS THOUGHTS AND FEELINGS WITH WORDS, AND AN OPTIMISTIC VIEW OF THE FUTURE, PEOPLE NEED TO LOOK BEYOND THEMSELVES, TO FIND WAYS TO BE EFFICACIOUS IN THEIR COMMUNITIES. Those who were victimized want to feel that the harm they sustained was acknowledged and redressed, but they also need to move beyond their experience of victimization, to feeling and behaving competently, and even generously. Having something valuable to give others is a clear indicator of recovery from past hurt and deprivation.

Those who did the victimizing must also go beyond mere self-control (mastery over outbursts of violence and acquisition of pro-social ways to obtain compliance from others) for meaningful recovery. They must empathize with their victim and the victim's family and community, all of whom suffered loss as a result of the victimizer's behavior. Their morality and social conscience must grow, and they must make meaningful restitution that benefits others and decreases the likelihood of recidivism.

Before the establishment of criminal justice systems, people owed debts directly to those they had wronged. People repaid their victims, not society, for stealing or other wrongdoing.

Today we have a sophisticated legal system. In this system, people who have committed crimes are prosecuted by district attorneys or attorneys general, are sentenced by a judge, pay restitution to a fund, and serve time in a county, state or federal correctional facility. This allows offenders to avoid serious consideration of personal responsibility for the harm they inflicted on others by focusing on the system and its treatment of them. Some see it as a zero sum game, the harm they did being cancelled out by the wrongs done to them in county jail or state prison, for example. Rather than using time served to contemplate the error of one's ways, develop a conscience, and come up with meaningful restitution to those harmed, many offenders avoid personal responsibility by looking outward at the shortcomings of the judicial and penal systems. Effective rehabilitation and reduced risk of recidivism depend on the opposite expenditure of energy, on people taking responsibility for their behavior and making restitution (Jenkins, 1990).

Community safety, ethical standards and due process benefit from the judicial and criminal justice systems, but victims often feel excluded or revictimized by the process. Their sense of being heard, of being restored to the position they were in before the crime, and of meaningful recognition and restitution by the offender are essential components of recovery.

Balanced and restorative justice (Bilchik, 1998) reconnects offenders to those they have harmed – victims, families, and communities – through reparative work and participation of victims (where possible and appropriate) in designing outcomes. Balanced and restorative justice emphasizes three components: accountability, competency, and community safety.

■ **Accountability**

Rather than emphasizing punishment, balanced and restorative justice holds people accountable for the effects of their actions in ways that facilitate moral development. People must appreciate how their behavior affected and harmed others and acknowledge they chose that behavior and could have chosen to behave differently. They must take action to repair the harm where possible and show the ability to avoid such behavior in the future. Accountability involves taking responsibility for behavior, including acknowledging the impact of the behavior on the victim's family and community, expressing apology and remorse, providing for repair of harm to the victim, making amends to the community, and making appropriate restitution (Bilchik, 1998, p. 9).

■ Competency

Balanced and restorative justice strategies build on strengths of offenders, their families, and their communities. All three take active roles to support productive behavior, a sense of belonging, and a sense of being useful. Balanced and restorative justice requires those who have victimized others to develop a number of key competencies: vocational skills, work experience, and service learning; cognitive, problem solving, and decision making skills; conflict management, dispute resolution and communication skills; emotional and behavioral control; citizenship and a social conscience; health management and recreational skills.

■ Community Safety

People must be accountable at home, at school, at work, while performing community service, and while recreating. Both through self-regulation and successful participation in academic, vocational, and community activities, they must demonstrate that they are contributing to a safe and harmonious society rather than disrupting it and putting others at risk.

Animal-assisted therapy programs provide the opportunity to demonstrate such contributions.

A number of children participating in the SHIP program in San Francisco have shown their progression from bystander or aggressor to protector by stopping friends from harassing animals. One child dissuaded boys from putting a dog in a clothes dryer in the neighborhood laundromat because of his confident and authoritative manner on matters pertaining to the safety and well being of animals. Several children have called the San Francisco Department of Animal Care and Control when confronted with more harmful behavior or an injured animal.

Animal-assisted therapy programs offer opportunities to consider the plight of other living beings, their needs for safety, competent care and affiliation. Many people too injured by or hardened to human concerns to respond well to human intervention will engage and enjoy working with animals. They will find ways to build ties, redress wrongs, develop a social conscience and give back to their community through humane programs. These programs can potentially benefit many people, not just those who have injured or killed animals in the past.

For these pro-social outcomes to occur, animal-assisted therapy programs need thoughtful, carefully developed structure and content. The tenets of emotional intelligence should be incorporated into all program content along with plans to help participants develop mastery, empathy, future orientation, literacy skills, and social conscience committed to balanced and restorative justice. The following chapter provides an example of a program incorporating these principles. Use the program as a model to see one application of these theoretical constructs, to gain ideas for your program, and to think about the unique ways your program design can incorporate emotional intelligence, mastery, empathy, future orientation, literacy, and balanced and restorative justice to meet your goals.

Chapter Five

Changing behavior and outlook
– the SHIP model

Overview

ALL YOUR PIECES ARE IN PLACE. You are prepared for the confidences children will bring you. You know how to structure your program by choosing appropriate settings, staff and volunteers, animals, and participants. And you know what skills to incorporate as you design your program.

But what does a completed program look like when everything is in place?

This chapter offers you an example of a completed and tested program called SHIP, the Strategic Humane Interventions Program.

As you read through SHIP's program rationale and design, think about the structural and design elements described in earlier chapters. Look for the guidance and concepts you've already studied to see how SHIP turns these concepts into a concrete, practical program.

You will see many familiar ideas as you read the SHIP rationale and design. You will recognize SHIP's choices of setting, staff and volunteers, animals, and participants and will see how these choices are critical to the program's success. You will see the program deliberately and relentlessly incorporating the five core skills: mastery, empathy, future orientation, literacy, and developing a social conscience and contributing to balanced and restorative justice. And you will see how a comprehensively planned animal-assisted therapy program provides the opportunity for real learning and growth that extends beyond the classroom.

What is SHIP?

THE STRATEGIC HUMANE INTERVENTIONS PROGRAM (SHIP), DESIGNED BY LYNN LOAR, WORKS WITH GROUPS OF THREE OR FOUR FAMILIES (CHILDREN AGE EIGHT AND OLDER AND THE PARENT OR GUARDIAN RESPONSIBLE FOR THEM) AND TWO OR THREE SHELTER DOGS UNDER THE COMBINED GUIDANCE OF AN ANIMAL BEHAVIORIST AND A SOCIAL WORKER. During a few one-hour sessions, the facilitators teach the families the basics of operant conditioning (clicker training; see below, pp. 85-89, for a detailed explanation of clicker training) so the families can teach the dogs – and each other – good manners and behavior exclusively by using positive reinforcement.

Each session is divided into two parts. For the first half, the families clicker train dogs to perform basic behaviors like sitting, coming when called and walking on a leash without pulling. For the second half, the families play the training game (see below, pp. 90-95, for a detailed discussion of the training game), clicker training each other to improve their ability to shape behavior through positive reinforcement. Families commit to a finite number of sessions and may sign up for a second series.

Karen Pryor describes the SHIP program (personal communication) as follows:

"The SHIP program is about learning. It begins with the families learning to teach the shelter dogs to sit, to make eye contact, to touch a held-out hand, and to respond when called. Children wielding clickers and treats can teach these simple behaviors and experience success (the dogs experience success, too, of course). Families witness and participate in the process. The techniques for interacting through positive reinforcement can be rapidly assimilated and transferred to interfamily processes, without verbal instruction."

By teaching stressed families to clicker train carefully selected shelter dogs, SHIP seeks to improve the relationships within the family at the same time that it increases the dogs' chances of adoption. To achieve these goals, SHIP focuses on developing cognitive, empathic, and behavioral skills that are the rudiments of emotional intelligence. SHIP makes these skills portable and transferable to diverse settings so that they are available to participants at home, at school, at work, and in the community both when times are good and when tensions build.

Created in San Francisco, SHIP has been implemented in San Francisco and Sonoma counties in California and also in Cincinnati, Ohio. In California, SHIP has been supported through a grant from the California Governor's Office of Criminal Justice Planning (OCJP), in collaboration with the Humane Society of Sonoma County, the YWCA of Sonoma County, and the San Francisco Department of Animal Care and Control. In Cincinnati, SHIP has been developed and supported under the sponsorship of the Childhood Trust at Cincinnati Children's Hospital, the Cincinnati YWCA Battered Women's Programs, and SPCA Cincinnati, funded in part by the Kenneth A. Scott Charitable trust.

San Francisco, a city of some 700,000 people, has the smallest percentage of children (16 percent) of any city in the United States. It is also one of the most expensive cities in the country, with housing the costliest in the nation. As a result, most people who choose to live in San Francisco are working adults, paying a considerable amount of their income each month to rent small apartments. When they become parents, many people move to the suburbs so they can afford a bigger apartment that comes with some grass and perhaps a play area for children.

Children represent a relatively invisible and underserved segment of San Francisco's population. Most of the city's children live in substandard housing in congested and dangerous neighborhoods. Many live in single-parent families, with that parent having to work well more than 40 hours per week to afford the rent. A considerable number of children live with grandparents or other relatives, their parents' lives having been destroyed by drug or alcohol abuse. Still other children – far too many – are homeless and drift with their parents endlessly from a homeless shelter to a vehicle, to a friend's couch, and into another shelter, ever on the move because the cost of housing is beyond their reach.

SHIP initially offered services to families living in a shelter for homeless families in the Tenderloin, an inner-city neighborhood that is home to the poorest and most troubled residents and to the greatest number of drug addicts and parolees. It then moved to a safer room in the same neighborhood, the community room in a large apartment building, and made the services available to all families in the Tenderloin.

At the same time, SHIP implemented services at an elementary school in Bayview-Hunter's Point, a marginalized neighborhood at the southern part of the city that is home to many of the families with children. The school has a history of family-based services and involving parents in their children's activities. Many of the school's children have been exposed to family and community violence; as a result, a sizeable percent live with grandparents. Quite a number of the children have experienced the death of a relative and have one relative – or more – serving time in county jail or state prison, or on probation or parole.

The participants in the Sonoma County component of SHIP are referred through the juvenile court, the department of mental health, or another municipal or not-for-profit organization or school providing services to at-risk children. Cincinnati SHIP works with families living in transitional housing following crisis intervention at the local shelter for battered women and their children. In all locations, SHIP integrates its work into school and family life through wrap-around services including crisis intervention, classroom support, referral to and coordination with other service providers, and individual and family counseling by one of SHIP's social workers. These services are reinforced through field trips to animal shelters and other places of relevance and interest.

With this target population (inner-city families exposed to family or community violence) wary of people in authority and of dogs, their contact largely being with dangerous dogs in housing projects, SHIP decided to introduce clicker training as an alternative to violence, to change behavior and outlook through humane work with people and animals.

SHIP works with its target population in a neighborhood setting familiar to its participants using carefully selected shelter dogs in programs co-facilitated by an animal behaviorist/clicker trainer who understands the animals, a social worker who understands the people, and staff and/or volunteers from the social service agency hosting the program. These structural choices provide a coherent platform from which to develop the content of the program. SHIP's content meets its goals by teaching the five core skills in context:

- Teaching Mastery through Clicker Training

- Teaching Empathy with the Training Game

- Anticipating a Better Future

- Literacy: Consolidating Gains by Putting Them in Writing

- Developing a Social Conscience and Contributing to Balanced and Restorative Justice

 ## Teaching Mastery through Clicker Training

SHIP'S DESIGN IS BASED EXCLUSIVELY ON POSITIVE REINFORCEMENT THROUGH CLICKER TRAINING. Clicker training is a form of operant conditioning in which the learner, or operator, experiences mastery by operating effectively on his or her environment, e.g., by offering behaviors that earn rewards. With clicker training, a trainer uses a marker signal – a click usually – and an accompanying treat to flag noteworthy behavior for the learner. Clicker training relies exclusively on this pairing of an acoustic marker with a positive reinforcer to pinpoint and build repertoires of positive behavior. A more detailed explanation of clicker training follows on Pages 85-89.

SHIP uses positive reinforcement in two ways. First, the facilitators use clicker training to recognize and promote desired behaviors. Second, SHIP teaches clicker training to participants to train shelter dogs and to play the training game (clicker training in which roles of trainer and learner are both played by humans; a detailed description of the training game follows on Pages 90-95). As a result, participants both receive positive reinforcement for newly acquired skills and learn positive reinforcement skills to use in relationships within and outside of SHIP. Clicker training is the vehicle for both reinforcing participants' positive behaviors and for teaching participants to master the skills and world view of positive reinforcement.

A look at SHIP's design from the perspective of the five core skills shows that SHIP promotes mastery of a number of behaviors through clicker training.

■ Mastery by Doing: The SHIP Vision

"If you desire to see, learn how to act."
— Heinz von Foerster

All living beings construct a sense of how the world works. From their experiences they generate a set of rules that allow them to navigate their way in the world, accomplish tasks, transact business of many sorts, develop relationships with others, and pursue a range of goals and activities. Because each world view is based on individual attempts at efficacious action, it is necessarily idiosyncratic, strengthened by experiences that conform to the rules invented by the individual, and challenged, and perhaps broadened, by experiences that do not conform. New experiences that challenge the established mindset present the opportunity for growth, complexity and innovation in self-image and outlook (v. Glasersfeld, 1984, 1995).

Children growing up in abusive or negligent homes may have been unable to explore their environments due to ambient danger, indifferent or impatient parents, and impoverished settings. Life-long developmental deficits may result from the failure to assimilate and accommodate novel and broadening experiences in formative developmental stages. By the time these children reach their teen years, their experiences may be so narrow that they no longer recognize a smile or other positive social cue. Instead, they overreact to even the mildest negative cue with a repertoire of angry and aggressive responses – and are reinforced for this antisocial posture because of the frightening figure they present to the world (Garbarino, 1999, p. 81). As adults, they may find their range of emotions, experiences and choices stiflingly restricted, with anger their main interpersonal style.

Using clicker training to teach mastery, SHIP gives people opportunities to practice benign observations and behaviors in authentic, positive settings. It helps them build a repertoire of safe, responsible actions, of techniques to enlist others and positive and appropriate ways to influence their behaviors. It introduces them to a support system of like-minded and like-behaving individuals.

This approach challenges clients' narrow and self-limiting sets of rules through the experience of joyful novelty designed to increase positive experiences and broaden the range of appropriately desirable options the individual would see. It reinforces them for positive interactions and expectations and helps them construct a pro-social set of rules for interactions with others. The aim of this approach is to promote mastery by making learning so interesting and enjoyable that clients want to incorporate these experiences into daily life and relationships.

SHIP uses clicker training to focus on positive exchanges. This approach teaches mastery of a number of behaviors: the ability to read positive cues in others, to break down a positive behavior into such small steps that success is assured (and mistakes along the way are ignored except as an indicator to the teacher to use smaller incremental steps), and to react positively during and immediately after every step toward the desired behavioral goal.

SHIP's loftier vision is that giving participants an exclusively positive experience in reading the cues of others and responding affirmatively and influentially will lead them to reconstruct their world view and sets of rules for effective interaction with other living beings in more flexible and humane ways.

To achieve its vision, SHIP integrates clicker training into an animal-assisted therapy program. This combines two powerful approaches. Animal-assisted therapy programs allow skills to be learned in safe and structured settings. But these skills must be truly mastered if they are to be of any lasting value. To be true alternatives to familiar abusive behaviors, skills must be readily available and applicable in times of stress and crisis. People must learn not only sufficient self-control to touch gently and speak positively in the animal-assisted therapy session but also to choose that behavior and language even when they are frustrated or angry at home or in the community.

Developing mastery of the basics of operant conditioning as part or all of the curriculum accomplishes that goal; it allows people to operate on their environment effectively and to elicit desired behaviors from others through the techniques of positive reinforcement. For this reason, SHIP promotes mastery through clicker training to combine the lasting impact of operant conditioning with the safe and structured setting of an animal-assisted therapy program.

■ **Positive Reinforcement: The Tool for Creating Mastery**

How does SHIP teach people to shape behaviors using clickers? SHIP relies exclusively on positive reinforcement for teaching and learning: this is a central tenet of the SHIP program and is fundamental to its approach to mastery.

Pryor defines reinforcement as "an event that (a) occurs during or upon completion of a behavior; and (b) increases the likelihood of that behavior occurring in the future. The key elements here are two: the two events are connected in real time – the behavior engenders the reinforcement – and then the behavior occurs more frequently…. What's critical is the temporal relationship between them" (Pryor, 1999, p. xi).

Positive reinforcers tend to be something immediately appreciated by the human or animal learner, an edible treat most commonly, but also stickers, points that can be cashed in for a larger privilege, minutes on a computer, or anything else the learner would be willing to work for. In social rather than structured settings, reinforcers like smiles, hugs, and compliments occur spontaneously and mark appreciated words and behaviors.

Some teachers and trainers believe that negative feedback is as important as positive feedback and will therefore tug leashes, dock points, take away minutes on the computer, or remove other privileges for unwanted behavior just as they add to them for desired behavior. SHIP does not use this approach. Instead, SHIP's curriculum is built exclusively around the use of positive reinforcement.

When positive reinforcement alone is used for teaching and learning, "the global behavior of the learner changes. A punished or correction-trained animal learns to give the minimum necessary in order to stay out of trouble. These learners are 'good soldiers': They do what they're told, and they never volunteer. Under this regimen, even if obedient, learners remain far more interested in their own doings and private life than in whatever you or any voice of authority might want. They are therefore not only vulnerable to distractions, they are hoping for distractions. Furthermore, when pushed too hard or punished too much, these learners get mad or quit. This is just the suite of behaviors we see in most household dogs, in many employees – and in kids in school" (Pryor, 1999, p. 174).

Not only disheartening, correction or criticism, however constructively intended, discourages creativity and experimentation and increases reliance on the instructor for guidance. Moreover, if the instructor's frustration builds or the correction becomes energized in any way, it takes on a menacing quality, suggesting that non-compliance will result in something aversive, perhaps even abusive. Confusion about the behavior or the trainer's expectation becomes highly stressful and warns the learner that a correction may be coming.

This uncertainty and the fear of impending consequences contaminate the learning process, even if praise predominates and corrections are few. The markers of progress become tainted, and may be cause for suspicion. The learner sees each marker, whether positive or negative, as another step taken anxiously toward a familiar, and familiarly negative, conclusion. Waiting for the other shoe to drop provokes anxiety and impedes learning. Gone is the eager and open-ended exploration in a totally safe setting. Rather, the learner inches along carefully and guardedly, focusing more on avoiding familiar pain than seeking pleasure in discovery of something new.

Trainers who use both positive reinforcement and correction or punishment may rely on positive reinforcement primarily until something unexpected happens, particularly something interpreted as disobedience or defiance. Then, the trainer punishes the learner. For the trainer, the ratio of rewards to punishments may be obvious, and obviously positive, but for the learner, an element of danger has entered the arena and will remain, the risk of punishment always on the learner's mind.

Thus, the introduction of an aversive has poisoned the learning environment and the relationship between the trainer and the learner. Learning is no longer a risk-free enjoyable opportunity to explore, figure something out, and earn reinforcement, but a task that can lead to either a good or bad outcome. "The shift becomes visible in the learner's attitude, which switches from attentive eagerness to reluctance, often with visible manifestations of stress. Even though successful response to a given discriminative stimulus is still followed by reward, if failure is now followed by punishment, you have made that discriminative stimulus ambiguous in terms of predictable outcome. It is no longer 'safe.' You have poisoned your cue" (Pryor, 2002).

People tend to underestimate the impact of punishment or correction – especially if they stop short of harshness – on learning, but it is readily apparent through observation. John Holt, an elementary school teacher, wrote two best-selling books in the 1960s chronicling his observations of children. The first, *How Children Fail,* explored the coping strategies – mumbling, daydreaming, grabbing for answers without thinking just to get one's turn over with – children used in elementary school classrooms that virtually ensured their failure, at least their failure to learn much. "They fail because they are afraid, bored, and confused. They are afraid, above all else, of failing, of disappointing or displeasing the many anxious adults around them, whose limitless hopes and expectations for them hang over their heads like a cloud" (Holt, 1964, p. 16). They fail to learn because they are "humiliated, frightened, and discouraged. They use their minds, not to learn, but to get out of doing the things we tell them to do – to make them learn.... [T]hese strategies are self-limiting and self-defeating, and destroy both character and intelligence.... [W]hen we make children afraid, we stop their learning dead in its tracks" (Holt, 1967, pp. 9f.).

In his sequel, *How Children Learn* (1967), Holt contrasted this plight of school-age children, whose love of learning had been poisoned, with the persistent eagerness for exploration and acquisition of skill seen in younger children. They learn through trial and error and have a high tolerance for failure. Toddlers, for example, initially fall a great deal while learning to walk. Their frequent failures do not discourage new attempts to master a task. Parents and other caregivers may lend a hand, but rarely try to "teach" a toddler how to walk. Like the toddlers learning to walk, children respond to objective feedback from the environment rather than punishment for errors imposed by people. "They have a style of learning that fits their condition, and which they use naturally and well" (Holt, 1967, p. 9). "What teachers and learners need to know is…: first, that vivid, vital, pleasurable experiences are the easiest to remember, and secondly, that memory works best when unforced, that it is not a mule that can be made to walk by beating it" (Holt, 1967, p. 10).

Correction and punishment exact a toll from the teachers and trainers who dispense them as well as from the learners who must cope with receiving them. Animal trainers, teachers of any sort, parents, grandparents, or people attempting to shape the behavior of another who use correction or punishment, even on rare occasion, damage the trust and rapport they once had with their learner.

They also get reinforced insidiously for their use of these aversives. "Animals" – and children – "soon learn to recognize the signs of coercion, and to respond to the hints. A lift of the hand is enough to move the herd or stop the dog from approaching; you no longer need to actually wave sticks, thump rumps, or yell. Thus the trainer is reinforced for diminishing effort, a natural shaping contingency. Another natural contingency, however, is that when an animal fails to respond to, say, a raised hand, the trainer's natural response, as a dominant individual, is to escalate the threat, and if that doesn't work, to apply physical punishment. This has two consequences. If the animal finally does comply, the trainer is instantly reinforced for using the punishment. Furthermore the longer it takes, the more reinforcing the final escalation. Hey, it worked, didn't it! The fact that punishment did NOT work at first, or quickly, is masked entirely. Eventual success reinforces the trainer's punishing behavior" (Pryor, 2000, p. 8).

Using positive reinforcement exclusively in teaching does not mean never saying "no" or meting out a consequence. No responsible adult would let a child or a dog run into traffic and wait to reinforce coming when called instead of lifting the renegade out of danger. Similarly, adults say "no" to a child reaching for a hot cup of coffee or a dog about to gobble a tray of hors d'oeuvres – but none of these sanctions occurs during training. When learning is the activity, the setting and the teacher or trainer must be safe so that free exploration is possible. During training, corrections are only likely to stifle curiosity and willingness to try something new. Without free exploration, mastery is not possible.

■ Event Markers: Clicking for Mastery

To promote positive reinforcement throughout the curriculum, SHIP uses acoustic event markers, called clickers, and treats.

An event marker is an artificial stimulus that coincides with a desired behavior. Most people choose an acoustic event marker rather than a visual marker so they can flag a behavior without requiring the learner's proximity. Using an acoustic marker, trainers can work from a distance, marking a behavior mid-jump even while the learner is facing away from the trainer. Dog trainers generally to use a child's cricket, a simple plastic box with a metal strip that makes a click when depressed. Thus, at least for dog trainers, acoustic marker-based training has acquired the name "clicker training."

The trainer begins by making the click and then giving the learner a treat. Very quickly, the learner realizes the acoustic marker or click means that the treat is coming. By marking selected desirable behaviors with the click, the trainer can identify a specific behavior and reinforce it, in essence saying "I like what you are doing in this instant and I will pay you for it." For instance, the learner figures out that sitting earns a click and a treat and begins to offer this behavior. The learner feels proactive: his or her behavior causes the click and treat. Encouraged by this prowess, the learner continues to offer the behavior. The learner has constructed a reality in which his or her behavior causes desired outcomes, reflecting mastery over behavior and environment and the ability to elicit a desired response from another.

Some dog trainers and other animal behaviorists use the phrase "clicker training without the clicker" to describe training that uses positive reinforcement primarily, if not exclusively, relying on language such as "yes" or "good" in place of a click or some other artificial sound to indicate approval.

For a number of reasons, "clicking" using language rather than an artificial signal such as a clicker results in less progress for both animal and human learners. Words said aloud take up more time than a brief acoustic marker such as a click. The reliance on spoken language with its lack of temporal precision in pinpointing incremental behavioral gains not only reduces learning but also represents the failure of the trainer to establish efficient and effective communication with the learner.

In addition, it is hard for animals to sort out spoken language. Domesticated animals hear speech around them all the time, little of it directed at them and less of it intelligible without the expenditure of great effort. Wild animals rarely hear human language at all. Animals' hearing is focused on sounds of members of their own species, of predators and prey, and of indicators of safety and danger. Recognizing the human speech sounds directed at them and figuring out what the sounds mean takes considerable work, more than learning the behaviors the verbal cues are intended to trigger.

Verbal commands often create obstacles for people too. Few people (roughly 3 percent of the population) are auditory learners. Children learn enormous repertoires of behaviors before they can produce language. Sequencing and retaining spoken information come much later in childhood. Children with any of the many common learning disabilities usually have difficulty following verbal directions. People who had harsh parents or teachers may also respond poorly to instructions given aloud, reacting emotionally with recollections of past insults or humiliations rather than focusing on the task at hand.

Thus, while omitting the clicker may be convenient for the trainer who now has a free hand, it makes the learner deal from weakness rather than strength, from confusion rather than clarity. The trainer may be equally positive and benign whether clicking or saying "yes," but the learner is clear in one situation and working at a considerable disadvantage in the other.

The marker signal provides a precise staccato indicator as the desired behavior occurs. Its sound carries clearly and distinctly above the surrounding din of verbiage. The brevity and specificity of communication with the marker signal cannot be equaled conversationally. Moreover, because the sound is extraordinary, it has a significant impact on both the learner and the trainer. Lacking tone of voice and intonation, qualities unavoidable in speech, the marker signal also comes across as an objective indicator of progress. Both participants are reinforced by the click, the learner for the act and the trainer for the well-timed click and the learner's new behavior.

Hearing "yes" or "good," the learner knows he or she has pleased the trainer. Hearing a click, the learner knows he or she got the behavior right. Vague praise, while nice, is not as useful for learning as the specific targeting of achievement – and may even be distracting if the learner attends to the social niceties that come with conversation. The click stresses the learner's role as the behaver rather than the trainer's role as the giver of praise. Thus, the relationship becomes more egalitarian, with both the learner and trainer trying to get the behavior and the communication right. The click reinforces the efforts and precision of both participants. The resulting shared experience builds a collegial rapport that transcends age, language, and species.

Perfect timing is required for efficient shaping of behavior with a marker signal. To achieve this, the trainer must be totally focused on and attentive to the learner's effort, understanding of the behavior being shaped, and level of frustration. A good trainer can anticipate possible misconstructions and streamline shaping so that the learner's energy is directed toward the goal with little effort wasted on irrelevant actions. The ability to anticipate the likely conceptualization of the learner, the desire to work swiftly to conserve the learner's energy, buoy enthusiasm, and encourage learning are skills that promote empathy. Clicking frequently creates an atmosphere of abundance and generosity as well as guidance.

The click works better for the learner because of the learner's innate auditory limitations and the click's clarity of communication. The click works better for the trainer because of the concentration and precision it requires from the trainer. The click works better for the relationship of the trainer and learner because it reinforces both of them, reduces the power differential between them, and increases the collaboration and enjoyment of a shared experience. Clicker training without the clicker compromises achievement; clicker training with the clicker maximizes learning and mastery (Loar, 2000).

■ Mastery through Marker-Based (Clicker) Training: Why it Works

Karen Pryor often remarks that people overestimate the intelligence of dolphins and underestimate the intelligence of horses. The primary reason for this miscalculation is each species' reaction to its different contact with humans. Dolphins cannot be restrained or taught by force. They must be allowed to swim freely to breathe and survive. If dolphins do not like the way they are treated, they just swim away. Because dolphins get their hydration through the fish they consume and not through drinking water, food cannot be withheld. So, dolphin trainers work non-coercively with a whistle or other acoustic marker and a bucket of fish to communicate (Pryor, 1995). Horses, on the other hand, are on leads, and further controlled by reins and a bit in their mouths. Riding crops and kicks are used to "communicate." Horse trainers talk about "breaking" horses as a necessary part of training.

Pryor concludes that the difference in attitudes toward people and toward learning readily observable in dolphins and horses reflect not so much the difference in their innate intelligence but their reactions to the way people treat them. Children – adolescents in particular – respond in like manner, generally amiable and eager to learn new things unless treated harshly. Pryor observes, "most dolphin trainers, who must develop the skills of using positive reinforcers in their daily work, have strikingly pleasant and agreeable children" (Pryor, 1999, p. xvi).

This viewpoint has led SHIP to design a curriculum based exclusively on clicker training. Why does it work? Behavior learned through marker-based training promotes

- Retention of skills acquired through marker-based training,

- Accelerated learning as a result of marker-based training,

- Learning without fear,

- Learning for fun, playful learning, and

- Creativity.

Retention of skills acquired through marker-based training

Behavior learned through marker-based training is readily retained. Effort does not go into remembering; rather, the learning just sticks. People remember for years an early or particularly challenging task in the training game, and animals remember skills taught but not practiced in the interim. Pryor gives a particularly compelling example of this retention, and the ability of a shaped behavior to function as interspecies communication:

"One night after dinner, to amuse my cousin's children, I taught their cat to play the piano.... I shaped the behavior of the cat sitting on the piano bench and plunking at the keys with one paw. (With most cats this takes about five minutes. Cats like to train people to produce treats predictably.) After that evening no one ever asked the cat to do it again, nor did the cat offer the behavior.

"One morning two years later my cousin called to tell me that the previous night they were awakened by ghostly sounds from downstairs: Someone seemed to be playing the piano. On investigation, he found that the living-room doors, as usual, had been shut to conserve heat. And inside the living room, the cat, who normally slept upstairs in the bedroom, was sitting on the piano bench. When, one presumes, the normal responses of meowing and perhaps scratching at the door didn't work, the cat offered a learned behavior to ask, not for food this time, but for its preferred sleeping place. The effort was a success" (Pryor, 1999, p. 169).

Accelerated learning as a result of marker-based training

Experienced clicker trainers will regale virtually any audience with stories of great strides in learning, unequalled in "clicker training without the clicker" or any other method of instruction. There are many hypotheses about why this happens: that the marker signal is processed in the amygdala, that the apersonal marker elevates it above competing quotidian concerns, that the clicker clarifies the confusion accompanying trial and error through its precision and specificity, and so on. Research has not yet explained why, but anecdotal evidence shows that marker-based learning is fast-paced and brings frequent windfalls. It also allows people with learning disabilities, language deficits or interpersonal difficulties to bypass their areas of weakness and build on strengths at a pace they choose.

Learning without fear

When positive reinforcement is used exclusively, the worst that can happen to a learner is that no reinforcement is forthcoming. Offering the desired behavior causes reinforcement; failing to do so is a non-event.

Learning for fun, playful learning

As a result of the risk-free environment, learners find the process of learning enjoyable and are willing to be playful and take cognitive and behavioral risks. Clicker dogs attending clicker training activities are famous for stealing clickers from open purses and bringing them to their owners to start a game. SHIP's clients eagerly request the training game, sometimes asking for an easy or especially difficult behavior depending on their mood. One of the families in the pilot group in San Jose made dazzling strides with their skills. When queried about their extraordinary progress, they replied that they had been playing the training game at home after dinner instead of watching television. The facilitator said, "There must not be any yelling in your home." The mother, visibly startled by this comment, reflected for a moment and replied, "I hadn't thought about it until you mentioned it, but we've been playing the clicker game for a couple of hours every evening just because it's fun and nobody has raised a voice much less a hand since we started doing that."

Creativity

In one marker-based program, Karen Pryor and her associates worked with dolphins at Sea Life Park in Hawaii, training them to exhibit a number of behaviors on cue. Once the dolphins had mastered the behaviors, Pryor began to click them for novelty. In these sessions the rule was that the dolphin would earn rewards for exhibiting behaviors the trainers had not seen before.

After running through the established repertoire, the dolphins figured out the challenge and began behaving creatively to trigger reinforcement. One dolphin, named Malia, "began emitting an unprecedented range of behaviors, including aerial flips, gliding with the tail out of the water, and 'skidding' over the tank floor, some of which were as complex as responses normally produced by shaping techniques, and many of which were quite unlike anything seen in Malia or any other porpoise by Sea Life Park staff. It appeared that the trainer's criterion, 'only those actions will be reinforced which have not been reinforced previously,' was met by Malia with the presentation of complete patterns of gross body movement in which novelty was an intrinsic factor. Furthermore, the trainers could not imagine shaped behaviors as unusual as some emitted spontaneously by the porpoise" (Pryor, 1995 [originally published 1969], pp.34f.).

It is the approach that generates the behavior; Pryor's marker-based training promotes playfulness and creativity rather than fear and suspicion.

There are two striking differences between most parenting skills classes and virtually all dog training classes. The first is that parents attend parenting classes without their children, while dog owners bring their dogs to dog training classes. Thus, the former relies on parental description of behavior problems, necessarily self-serving and limited in perspective, while the latter allows the trainer to observe interaction and address problems as they occur.

The second difference is the homework assigned at the end of the first class. Parents are usually given some directive about managing misbehavior the next time it occurs. Dog owners are told to figure out which kind of treat their dog enjoys the most and would be willing to work the hardest to earn, and to use that treat to reinforce a positive behavior.

As a result, the parent goes home looking to manage misbehavior while the dog owner goes home looking to gauge enjoyment. Effectively applying the parenting advice, parents will focus on negatives, the misbehavior and its management. Effectively applying the dog training advice, owners will see and reward their dog's good behavior and the proffered treats will result in a positive interaction between owner and dog. The child will be more or less well managed when misbehaving; the dog will have skills to manage his or her environment.

Parents and dog owners generally want similar things from their charges – mastery of impulsivity and good manners around people, food, and possessions. SHIP uses positive reinforcement exclusively, relying on clickers as event markers to teach parents and children to train dogs in mannerly behavior both for the betterment of the dogs and to teach the humans positive shaping techniques and the ability to break desirable behaviors down into small and learnable increments. This approach to mastery, presented in a safe animal-assisted therapy program, is intended to create mastery that can be retained and applied once the program is over and participants need these skills to respond to the ongoing difficulties of their everyday lives.

Clicker training teaches people to master the skills of teaching and learning, to break things down into very small increments and build a more complex behavior. Of necessity, it requires considerable tolerance for frustration and the ability to think and sequence behaviors while aroused or anxious. Both the learner and the trainer must construct meaning out of clicks, figure out what movement is causing the click and how to create a meaningful behavior out of it. Both learn to play by the rules and pace the work to facilitate learning and partnership. The trainer must constantly reflect on the learner's response to the click and what the learner thinks he or she is being clicked for doing. This is the beginning of empathy and responsibility.

Teaching Empathy with the Training Game

■ The Training Game

"Clicker Training gets your timing right so you can comfort a sick child" observed Karen Pryor (Boat, Loar and Pryor, 2001, p. 9). Timing is a way to break down empathy into teachable skills, skills that improve behavior and rapport between teacher and learner, parent and child, trainer and animal, or any other dyad.

SHIP divides its hour-long sessions in half, with 30 minutes devoted to clicker training animals and 30 minutes to clicker training people, the latter called the Training Game. Two people volunteer, one to be the trainer and the other the learner. The learner chooses the treats he or she would like to work for and then goes far enough away to avoid hearing the group select the behavior to be shaped. Depending on the safety of the setting and the age and maturity of the learner, the spot to wait can be outside the training room or at the far end of the room with the learner's back to the group. In subsequent rounds of the game, the learner becomes the next trainer. This order promotes generosity in the trainer: somebody who has just been the learner will vividly remember the uncertainty involved and how encouraging and informative frequent clicks were.

Few supplies are needed for the training game: a clicker and lots of treats. SHIP also gives participants fanny packs so they can feel the weight of their earnings. They also can keep their clickers in them and attach the Clicker Promise (see Appendix 1, p. 195) to the straps.

These rules must be followed when playing the training game out of respect for people and property:

1. Choose a task that is not embarrassing or difficult.

2. Choose a task that does not involve touching other people, animals or personal possessions.

3. Always look at the learner and have the learner come toward you (the trainer). If you cannot see what your learner is looking at, you might unintentionally shape a behavior you cannot see. And, you don't want to reward somebody for moving away from you, making rejection pay.

4. Take turns: the learner becomes the trainer in the next round.

5. Be generous – click often; use more treats per click to communicate enthusiasm, e.g., 1 click and three treats to show a big stride toward the goal, 1 click and a jackpot (a generous handful of treats) for an exceptionally big stride.

When the learner has left the group, the group must settle on a task such as sitting in a designated chair, touching an object in the room, or turning in a circle. As Hilary and Evelyn, 10-year-old authors of *Teaching with a Clicker: How to Train People and Animals with a Clicker and Treats* (see Appendix 1) instruct, "Pick something easy at first. Click for an easy task, and then go to a harder one. When you start, click for a step in the right direction. Remember, the learner's a beginner!"

Groups often have a hard time with this, proposing as a first task filling a glass with water, erasing a blackboard or some other multi-step behavior, a behavior chain in reality. When the facilitator points out what's involved: 1. going to the glass, 2. touching the glass, 3. lifting the glass, 4. carrying the glass, 5. to the faucet, 6. turning the faucet on, 7. placing the glass under the stream of water, and 8. turning the faucet off, attendees, especially parents, are amazed at the complexity of such a seemingly simple task. Parents begin to realize why saying "clean your room" to their child yields such poor results. The group must agree on a simple task, touching the glass for example. Learning to break a complex behavior down into its components and settling on accomplishing only the first step as a finite and rewarding activity teaches parents to set more realistic goals with their children – and themselves – in other settings. Appropriate and manageable expectations increase the likelihood of success. They also reduce the risk that failure to do the impossible would be misinterpreted as disobedience and noncompliance.

Once the group agrees on an appropriate task, somebody invites the learner to come in and the game begins. Neophyte trainers tend to expect too much before giving their first click. The learner, getting no feedback, becomes discouraged and stops moving. Frequently, the frustrated learner will stare intently at the trainer in the hopes of eliciting some facial cue or verbal guidance (among the strategies John Holt noted that children used when trying to circumvent a task). To prevent this, the facilitator should ask the trainer as soon as the task is decided (before the game begins) to list the first few increments that might be clicked as soon as the learner enters the training area. For example, if the task is to raise one's hand above the head, the first click could be for the arm that swings automatically as the learner walks into the room. It could be for a glance upward as the learner scans the room.

Therapeutic gains from playing the training game

The training game results in a number of gains that promote empathy. These include:

- Creating an atmosphere of abundance,
- Replacing stinginess with generosity,
- Gentle touching,
- Concern for the welfare of others,
- Teaching people to – and how to – reward good behavior,
- Teaching people to – and how to – observe good behavior,
- Teaching timing to evoke empathy, and
- Clicking for positive affect.

Creating an atmosphere of abundance

SHIP's families are poor and typically come from generations of impoverishment and emotional deprivation. They face economic stress daily and contrast their poverty with the affluence depicted on television. Facilitators make sure that there is always plenty of candy so nobody has to worry about there being enough.

Replacing stinginess with generosity

An initial challenge is getting novice trainers to click and treat often enough. Progress can be made by getting people to articulate how it felt to be the learner waiting for a click as they are about to become the trainer, and by getting them to list lots of first steps they could click for. However, there is an underlying reluctance to click and treat often which seems to reflect the clients' generalized experience of insufficiency at least as much as their inexperience as a trainer.

Initially the children are thrilled with the training game because they earn candy – and they earn lots of it. Frequently the parents complain about the candy. The group discusses the need for rewards to be things the learner really values and will work hard to earn, candy the obvious currency for most children. Facilitators remind the parents about how things go at Halloween, first a great focus on all the candy and then a waning of interest as time goes on. After their early objections, parents tend to get very interested in earning candy themselves (usually by the third week), allowing the program's abundance to reduce their own sense of deprivation. A couple of weeks later, the candy is of passing importance for most children and adults and many return some or all of their earnings to the candy jar before leaving.

Gentle touching

One startling thing leaps out when parents and children play the training game – many of the parents go to great lengths to avoid touching their children. Participating parents drop the candy into their child's hand from a few inches away or encourage the child to unzip the fanny pack so they can drop the candy into the pouch. To overcome this behavior, the facilitator insists on the candy being placed in the recipient's hand. After a few sessions, the transfer of candy happens easily with hands touching momentarily in passing. For some children, this may be the first non-abusive touch from the parent's hand in quite a while.

Concern for the welfare of others

The edginess around handing candy and the clumsiness of children in general result in candy occasionally falling to the floor. Initially, people retrieve candy intended for them but tend to ignore candy other people have dropped. This provides an opportunity to focus on the welfare of others, in this case, the SHIP dogs. Despite reasonable precautions, the dogs inevitably manage to get a few of the scattered treats. Therefore, for the first few sessions, treats for people are fruit-flavored hard and soft candies, things that are not toxic for the dogs. After a while, participants get better at handing rather than dropping the treats and more ready to pick up treats – including those somebody else dropped – demonstrating concern for the welfare of the dogs rather than a narrow notion of justice requiring only that each person pick up treats that he or she dropped. Facilitators acknowledge those who promptly pick up treats they dropped; they give profuse thanks, usually including a click and more treats, to people who pick up treats somebody else dropped in the interests of the welfare of the dogs.

At the end of the session in which treats are well-monitored by the participants, the facilitator asks the group to consider an important question requiring reflection and consensus: "You have been doing excellent work and have learned a lot. I would like to recognize the quality of your accomplishments. Clicker trainers usually do this by offering better treats. For people this most often means chocolate. But there is a problem with this because chocolate can make dogs very sick. So, you need to decide if you can make it safe for me to bring chocolate. Can you guarantee that if I bring chocolate next time no dog will get any of it? That means you will keep a watchful eye out at all times to keep the dogs and the chocolate apart, regardless of whose chocolate it is and who dropped it. Take a minute and think about it."

In several years, only one group decided they were too scattered to monitor the chocolate adequately and asked for the fruit candies to continue. They were praised for their mature assessment of the situation and for their willingness to put their altruistic desire to keep the dogs safe ahead of their own sweet tooth. All the other groups have eagerly accepted the responsibility of becoming vigilant on behalf of dogs in proximity to chocolate.

They then are given the Dog Protection Promise to sign. At the beginning of the next session, the participants receive their copy of the signed and dated Dog Protection Promise in a nice frame. Another copy is kept in their file (see Appendix 1, p. 196).

Teaching people to – and how to – reward good behavior

People tend to be much more used to giving and receiving criticism than praise. They need to be coached to reward good behavior in every aspect, clicking frequently, treating generously and by actually handing the treats to the recipient. The facilitator often creates a parallel dyad, shaping the generous behavior of the trainer toward his or her learner.

Teaching people to – and how to – observe good behavior

Sometimes the problem with giving positive reinforcement for good behavior goes beyond reluctance to praise. The trainer may be so engulfed in negatives that he or she simply does not see positives. People cannot respond with empathy to behavior they do not see. As a result, SHIP teaches participants to see positives as part of the effort to teach empathy.

A common problem in group activities is getting the audience to watch attentively, in this case to observe training and learning styles. A way to address that problem and also to teach participants to see positives is to give somebody a clicker and treats and ask him or her to watch the audience and click and treat people for paying attention, for smiling, and other positive behaviors. Empowered by the clicker and feeling some urgency to use it, people begin to notice postures and facial expressions indicating attentiveness and enjoyment.

Teaching timing to evoke empathy

Accurate timing of the click is the key to conveying information to the learner. Click too late and you reinforce the wrong behavior. Click too infrequently and you frustrate your learner, and appear mean spirited and untrustworthy to boot. Accurate timing requires that the trainer focus not only on the moves the learner makes, but on the definition of the task the learner is constructing, to reinforce on-target moves and ignore tentative forays that could, with only an errant click or two, send the learner off on a dead end. This means more than the sculptor's envisioning a statue in the block of marble. It means the trainer seeing with the learner's eyes the learner's vision of the statue in the block of marble.

In one round of the training game, the learner, in this case a humane officer with the Humane Society of Santa Clara Valley, entered the training area and got clicked. She took another step and got clicked again. She thought she was moving in the right direction toward an object or other target. Actually the task was to stand on one foot. How would the trainer communicate that to the learner who with another click or two would be sure she was heading in the right direction across the room? How do you break the task down and slow the walker down?

You do this by dividing the task into smaller steps. Standing on one foot really means lifting the other. Walking involves forward motion; standing does not. Could the trainer click early enough for the learner to realize the click was for the heel leaving the ground, not for forward motion? The audience was astonished at the complexity of the problem. From their perspective, things went quickly and linearly from entering to focusing on feet to standing on one foot. It looked this way to them because they knew ahead of time what the goal was. Everything they saw was in this goal-oriented context. Not so for the learner who had no idea what was expected.

In another session, an experienced and confident learner bounded in offering all sorts of behaviors and exhausting herself in the process. For her considerable efforts she received few clicks from an inexperienced and unempathic trainer. After a minute or two of jumping, turning, moving first one limb then another to see what would earn a click, she turned to the trainer and said, "I'm out here working myself to death for you and you're not giving me anything back. Frankly, I don't like you and I don't trust you!" (Boat, Loar & Pryor, 2001, p. 7).

Barbara Boat was so taken with her responsibility for the learner's emotional well being that she referred to her first learner as her learner-victim! When Boat had her turn as the learner, she had a very experienced trainer. She felt smart and capable: "My coach was very skilled and I soon was turning in circles, picking up my rewards (pennies) after each click that my coach used to inform me that I was doing a fabulous job and was a very smart learner. Now it was my turn to be the coach. The designated behavior for my learner-victim was to walk several steps to a table and touch the mat on the table with her hand. As soon as my learner started offering me behaviors I was overwhelmed! Should I click and reward that step or that turn or – oh no! I accidentally clicked as she sank down on one knee. How am I going to get her off the floor? I was mortified. My poor learner-victim was hopelessly confused and I was the cause! My sense of responsibility to create a positive outcome for my learner amazed me then and still does!" (Boat, Loar & Pryor, 2001, p. 7).

Timing is a way to break down empathy into teachable skills. It does not correct or give advice. Precise timing truly helps both the problem and the relationship.

Clicking for positive affect

Many child and adult participants in SHIP have experienced numerous losses and frightening traumas in childhood. As a result, they have shut down emotionally. Continuing to feel would mean continuing to feel pain; being numb seems preferable. However, such adaptation to trauma is costly, as Garbarino explains:

1. Children become hypersensitive to negative social cues.

2. Children become oblivious to positive social cues.

3. Children develop a repertory of aggressive behaviors that are readily accessible and can be easily invoked.

4. Children draw the conclusion that aggression is a successful way of getting what they want. (Garbarino, 1999, p. 81)

Garbarino cautions, "empathy is the enemy of violence, depersonalization is its ally" (Garbarino, 1999, p. 114). Through the training game, as learner, trainer, observer, and reinforcer of observers, people regain their ability to see the behavior and affect of others, to "repersonalize."

Barbara Boat concluded from her first experience as the learner and the trainer in the training game: "Clicker training focuses the trainer's attention on the learner, with respect for the learner's abilities, frustration, and fatigue. This accurate assessment that is essential for clicker training is empathy – in a way that can be learned through repetitions of the training game. Trainers always want their learners to succeed – the trainers' success depends on the learners' achievements – so they are very helpful. They streamline things and break tasks down into small and manageable steps. They make learning fast and fun through frequent clicks and generous treats. They come across as kind and encouraging trainers, and their students as avid and enthusiastic learners" (Boat, Loar & Pryor, 2001, p. 9).

Anticipating a Better Future

SHIP's DESIGN ENCOURAGES PARTICIPANTS TO HAVE A MORE POSITIVE FUTURE ORIENTATION. Through their work with dogs, SHIP's participants can feel hope first for the dogs and then for themselves.

People eagerly participate in training SHIP's dogs both for the pleasure of the activity and in the hope that the socialization and skills acquired will give the dogs a chance for adoption and a better life. People who feel boxed in, exhausted or defeated, will nonetheless express optimism for the dogs they have worked with. And, they are willing to work hard for the dogs to have a better future.

Over time, participants' optimism for the dogs' futures begins to spread to their own inchoate and very fragile hopes. Safety still lies in pessimism and danger of disappointment; additional hurt still lurks in raised expectations. But through their work with SHIP dogs, participants begin to experiment with optimism by using the animal as a proxy. They point out similarities between the animals and people as they express their hopes that the animals will have a better life. Poems from children in Pam Raphael's humane education classes illustrate this dynamic well:

Cats and dogs are living beings like us,
So treat your pet the way you want to be treated.
Lots of animals starve or are killed by cars.
You have to be responsible for your pet.
Understand them like we understand each other.
Animals suffer without food.
Feel for your pet, so care for your pet.

Alanna, Grade Five (Raphael, 1999, p. 36)

I was walking down the street one night
When I spotted a kitten, gray and white.
He was hungry and very sad.
He looked like a good kitten, not bad.
He was playful but liked to roam.
So I did a good thing and took him home.

Valentina, Grade Five (Raphael, 1999, p. 39)

Dogs and cats, like us, have feelings.
They cannot be abused or treated unfairly.
Please treat your animals the way you
Want to be treated.

Cassie, Grade Five (Raphael, 1999, p. 20)

Animals make me happy and feel good.
I have a cat and when I feel sad he
Comes to me and cheers me up.
Animals are so loveable.
People should b loveable to the animals.
Animals help people and we should help them.
You should never hit an animal because they are just like us.
Dogs and cats have feelings, too, like us.

Veronica, Grade Five (Raphael, 1999, p. 20)

I think you should treat animals the way you want to be treated.
If you treat them the right way, they will warm you.

Shoshanna, Grade Five (Raphael, 1999, p. 21)

These poems demonstrate the connections SHIP's structure and design seek to create. Program participants learn that responsible, nurturing treatment is possible for animals and for people, and that this treatment opens the door to a more optimistic view of the future.

Literacy: Consolidating Gains by Putting Them in Writing

MANY OF THE CHILDREN PARTICIPATING IN THE STRATEGIC HUMANE INTERVENTIONS PROGRAM IN SAN FRANCISCO ARE BILINGUAL, PRIMARILY CANTONESE/ENGLISH OR SPANISH/ENGLISH. Although they appear fluent in both languages, many actually speak each language less well than they should at their ages. Their parents tend to be limited speakers of English or monolingual in their native language.

As a result, their children's English does not develop through conversation at home as it would in an English-speaking family. Between extended work schedules, limited education, and the children acculturating faster than their parents, the parents often speak only perfunctorily to their children in their native tongues, usually about chores, routines, schedules and the like. Thus, these bilingual children do not develop a mature fluency in their primary language, or in English, which they get largely from equally limited peers and television.

This conundrum of speaking two languages, but neither of them at an increasing level of complexity and subtlety, creates problems in comprehension and expression, in being able to negotiate the children's necessary journey in two cultures. It also restricts their ability to express feelings, frustrations, and the more complicated concerns children face as they approach their teen years.

The writing projects that SHIP uses are designed to focus on the details of effective communication, on translating the keen observation that comes with clicker training into equally clear written expression, and on bridging language and cultural gaps. They involve attention to detail, managing time and effort to work on a complicated project in small pieces, eliciting the advice of others, and empathic writing, choosing idioms and phrases that will resonate with the project's intended audience.

The results have been remarkable. SHIP's literacy component has promoted mastery of writing, and the work to achieve mastery of writing has promoted empathy, an optimistic view of the future, and the chance to contribute to society. *Teaching with a Clicker: How to Train People and Animals with a Clicker and Treats* (see Appendix 1, pp. 186-187) demonstrates one such project; dog resumes are also used in SHIP to promote literacy. In addition, SHIP uses a number of written documents to maintain enthusiasm and motivation. These tools also have the benefit of promoting reading as well as writing, the two components of literacy.

■ Teaching With a Clicker: How to Train People and Animals with a Clicker and Treats
(see Appendix 1, pp. 186-191, for the English, Spanish and Chinese versions of the brochure).

This piece was written by Hilary Louie and Evelyn Pang (names used with their and their parents' written permission, and proudly because of the excellence of their work). Hilary and Evelyn were both ten years old when they joined the SHIP program. After having participated in SHIP sessions for a number of months, they expressed a desire to do an extra project. Bilingual, they decided to write a children's guide to clicker training in English and then translate it into Chinese. With the author's permission, they adapted Karen Pryor's *15 Tips for Getting Started with the Clicker* for children.

The girls met weekly for several months and worked diligently, wrestling with clarity of wording and sequencing of ideas. Pryor is a clear and accessible writer, but her tips are written for an adult audience. The girls figured out the meaning and connotation of every word and phrase in Pryor's text, its impact on behavior and the relationship between the trainer and the learner, and then explained each concept in language that would be accessible to children their own age and a bit younger. Finding words readily understood by 8- to 10-year-olds for "successive approximation" or "incremental steps toward a goal" is not an easy task. The children came up with wonderful language: "Pick something easy at first. Click for an easy task, and then go to a harder one. When you start, click for a step in the right direction. Remember, the learner's a beginner!"

Then, Jane Tamagna, the editor of this book, its predecessor (Raphael, 1999) and several other projects for the Latham Foundation (e.g., Sternberg, 2002), reviewed the girls' draft and made some suggestions about headings and organization. The children studied her suggestions and spent an evening focusing on sequencing ideas and concepts. They revised their work using headings for the now-discrete parts, created a welcoming introduction and a "Do and Don't List" for the conclusion. They drew pictures to illustrate their text.

Next they translated their draft into Chinese with the assistance of Jackie Kan, a bi-lingual staff member in their building. They learned the difference between a literal and an idiomatic translation, and they began to appreciate the different cultural and conceptual ideas about relationships and behaviors and how to express notions of positive reinforcement and respect for learning in two dramatically different cultural contexts. They became able to distinguish between literal meaning and culturally-based interpretation. They grew in expression in both languages, and in sensitivity to the values conveyed by idiomatic usage in each language. They became more conscious of differences in expectations and standards for greetings and manners and the divergent value systems underlying them. They matured not only in command of language and in translation skills but also in precision of expression and empathy for others facing the challenges of acculturation

Hilary and Evelyn worked for almost a year, meeting weekly in their free time. As they were proofreading the final version of their brochure, they announced, "We are not done. We have written how to teach with a clicker, but not what to teach." Thus, they plunged into "Teaching With a Clicker: How to Teach Your Dog Good Manners and Tricks." The English version appears in Appendix 1, pp. 192-193. The girls were busily at work on the Chinese translation as this book went to press. It and the Spanish translation by Lina Tam-Li will be available at www.Pryorfoundation.com in 2004. Hilary and Evelyn have asked the authors to alert the book's readership that their subsequent works will be made available through this web site. Next on their agenda is Pryor's "Poisoned Cue" (Pryor, 2002) from the girls' perspective.

Hilary and Evelyn developed the ability to commit to an involved project, to break it down into small segments and proceed incrementally toward their goal. They also learned to incorporate the suggestions of an outside reviewer, to reflect on the advice received, and to revise their work accordingly. Their brochures are given to all new participants in SHIP. Monolingual parents are especially appreciative of work done by their children's peers that is accessible to them and explains the activities of SHIP's sessions.

It was fun to reinforce the girls' work. Each week after the session, the facilitator would type up and mail to the children the meeting's output. She would add praise and a few questions to think about for the upcoming session. Letters complimenting the girls' efforts were sent periodically to parents and teachers. When their draft was completed, it was sent to Barbara Boat and Karen Pryor for review. Both responded enthusiastically and began using it in their work. Pryor also gave each girl an autographed copy of *Clicker Training for Dogs* (1999) to the girls' great delight.

The Spanish Translation:

(see Appendix 1, pp. 190-191, for the Spanish translation of the brochure)

A bilingual mother-daughter team, Maria Garcia and her 11-year-old daughter, Priscilla Galvez, and a 13-year-old friend of the family, Lina Tam-Li, translated the text into Spanish (again, names are used proudly with permission). The Galvez family speaks both English and Spanish at home, but their children, in English-only classes at school, are favoring English and not continuing to grow in their command of Spanish. Lina, fluent in Chinese, her mother tongue, and in Spanish from several years living in Panama, was new to America and needed to learn English. The group met weekly throughout the summer of 2003, with Lina taking the bus from the far end of the city to attend. They were joined by Dinora Castro, a bilingual SHIP volunteer. The facilitator marveled each week that the girls would come during their summer vacation and work diligently. Another marvel was the collegiality of the group, made up of three adults and two children, the adults having a greater command of the languages but the children having a greater sense of suitability for the project's intended audience. Everybody had a clicker and a supply of treats to mark a good translation or clever wording by somebody else.

The group reviewed the English draft Hilary and Evelyn had written and got into productive discussions about the concepts and techniques involved. By translating the text into Spanish, the participants learned how to make themselves clear in both languages. They became more comfortable speaking and reading in each language and more skillful in translating from one language to the other, a new technique for them. To make sure the meaning was clear in both languages and to everybody, the group would translate from English into Spanish and then at the end of the hour go from the new Spanish text back into English to make sure nothing had been lost or distorted.

Cultural nuances and differences emerged as the group searched for the right words. Pryor's text implies, and Hilary and Evelyn's text makes explicit, notions of respect for the learner that are essential for clicker training: "If the trainer looks away, the learner will be frustrated and not want to do it again." "Pay attention. Don't get distracted. When the learner is trying, be nice, give more time and extra treats. Don't be bossy. You will seem mean and the learner will think he or she is bad."

Showing respect for others is a universal concern that is implemented differently in different cultures. Discussions of ways to show respect in Hispanic and American cultures helped clarify areas of confusion and facilitated acculturation for Lina. The children became increasingly confident and capable in asking for clarification and in suggesting how people from different backgrounds might react. These skills will allow them to feel confident facing new settings, new intermediate schools for both girls as it happened, to be clear in explaining their own concerns and in eliciting the help and advice of others. They are much more sensitive to the culturally bound expressions and connotations of both languages.

Dog Resumes

Another way to encourage writing, a future orientation, and a social conscience is to have the children write about the animals they have met and trained in the sessions to increase the dogs' adoptability. Children readily see that dogs with good manners have better prospects than those jumping and barking at prospective adopters. They get a sense of larger purpose when they teach dogs needing homes to sit despite distractions, to come when called, and to exercise impulse control around food. After working with a dog, children can write up what and how they taught the dog. This exercise reinforces the learning and makes the children reflect on technique and incremental progress. It also gives them a face-saving way to reflect on their own impulsivity and review techniques to master it. Their write-ups and accompanying drawings can be posted on the animals' cages in the shelter to encourage adoption. The format SHIP uses is written from the dog's point of view and involves a good assessment of the animal's behavior and learning style.

My name is _____ .

I am _____ months/years old.

I am _____ (breed, heritage).

Here's what I can do:

_____

_____

_____

Here's how I learned these skills: (description of clicker training)

_____

_____

_____

This is my learning style: (description of animal's attention span, tolerance for frustration and other observed quirks)

_____

_____

_____

A full reproducible version of the Dog Resume is given in Appendix 1, p. 194.

Written and Photographic Reinforcers

Progress must be reinforced in many ways and at many times to maintain enthusiasm and motivation. Rewards and jackpots are great during sessions. Polaroid photos taken of displays of excellence are especially powerful reinforcers. People enjoy looking at all the photos at the end of each session, and tend to point out what they like about the behavior captured on film. It is a way for people to pay and accept compliments free of the usual shyness and embarrassment. The photographs can be posted on refrigerator doors, bulletin boards, and other sites of serious recognition. For programs working with poor families, these may be the only photographs the families have of their children, cameras and film being a luxury beyond their reach.

Written reinforcers serve two functions: they reinforce behavior and they introduce reading into the curriculum. SHIP uses a number of written reinforcers. These include

- Letters of praise,

- The Clicker Promise,

- The Dog Protection Promise,

- Certificate of attendance,

- Consent forms, and

- Thank you notes.

Letters of Praise

Letters of praise sent to participants in between sessions are welcome reinforcers, especially to children who rarely get mail. The letters should be very specific, praising a laudable behavior and elaborating on its significance and generosity. Three examples of other written documents that carry great weight and can be used to strengthen inchoate behavior and values are provided in Appendix 1, pp. 198-200.

The Clicker Promise

The Clicker Promise addresses impulse control. Participants promise only to use their clicker when training and not at other times. Although this may not be much of a problem for busy adults, fidgety children find it difficult to ignore the clicker readily within their grasp. Getting in trouble in class for clicking and disrupting instruction would offset progress made in the animal-assisted therapy session. Having and not clicking a clicker is a challenge worth mastering. Participants take the Clicker Promise very seriously, especially if they are asked to read it aloud, pledge fidelity, sign the pledge, laminate it, post it in a prominent place, and create a small version (about the size of a business card) to laminate and attach to the wrist strap of their clicker. The Clicker Promise can be reproduced from the model given in Appendix 1, p. 195.

The Dog Protection Promise

The Dog Protection Promise reinforces concern for others, in this case the SHIP dogs. Chocolate is a highly valued reinforcer for people, but it is toxic to dogs. Irresponsible handling of chocolate can prove deadly to dogs. As a result, SHIP participants are asked to decide when they are ready to introduce chocolates as a treat. Once the decision is made that the group is responsible enough to assure the dogs' welfare, each participant is asked to read and sign a promise to handle the chocolate in a way that shows concern for and protects the SHIP dogs. It states that the signer will make sure no dog manages to get any of the chocolate being used in the session, and further that the signer will keep a watchful eye out for the safety of dogs and others in general.

Participants are then given the Dog Protection Promise to sign. The promise has room for their date of birth, the date of their signature, and for names to be printed and signed; as much detail as possible is included because this emphasizes and solemnifies the commitment. At the beginning of the next session, the participants receive their copy of the signed and dated Dog Protection Promise in a nice frame. Another copy is kept in their file. The Dog Protection Promise can be reproduced from the sample provided in Appendix 1, p. 196.

Certificate of Attendance

At the end of the six-week course, people graduate and are awarded a certificate of attendance. There is room in its center for a photograph. Few of the older relatives of SHIP's participants have completed high school; virtually none has gone to college. Therefore, certificates of completion are especially important to show that people can finish classes. Combined with a now-well developed future orientation, these certificates should take on a predictive as well as a reinforcing value. A Certificate of Attendance that can be customized and reproduced is given in Appendix 1, p. 197.

Consent Forms

It is necessary to obtain permission, that is, informed consent, from parents or legal guardians before they or their children participate in any program and before any photographs are taken or videotapes are made. If a court is involved with the family, a court order may be needed as well. SHIP's consents are included in Appendix 1, pp. 201-206.

SHIP has children as well as parents/guardians sign consent forms even though they are not legally required to do so. Asking the children to give permission is empowering and validating especially to children who feel slighted or ignored.

Because signing permission slips is so reinforcing to the children, SHIP uses several of them instead of a comprehensive form. Each one is used to mark a milestone. The general consent to reproduce artwork and writing for professional audiences was supplemented by a specific consent to reproduce work for this book, the Latham and Pryor Foundation web pages, and a further consent for use by Karen Pryor, Sunshine Books and www.clickertraining.com. Each child and parent signed a copy of every consent form. The children asked enthusiastically for weeks when they would get to sign their form, and it provided an opportunity to praise their work and show how it would help others. The form for parents allowed the author to tell the children's parents how excellent their children's work was and why it was being included in this book.

The following consent forms are provided in Appendix 1: participation and permission to videotape, permission to reproduce artwork and writing, and a court order allowing videotaping and photographing (pp. 201-206).

Thank You Notes

Thank you notes are another way to highlight and reinforce gains. Not only can facilitators and other adults write them to participants, but the participants can also reinforce the behavior they like as well. Included in Appendix 1, pp. 198-200, are a thank you note and certificate written for Hilary and Evelyn by Hugh Tebault, president of the Latham Foundation, upon the publication of their brochure, and a thank you note Hilary and Evelyn wrote to Lynn Loar – which she found so reinforcing that she offered the praised behavior in much greater quantities!

The literacy component is an important part of SHIP. Integrating reading and writing into the program gives participants a chance to reflect on their learning, develop literacy, and recognize the mastery they have gained. The poems and writing scattered throughout this book are all the work of children participating in humane education or animal-assisted therapy programs that, like SHIP, integrated the core skill of literacy into the design of the program.

Developing a Social Conscience and Contributing to Balanced and Restorative Justice

THE LAST CORE SKILL, BALANCED AND RESTORATIVE JUSTICE, IS ALSO INCORPORATED INTO SHIP'S PROGRAM DESIGN.

Some people who have been hurt in childhood or who have hurt others often have a profound urge to "give back" to their community. Other people may be required by their school or by a court to perform community service. Whatever the reason, people who perform public service realize that they have skills to help others and can make a difference in their communities. Finding ways to put new skills to use for the betterment of others is crucial to the lasting impact of the intervention.

We've already seen one example of SHIP participants, Hilary and Evelyn, who took their newly learned skills and applied them to work that would benefit others. The outcome of the girls' efforts are training tools that are now used with young people across the country. And beyond the specific product, Hilary and Evelyn drew others into their work in ways that contributed positively to their lives.

Most families involved with SHIP are regular recipients of social services; few develop the skills or have the opportunity to give something to others. Unfortunately, people who are long-term clients can become very dependent on systems and too needy to maintain a support system of their own creation. SHIP therefore emphasizes volunteer internships at the local animal shelter or other appropriate organizations so that clients can graduate from recipient of services to provider. They come with respectable skills and have something to contribute.

SHIP alumni work along with other volunteers and paid staff at the animal shelter. Their budding social conscience is nurtured by their colleagues, and they see others for whom voluntary community service is a chosen activity, an avocation they stick with for years. They also learn about the skills needed for employment and can set their sights on a meaningful career in animal welfare if they desire.

The SHIP program serves as a model of an animal-assisted therapy program that integrates effective structural and design requirements. Starting with the structural requirements, SHIP's designers selected their setting, staffing, animals, and participants. The result? A program held in familiar, neighborhood locations; staffed with both an animal trainer and a social services professional; using carefully selected shelter dogs; targeted to at-risk inner-city families.

With these decisions in place, SHIP used the five core skills to design a successful program. SHIP teaches mastery and empathy relying exclusively on positive reinforcement. As trainers teach participants to clicker train, the learners are both learning and then teaching, a combination that reinforces the mastery of operant conditioning and the empathy required to successfully get a dog to sit or a child to respond.

SHIP creates an optimistic future orientation through the dogs' training: a trained dog becomes much more adoptable and faces a more optimistic future. SHIP's clients, then, become responsible for the optimistic future for the dog and can begin to imagine having some control over their own future.

Through literacy, SHIP gives clients the opportunity to reflect on their learning and to express fearful ideas they may hold about their own lives through poems and stories about pets.

And finally, SHIP stresses balanced and restorative justice. Through SHIP, participants learn skills that can contribute to the well being of others. They can work at a local shelter or create tools that can help train future clicker trainers. They can become positive and productive contributors to their society in specific and practical ways that enhance their own possibility for employment.

The SHIP program is one of many successful animal-assisted therapy programs. Although these programs vary greatly, they share a common commitment to structural and design requirements that result in successful programs.

The program you create may be very different from SHIP or other existing animal-assisted therapy programs. You are addressing a specific problem, serving a specific group, and developing a specific approach. Take what appeals to you from SHIP and other programs and create the rest. Whatever approach you take, adhering to the structural and design requirements will lead you to a successful program. The next chapter gives you some examples of the applications of these principles of structure and design to six different problems.

Chapter Six

Applying animal-assisted therapy to special problems

Overview

ANIMAL-ASSISTED THERAPY CAN SERVE A VARIETY OF CLIENTS. SHIP, for example, targets families exposed to violence at home or in their communities. Other programs address issues faced by teen parents, people with developmental disabilities, or other clients with particular concerns. You may already have a need and population in mind for your animal-assisted therapy program. Whatever group you target, you will need to design your program to meet specific concerns. This chapter provides guidance about unique design issues raised by six target populations:

- Pregnant teens and teen parents,

- Youth seeking employment,

- People with disabilities,

- Children who have hurt animals,

- Youthful offenders, and

- Parents ordered by a juvenile or family court to have supervised visits with their children.

This chapter will look at situations in which animals have helped improve the psycho-social functioning of each of these groups and will define special issues of the particular population, the skills that need to be developed in the program, and reasons why animal-assisted therapy using clicker training may be a particularly good intervention.

Pregnant Teens and Teen Parents

SOME ANIMAL-ASSISTED THERAPY PROGRAMS SERVE TEEN PARENTS, PREGNANT TEENS, OR TEENS AT RISK FOR PREGNANCY. If you are interested in designing a program for these clients, you will need to build a program that helps them master practical skills and develop empathy using techniques appropriate for the teens' maturational level.

Teen parents are above all still teenagers, moody and impulsive young people who have difficulty deferring gratification and putting the needs of others ahead of their own. Parenting, particularly of infants and toddlers, requires constantly putting the needs of a demanding and dependent creature ahead of one's own needs and wishes. Teen parents' maturational level is at odds with the responsibilities of parenting an infant or toddler.

Teen parenting programs tend to focus on caring for the infant, feeding, bathing – all good things, but cognitive. For teen parents to implement the skills acquired in the parenting program, they must master their impulsivity and markedly increase their tolerance for frustration. They must subordinate their own desires and put the needs of their infant first.

In pregnancy prevention programs, the realistic burdens of caring for an infant are focal. Teens are asked to tend to an egg or a baby doll programmed to cry at odd hours around the clock for a week or more. These comparatively minimal demands impress on many youth the sacrifices they would have to make if they were to become parents. Ironically, these same skills are rarely the focus of programs for teens who are already parents.

Caring for and clicker training animals and children provide the practical skills teen parents and teens at risk of becoming parents need in order to be able to care for their own children. Because of the inherent appeal and pleasure in working with animals, teens are more likely to stick with an animal-assisted therapy program than they are to care for an egg and attend a child development course. They are also more receptive to advice on bottle-feeding a baby goat or pig than to advice about their own behavior toward their child. Besides their greater receptivity, they can broaden their perspective to appreciate the demands all infants of every species make in order to survive and grow. This breadth of experience also helps reduce the feelings of persecution overwhelmed parents often feel, mistakenly believing their child is making demands out of malice or vengefulness rather than just crying and testing limits the way any small creature does.

Reproduction and adoption are topics that come up frequently at animal shelters and humane organizations. Teenagers can garner information about conception, pregnancy and birth, and also learn about standards for adoption, without feeling defensive or overtly talking about their own situation. These programs offer a good way for teens to get accurate information from knowledgeable adults without personal embarrassment.

Youth Seeking Employment

PROGRAMS THAT CONNECT TEENS WITH ANIMAL ORGANIZATIONS CAN HELP THE YOUTH, THE ORGANIZA-TION, AND THE ANIMALS. These programs are particularly effective in developing an optimistic future orientation and providing for balanced and restorative justice.

Many teenagers want to work while they attend high school. Some may earn academic credit through a work/study or service-learning program. Some may want to earn money by working afternoons, weekends, and vacations. Others may perform community service on their own or as part of a youth or church group. Still others perform community service as part of a diversion program, the disposition of their delinquency case.

Animal shelters and humane programs can offer many appealing internship opportunities. Collaborations with youth service organizations can allow placements that introduce meaningful career opportunities as well as attainable entry-level jobs to high school graduates. The success of these internships depends on well thought out plans and clear delineation of roles among the animal service staff and staff responsible for supervising the youth. Collaboration is essential – and wariness on the part of the animal welfare staff should be anticipated. Courts do, on occasion, order people to perform community service at animal shelters without regard for the demands for supervision this makes on shelter staff. For these placements to work, the youth serving agency must take primary responsibility for the youth and develop a team approach that does not unduly burden the already overworked staff at the animal shelter.

Animal shelters offer a number of jobs that people with basic clicker training skills and a good mentor could master. These jobs would improve quality of life for the animals, improve their prospects for adoption, and be appreciated by the staff who routinely have more work to do than is humanly possible. Such jobs include teaching dogs to come to the front of their kennels and sit quietly when people approach or walk by, teaching basic obedience skills to dogs, walking dogs, socializing cats, and assisting adoption counselors in their work. Many youth are also very interested in the work humane and animal control officers perform and welcome chances to learn more about these roles and activities.

With a high school degree and relevant experience, these youth would be highly competitive candidates for jobs in animal shelters, kennels, dog walking, pet sitting services and similar organizations. In addition, shelters operate seven days a week and can frequently accommodate schedules of people taking college classes. Community colleges offer AA degrees in veterinary technology, law enforcement, social services, and business administration, any of which would boost marketability in animal welfare careers. Mentorships that encourage high school students to pursue humane careers and enable them to qualify for responsible and meaningful jobs upon their graduation are key to successful outcome.

People with Disabilities

PEOPLE WITH DISABILITIES OFTEN SPEND A LOT OF TIME IN PHYSICAL AND OCCUPATIONAL THERAPY PROGRAMS PERFORMING REPETITIVE MOVEMENTS IN RELATIVELY MEANINGLESS TASKS, E.G., PINCHING CLOTHES PINS OR STACKING CONES, TO GAIN GROSS AND FINE MOTOR CONTROL. Animal-assisted therapy programs can turn these mindless tasks into activities that promote mastery and motivation while benefiting the clients and the animal. One type of animal-assisted therapy for people with disabilities teaches the techniques of dog grooming or basic training. Motivation is much higher and much more effectively reinforced through work with an animal. The desire to get the timing of the click right and to deliver the treat promptly to the eager animal inspires people to master motor control. In addition, the ability to keep all of one's body still except for the hand extending as the target or the arm brushing the dog involves using one muscle system for motion while maintaining stable control over the rest of the body. Well chosen tasks in the training game could further such control and self-regulation.

A second animal-assisted therapy program that targets people with disabilities teaches the clients to clicker train service dogs, often their own dogs. Clicker training is increasingly being used to train service dogs for all sorts of activities (see www.clickertraining.com and www.Pryorfoundation.com for more information on clicker training service dogs). These dogs are safer and more personable than traditionally trained dogs, having only positive experiences with humans to draw on. A promising new trend is for a person with a disability to work with a clicker trainer to select and train a service dog specifically for the needs of that individual. This approach allows for better match between the dog's talents and the owner's needs. It also allows the dog and owner to develop a bond while they shape behaviors together. And, the dog is spared an extra move from a temporary home to a permanent one.

Children Who Have Hurt Animals

SOME ANIMAL-ASSISTED THERAPY PROGRAMS PROVIDE SERVICES FOR CHILDREN WHO HAVE HURT ANIMALS. These programs are effective at promoting mastery, empathy, and balanced and restorative justice, but they raise a number of special concerns. If you are considering this group as your target population, you must ensure the safety of the animals, provide adequate supervision at all times, and insist on strong reporting procedures of abusive or negligent behavior toward humans and animals.

Children may have hurt an animal accidentally, impulsively, out of curiosity, or with intent. Before allowing any child who has hurt an animal to participate in a humane education or animal-assisted therapy program, risk must be thoroughly evaluated and adequate supervision ensured. Boat's inventories (see Chapter 7, pp. 124-132) allow for an increasingly focused discussion of exposure to animals. Lockwood's instruments (see Chapter 7, pp. 133-138 and 150-154) assess risk and give an indication of the danger the child (youth or adult) currently poses, and Loar's family-based risk assessment (see Chapter 7, pp. 138-149) puts the individual's behavior in interactive context.

Safety measures described in Chapter 3 are essential but insufficient when a child has hurt an animal. In addition to all the caveats presented there, five additional precautions must be taken when a child who has hurt an animal is involved in an animal-assisted therapy program.

1. Always have one person dedicated to manage the animal.

2. Always provide one-to-one supervision for each participant.

3. Require all participants and staff to agree in advance that any violence, threat of violence, or other dangerous behavior will immediately cause the animal to be removed from the session.

4. Require all staff to agree to report to appropriate animal control authorities any abusive or negligent behavior that becomes known.

5. Give appropriate notice in advance to adults and authorities since this is not a mandatory report and the reporter may not have immunity when reporting animal abuse or neglect.

Clicker training is a particularly useful tool for animal-assisted therapy programs serving children who have hurt animals because clicker training allows the trainer to shape a behavior from afar. A person can click and toss treats into a cage or kennel to teach sitting, looking up at the person in front of the cage or kennel, lying down, and many other behaviors. Thus, safety can be ensured while skill develops. Empathy must be vouchsafed as part of this intervention. The human client can learn to recognize the animal's feelings, enthusiasm, frustration, confusion, and fatigue while clicker training safely from the other side of the cage.

Contact with the animal must be gradually introduced, after basic skills have been mastered and genuine concern for the animal developed. This must include the client's awareness of his or her ability to scare or injure the animal combined with the motivation and ability to choose safer behaviors instead. Initial contact should be brief and pleasant to both human and animal, restricted to contact such as a gentle pat on the animal's shoulder. The client might then begin brushing and grooming the animal with the aim of learning what pleases the animal and using that amount of pressure and length of stroke. These are mutually beneficial activities that combine skill and empathy.

Youthful Offenders

WORK WITH YOUTHFUL OFFENDERS REQUIRES EVEN GREATER VIGILANCE AND SUPERVISION THAN DOES WORK WITH CHILDREN WHO HAVE HURT AN ANIMAL. Supervision and adequate staffing must be guaranteed at all times. In addition, clinicians must anticipate and plan to handle a number of serious dynamics before they introduce an animal into work with youthful offenders.

The selection of the animal is particularly important in these programs. Will it weigh about as much as or be roughly the same size as the offender's victim? What will its submissive behavior provoke? Will it evoke predatory behaviors? What if it growls or barks at the offender? What if it shows fear? Aggression? Will it sexually arouse the offender if it lies on its back and exposes its underbelly and genitals? If it licks its genitals? Will the offender focus on the animal's genitals? What if the dog gets an erection? What if the size of the dog's penis provokes the offender? If the dog has been neutered, what sort of reaction will the castration evoke?

Clicker training offers the therapist a constructive way to focus the youthful offender's attention on the behavior rather than on the physicality of the animal. Dynamic and fast-moving, clicker training demands full concentration. The offender can learn to respect the animal as a thinking and feeling being. Moreover, if he or she embraces the role of the trainer, he or she will feel responsible for the learner's accomplishment. Clicker trainers want their learners to succeed; they pace things for the learner's success. Rather than being coercive or dominant, trainers form an egalitarian learning and training partnership.

Parents Ordered by a Juvenile or Family Court to Have Supervised Visits With Their Children

ANIMAL-ASSISTED THERAPY PROGRAMS OFFER A POSITIVE WAY FOR PARENTS AND CHILDREN TO INTERACT DURING A SUPERVISED VISIT. These programs can promote mastery and empathy while giving the parents and children a common, enjoyable experience. They can alter the strained experience of most supervised visits, which do little to help parents master parenting skills or strengthen the parent-child relationship.

Juvenile and family courts order that visits between parents and children be supervised when the courts have concerns about parents' abilities to behave safely with their children. Supervised visits ensure safety and maintain contact between parents and children while affording parents time to gain the skills necessary for greater responsibility. Sometimes, children live with one parent and visit the other parent. At other times, children live with a relative or in a foster or group home and have visits with one or both parents. If parents have a history of domestic violence or have behaved dangerously while exchanging their children, often following a heated divorce and custody battle, a court may order that the exchanges be made at a visiting program. These programs typically allow one parent to drop off their children 30 minutes before the other parent arrives to pick them up. The programs provide activities and support for the children in the interim.

Supervised visits between parents and children tend to be strained. It may be because they are held in buildings – departments of social services or courthouses – that evoke shame and humiliation for the parents. It may be because the presence and duties of the supervisor add artificiality and tension to the visits. It may also be because the parents and children do not have recent positive experiences with each other to draw on.

While necessary to ensure safety and reduce the risk of abuse, supervision is not sufficient to create positive interaction between limited parents and their children. Parents ordered by a court to have supervised visits usually need guidance to engage in age-appropriate activities and conversation with their children, something the supervisor may not be able to provide. At its most basic, parents may actually need to learn how to enjoy their children's company and how to play with them.

Effective visiting plans focus on an enjoyable skill-building activity within the current capabilities of both parents and children, giving them something to do together that is pleasurable and purposeful and that also structures their time together. Matters of discipline and limit setting recede in importance because of the positive and organized activity. The most stressful times, the beginnings and endings of visits, are incorporated into the activity, typically with a ritual greeting and parting. As parents and children develop common interests and skills by experiencing safe and productive time together, risk decreases and rapport increases (Loar, 1998, pp. 51ff.).

Animal-assisted therapy programs offer activities particularly well suited to supervised visits. Parents and children can learn together the essence of respectful, nurturing, and empathic interaction with another living being. They can be taught to pace their involvement based on the tolerance and attention span of the animal. They can master safe and gentle touching, feeding, bathing, grooming, and other ingredients of care-giving without feeling criticized about family matters.

Clicker training provides the methodology to break down these essential skills into manageable increments. Through a combination of work with the animals and people, particularly in the training game, parents and children can begin to learn about each other, about their learning and teaching styles, and about being respectful and generous, initially with frequent clicks and treats. Even the most limited parents whose interactions with their children have been overwhelmingly harsh and punitive can excel at rapid clicking. The learner experiences that trainer as reliable and generous. This abrupt switch to positive interaction introduces a new way of relating, one that is mutually reinforcing because the trainer's success depends on the learner's accomplishment. Both are heartily reinforced by the frequent clicks and the learner's achievement.

■ Playing the Training Game with High-Conflict Families

It is wise to build skills carefully and safely. SHIP's practice with high-conflict families has been to phase in parent-child interaction incrementally through the training game. Each group consists of three to four families, about eight to 10 people in all. Everybody gets to learn from and train both a child and an adult in the training game. For the first few weeks of each series of sessions, SHIP has parents work with other adults and non-related children so they can gain skills in situations where they can be relatively objective. Once they can get information from the click when they are the learner and can break skills down into small increments and click with accurate timing as the trainer, SHIP pairs parents with their own children as learning and training dyads. Thus, both parents and children are dealing from strengths as they work together as a learning and training team.

SHIP has noticed a number of interesting dynamics in the process of playing the training game with high conflict families. Some parents are initially unable to look at their child for any length of time, both when shaping a behavior and as an observer in the audience. Others will look at their child when he or she is the learner, but ignore other children during their turns even to the point of starting conversations with other parents and distracting the group from the task at hand.

SHIP has found the following interventions useful:

1. *Click for paying attention and for positive affect*

Parents and children alike in SHIP's programs often need to learn how to pay attention as learners, trainers and as observers.

The learner

Deriving information from the click requires total concentration. The learner must know what parts of his or her body were in motion at the time of the click, which is challenging for beginners and especially difficult for angry, impulsive and distracted people. Focusing on what was moving and what was still helps people gain mastery over impulsivity and inattention. Experienced learners will walk into the training area and initially figure out whether they are being clicked for moving in a direction or for moving a part of their body. If the former, they continue in that direction; if the latter, they then offer first one limb then another to identify the motion more specifically. Eventually, they offer more specialized movements and refine the behavior.

For example, if the learner's task is to wave to the audience, the trainer might initially click for the arm swing that automatically accompanies walking as the learner enters. It will take a few clicks for the learner to figure out that the clicks are for the arm movement and not the steps. After that, the learner would receive clicks only for the arm moving upward, eventually only for above the shoulder, and so on until the wave is shaped.

Learning to focus on moving one part of the body also requires keeping the rest of the body still. Self-regulation at this level of control gives people confidence to face the challenges and rules of decorum required by many social, academic and work settings. Instead of feeling overpowered by sudden impulses to strike out, people can select their movements, in effect choosing their reactions to stimuli.

The training game is hard at first. People experience uncertainty, confusion and frustration. Sometimes, and most of the time after a bit of practice, the learner can figure things out. Occasionally, though, a little assistance is needed. When the learner gets stuck or loses patience or focus, questions like these are useful:

- ◆ "Where were you when you heard the last click?"
- ◆ "What part of your body was moving when you heard the last click?"
- ◆ "What else were you moving when you heard the last click?"
- ◆ "How might you test to see if you are getting clicked for moving your arm or leg?"
- ◆ "What do you know so far?"
- ◆ "How did you figure that out?"
- ◆ "How could you make that movement bigger?"

The trainer

The trainer must always look at the learner, out of respect for the learner's hard work, to gauge frustration and concentration by the learner's facial expression, and to prevent inadvertent error by clicking a hand movement or glance the trainer cannot see. Additionally, in a clinical population, it would be inadvisable to click for motion away from the trainer, tantamount to making rejection pay.

Beginning trainers tend to be stingy with clicks. They click infrequently, and thereby fail to give adequate information to their learner. They expect too much of the behavior for the first click. Therefore, it is helpful before the learner begins to have the trainer consider all the little things that the trainer could click for at the outset and then shape into the desired behavior.

"What is the learner likely to do at first that you could click and build on?" is a helpful question. Answers should include looking in the right direction, stepping into the room, moving an appendage, and the like.

Facilitators find that they also have to remind the trainer to watch the learner. Questions that help the trainer appreciate the learner's awareness are important and help focus attention:

◆ "What does your learner know so far?"

◆ "How can you tell?"

◆ "How is your learner feeling right now?"

◆ "How could you make it easier for your learner?"

The observer

Observing the shaping of a behavior can be fascinating. The observer can see the learner's growing understanding, the increments the trainer selects and the communication that develops between the two. As a less active role, however, it takes more discipline. Here are some techniques that can assist people in becoming good observers:

a. Divide the observers into two groups, one group knowing the behavior being shaped, the other not. When either the learner or the trainer could use a suggestion, have members of the corresponding group volunteer suggestions. If a learner or trainer is stuck or very frustrated, have somebody from the corresponding group switch roles.

b. Have somebody who needs to learn to pay attention or to recognize positive affect click and treat observers when they are attentive or smiling.

2. Put the treat in the (human) learner's hand

People from harsh or abusive families need to learn how to touch each other safely and appropriately. SHIP discovered that many of the participating parents would go to great lengths to avoid the incidental touch of hands that accompanies the giving of the treat. Instead, they would drop the treat into the learner's hand – resulting in many treats dropping on the floor – or gesture for the learner to open his or her fanny pack so the trainer could drop the treat in it and avoid the passing touch of hands. The learners abetted this dysfunctional behavior by opening their fanny packs to catch the candy much as children extend their sacks on Halloween to receive candy.

Using the safety of the dogs as the motivation, SHIP staff insists that candy be placed carefully in the center of the learner's hand. The Dog Protection Promise is a landmark in the journey from avoiding touch to tolerating it. Initially tense and awkward about handing candy to others, especially parents to their own children, people become efficient and effective, replacing choppy and anxious stabs with streamlined and relaxed movements of hands and arms. Not coincidentally, rapport grows and parents begin occasionally to touch their children spontaneously in small, appropriate and gentle gestures.

Somebody handy with a clicker can also acknowledge good behavior whenever it occurs – picking up a dropped candy, smiling at somebody, saying something nice to somebody, doing something helpful. A wonderful and altruistic moment is when a member of the group spontaneously clicks somebody else for a positive behavior thought worth marking, and uses his or her hard-earned candy as the treat.

In the English-Spanish writing project, all the translators had clickers and access to a big bowl of candy in the middle of the table. Whenever somebody thought a word or phrase was particularly well rendered, he or she would acknowledge that excellence with a click and treat. Younger siblings waiting rather than interrupting or raising a hand and waiting to be acknowledged also earned clicks and treats. Democratizing the clicking also allowed the facilitator to ask why the person clicking thought the translation was particularly apt. This led to interesting discussions about multiple perspectives and cultural differences.

Fluency in marker-based shaping can also redirect verbal confrontations back to positive behaviors. At the end of one SHIP session, the group was drinking juice before adjourning. One child defiantly dropped her empty paper cup on the ground. Her mother told her to pick the cup up and put it in the trash. The child adopted a hostile pose and refused. A SHIP facilitator took a couple of steps toward the child who turned to look at her. The facilitator clicked and treated the child for looking her way. The child promptly looked down to avoid the eye contact, although she managed to accept the candy nonetheless. Looking down meant she was looking at the paper cup on the ground, so she was clicked and treated for that. Annoyed, she looked back at the facilitator who again clicked and treated her for gazing her way. A frustrated shuffle of feet, just short of stamping, inadvertently put the child an inch closer to the cup on the ground earning yet another click and treat. At this point the child began to giggle and bent down to pick up the cup. She earned a jackpot for this. Playfully then, she strode deliberately, cup in hand, toward the garbage can, getting clicked and treated along the way, first every step and then intermittently. With a great flourish, she dropped the cup into the garbage can to a round of applause from the group and a click and treat from the facilitator. She and her mother walked off arm in arm laughing and in good moods.

3. Pick a simple task

At the beginning of each round of the training game, the learner goes outside the room so that the group can select a behavior to shape out of the learner's earshot. Despite instructions to pick a simple task, people – particularly adults – tend to propose complicated behaviors. They will suggest having the learner fill a glass with water or a similar multi-step behavior. The facilitator must explain that such a behavior will require many trials to build, because it entails (1) going to the glass, (2) touching the glass, (3) picking up the glass, (4) carrying the glass (5) to the faucet, (6) lining the glass up under the faucet, (7) turning the faucet on and, finally, (8) turning the faucet off. Then the facilitator has to urge the group to agree on shaping step 1, touching the glass for the first round of the game.

The skillful facilitator can introduce an analogy at this point, the enormous number of steps involved in cleaning one's room and suggest that the group would surely know to stop at putting a sock or two in the hamper as a first step in this arduous journey. For court-ordered parents, such information is vital and can be presented in terms of language and rules the parents are now familiar with and willing to use.

Humor helps too. The facilitator could develop the analogy by suggesting that the parent introduce the child and the clothes hamper to each other with a ritual greeting. "Johnnie, this is the clothes hamper. Clothes hamper, this is Johnnie." Then the parent and child might explain to the hamper what would happen, and reassure the hamper that the child would be careful and gentle so the hamper would have no cause for alarm. Parent: "Hamper, Johnnie will be putting dirty clothes in you. You don't need to worry about this or be scared. Johnnie will be careful and gentle and only put clothes in you." Then the parent might ask the child to reassure the hamper similarly. Next the parent would introduce the child to a sock and the sock to the child. Similar reassurances would be made about the safe and gentle transport of the sock and the pleasant destination awaiting it in the hamper. The parent would then click and treat the child for picking up the sock and carrying it to the hamper. The child would earn a jackpot for putting the sock in the hamper. The game should stop there for the first night – although the hamper could thank the child for being so careful and say it was looking forward to receiving more clothes from him or her the next day. Within a few days, "put your laundry in the hamper" will have become an accurately understood cue that triggers reliable behavior. Then, and only then, can the parent move on to the next category of items to be put away – and must go back to the very basic first step with the new category.

Animal-assisted therapy programs can serve a variety of clients dealing with a broad range of concerns. As you design your program, consider the core skills and challenges specific to your target population. Some groups require high levels of supervision to ensure safety; some require a strong focus on empathy, mastery, or another of the core skills; yet others require serious attention to the selection of the therapy animal. With well structured and carefully designed programs, all participants in animal-assisted therapy programs can grow in mastery through the rigor and objectivity of clicker training and in empathy through meaningful activity with animals.

As you consider the design of your program, you may decide to serve one of the groups described here or some other population. Animal-assisted therapy programs, especially those that integrate clicker training, can be successful with a wide range of clients and needs; if you see a need, it is likely you can respond effectively to that need through a carefully constructed animal-assisted therapy program.

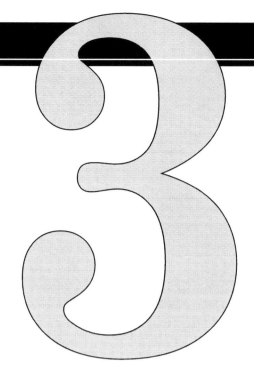

 Tools
for your
program

Tools for your program

Overview

ANIMAL-ASSISTED THERAPY PROGRAMS ARE RELATIVELY NEW. Like many emerging programs, animal-assisted therapy grew from a few early successes. Drawing on valuable anecdotal information, new programs built on the success of the original few.

We now know enough to move from shared anecdotal learning to measured success. Increasingly, programs developed by hospitals, humane societies, family counseling centers, and others have created both qualitative and quantitative tools to assess the effectiveness of animal-assisted therapy. These tools have allowed the field to share best practices and standardize successful approaches, learning from success and discarding what does not work.

This section provides three types of tools for use in your program:

- Tools for assessing risk,

- Tools for assessing individual progress, and

- Tools for assessing the effectiveness of programs.

Animal-assisted therapy programs must ensure the safety of all participants.

Chapter 7, Tools for Assessing Risk, provides instruments to help you select safe and suitable animals, measure the risk participants may pose to both the animals and people in the program, and identify the level of supervision needed in the sessions for safety's sake. These tools will help you get the right people together with the right animals with the right level of supervision for safety and success.

Chapter 8, Tools for Assessing Individual Progress, will help you measure gains for each participant in your program, allowing you to focus and adjust efforts along the way. This level of measurement also supports program evaluation and development.

Chapter 9, Tools for Assessing the Effectiveness of Programs, will help you make programmatic changes, justify funding requests, and assure maximum progress of participants.

Chapter Seven

Tools for assessing risk

Overview

AS YOU DESIGN YOUR PROGRAM, YOUR GREATEST CONSIDERATION MUST BE FOR THE SAFETY OF ALL PARTICIPANTS, BOTH HUMAN AND ANIMAL. The tools in this section help you ensure that your program will provide a safe environment by giving you a way to assess the suitability of the dogs and people for your program.

This chapter provides assessment tools to help you select suitable animals for the program and participants who will benefit from the program and not endanger the safety of others. The tools also help you determine the level of supervision needed in each session and understand which problem the program will address.

Six assessment tools are included in this chapter.

■ **Duford's Safe Dogs** - is a checklist derived from the suitability assessment provided in Chapter 3 to assess the suitability of dogs to participate in your program.

■ **Boat's Inventories on Animal-Related Experiences** - are questionnaires that explore a potential participant's experiences with and behavior towards animals. Both short and long versions of the questionnaire are provided.

■ **Lockwood's "Animals at Risk" Thematic Apperception Test** - is a projective test based on drawings that prompt responses about individual and family functioning including behavior and attitudes toward animals.

■ **Loar's Family-Based Risk Assessment** - is a numeric assessment of how likely a participant is to pose a risk to animals or family members.

■ **Lockwood's Factors in the Assessment of Dangerousness in Perpetrators of Animal Cruelty** - is a checklist that evaluates dangerous behavior directed toward animals.

■ **Eckert's Risk Assessment** - is a suite of tools to assess ongoing risk in teens and adults already known to have committed sexual crimes against minors.

Review these tools; select and modify those that will best help you focus your program on a common issue, select participants who can benefit from your program, select animals who will work effectively with the participants, and ensure safety for all.

Risk Assessment Tool 1: Safe Dogs

Donna Duford developed this tool to help program designers select animals who will further the program's goals, work effectively with participants, and ensure a safe environment. The checklist includes questions relevant to most settings. Beyond the general questions about the animal's behavior and affiliation, questions help you find an animal who can handle the stress, travel, and excitement typical of animal-assisted therapy programs. In addition, the questionnaire brings up issues that may interfere with the program's success, the appearance of the dog, for example, which can be a factor in a session's success or failure. The questionnaire relies on the detailed explanation provided in the corresponding section (pp. 48-51) of Chapter 3.

Safe Dogs: Screening for Suitability to Participate in a Humane Education or an Animal-Assisted Therapy Program

Note: Instructions are in italics.
If at any point you answer "no" to the question "Can you proceed?" **stop.**
The dog is not suitable for your program.

Complete at least one part of the test in an environment unfamiliar to the dog.

1. **History, especially of living with and liking children:**

   _____

   _____

2. **Current Behavior:**
   Observe dogs as children walk through the kennel.
   - Does the dog readily approach the front of the run with an open wag?　_____ yes _____ no
   - What else do you notice

   _____

   _____

3. **Affiliation, Round One:**
   Walk through the shelter.
   Stop at each kennel and face the dog, using benign facial expression and body language.
   - Does the dog approach you?　_____ yes _____ no

   If not, talk to the dog in a friendly tone of voice.
   - Does he or she approach you?　_____ yes _____ no

   If "yes" is checked in either line above, proceed.

4. **Interest in Food:**
   Offer the dog a treat. Choose dogs who eat readily.
   - Does the dog eat eagerly?　_____ yes _____ no

   If "yes" is checked, proceed.

5. **Affiliation, Round Two:**
Take the dog to the testing area with as little interaction and handling as possible. Sit or stand silently, holding the leash, and observe the dog. Ideal candidates orient and initiate interaction immediately, good candidates within 30 seconds, and acceptable ones in under a minute.
- How long does it take the dog to initiate interaction?   _____under a minute   _____over a minute

If under a minute, proceed.

Watch for these positive behaviors and check all that apply:
- Friendly approach with soft eye contact _____
- Open or circular tail wag   _____
- Leaning, nudging, licking   _____

Talk to and pat the dog for 30-60 seconds. Observe the dog's reaction. Watch for these positive behaviors and check all that apply:
- Prolonged physical contact   _____
- Increased tail wagging   _____
- Soft eye contact   _____
- Licking   _____
- Leaning   _____

Proceed if the dog exhibits at least one of these behaviors.

6. **Tolerance for Handling:**
Do the following tests, in order. Stop any time you feel uncomfortable – the dog is not suitable.
- Pat the top of the dog's head and down the back.
Dog's reaction:

_____

- Pat down the dog's back and tail, pulling the tail firmly and evenly (no yanking).
Dog's reaction:

_____

- Firmly grab back.
Dog's reaction:

_____

- Firmly grab a handful of skin on the dog's flank.
Dog's reaction:

_____

- Lift the dog's lips as if to look at the teeth. If the dog pulls away, let go. Repeat 5 times.
Dog's reaction:

_____

- Poke the dog with the pressure of a child in the head and on various parts of the body.
Dog's reaction:

_____

Ideal candidates will have no reaction, or only look in your direction. With the dog's lips, if the dog pulls away each time, but does not escalate the behavior, this is fine.

Good candidates may flinch, startle or get slightly excited, but recover quickly and seek your attention – as in the Affiliation tests – within a few seconds.

Dogs who react in other ways, biting, growling, pulling away or other similar behaviors, are not suitable.

Do not proceed if you see these behaviors.

7. **Tolerance for Movement and Noise:**
   Do kid-like things:
   * *Run*
   * *Squeal*
   * *Yell*
   * *Point in the dog's face*
   * *Wave your arms in the air*
   * *Wave your hands in front of the dog's face*
   * *Click the clicker once, pause, then click a few times*
   Dog's reaction:

   _____

   Ideal candidates will seem unfazed, remaining sociable with you. Good candidates may get slightly excited or apprehensive, but without barking, chasing or mouthing, and should settle and connect with you when you stop.

   Dogs who bark, chase, mouth, or do not settle or remain social with you are not suitable.

   Do not proceed if you see these behaviors.

8. **Resource Guarding:**
   Feed the dog a few treats sequentially from your hand. Drop a dozen treats on the floor, then try to move them with a fake hand (to protect your own hand). Try to push the dog's face away from the treats.
   Dog's reaction:

   _____

   Ideal candidates will stop eating to look at you softly or continue eating in a relaxed manner. Good candidates may eat slightly faster, but not race you to the food.

   Dogs who race you, resist your pushes, get stiff, growl, snarl, snap, or bite are not suitable.

   Do not proceed if you see these behaviors.

9. **Stress in New Environments:**
   During the testing, notice the dog's reaction when in a new environment.
   Ideal candidates appear confident.
   Good candidates may be cautious at first, but begin to relax and act more confidently quickly.
   Dog's reaction:

   _____

   Dogs who do not acclimate quickly to a new environment are not suitable.

   If the dog does not acclimate, do not proceed.

10. **Stress in Vehicles:**
    If the dogs are to be transported, take them for a brief ride to make sure they are not overly stressed by car travel.
    Dog's reaction:

    _____

    Dogs who cannot handle the ride without undue stress are not suitable.

    If you see high levels of stress, do not proceed if the dog must be transported for your program.

11. **Dog-to-Dog Behavior:**
    If you will be using more than one dog and they will be in the same space while training or awaiting turns, test them for friendliness with each other. Ideal candidates are friendly, but not preoccupied with each other.
    Dog's reaction:

    _____

    Dogs who are overly preoccupied with each other or do not exhibit friendly behavior are not suitable.

    If you see this behavior, do not proceed if you will be using more than one dog in the same space.

12. **Exuberance:**
    Watch for the dog's level of exuberance when you interact.
    Dog's exuberance:

    _____

    Exuberant dogs who can focus on treats are great. Avoid exuberant dogs who cannot settle.
    If your clients are afraid of dogs, you may want a dog with a little less oomph.

    If the dog cannot settle or is too exuberant for the program, do not proceed.

13. **Barking:**
    What have you noticed about the dog's level of barking during the testing?
    Dog's barking:

    _____

    Avoid overly vocal dogs. Incessant barking can be scary for some people, and can inhibit training. Dogs who bark occasionally and/or only at specific triggers like other dogs running by the kennel, may be fine in the training setting.

    If the dog is overly vocal, do not proceed.

14. **Wounds and Scars:**
    Examine the dog for wounds or scars.
    Dog's appearance:

    _____

    If possible, avoid dogs with obvious wounds or scars, cropped ears or tail.

    Is the dog neutered? Consider the impact of the dog's genitalia on participants.

15. Mouthiness:

What have you noticed about the dog's tendency to be mouthy as you interact?

Dog's mouthiness:

_____

Dogs who are mouthy in play or out of frustration are not suitable.
If the dog is mouthy, do not proceed.

16. Food Grabbing:

What have you noticed about the dog's tendency to grab food?

Dog's care when taking treats from a hand :

_____

If the dog grabs food hard, do not proceed.

Risk Assessment Tool Two:
Boat's Inventories on Animal-Related Experiences

BARBARA BOAT, PH.D., IS THE DIRECTOR OF THE CHILDHOOD TRUST AND THE PROGRAM ON CHILD-HOOD TRAUMA AND MALTREATMENT AT THE UNIVERSITY OF CINCINNATI'S CHILDREN'S HOSPITAL MEDICAL CENTER. She also serves as the Vice President and Secretary of the Pryor Foundation. Dr. Boat developed a long and short version of a questionnaire designed to elicit information about people's exposure to animals. The inventory explores the history of owning pets, of experiencing animals as a source of support, of losing animals, of fear of animals, of cruelty to animals, of using animals to coerce or control others, and of sexual interactions with animals. By starting with neutral and positive questions and progressing to more problematic ones, the questionnaire is designed to put people at ease and elicit increasingly difficult material as the interview progresses.

This tool will help you assess the suitability of participants by giving you information about the risk they pose to animals and people in your program. This tool will also help you determine the level of supervision you will need for a safe, effective program.

Animal-Related Experiences
9 Screening Questions for Children, Adolescents and Adults

1. **Have you or your family ever had any pets?** .... Y N

   How many?   **How many?**
   a. Dog(s) _____
   b. Cat(s) _____   **f.** Turtles, snakes, lizards, insects, etc.   _____
   c. Bird(s) _____   **g.** Rabbits, hamsters, mice, guinea-pigs, gerbils   _____
   d. Fish _____   **h.** Wild animals (describe) _____   _____
   e. Horse(s) _____   **i.** Other (describe)   _____   _____

2. **Do you have a pet or pets now?** .... Y N

   How many?   **How many?**
   a. Dog(s) _____
   b. Cat(s) _____   **f.** Turtles, snakes, lizards, insects, etc.   _____
   c. Bird(s) _____   **g.** Rabbits, hamsters, mice, guinea pigs, gerbils   _____
   d. Fish _____   **h.** Wild animals (describe) _____   _____
   e. Horse(s) _____   **i.** Other (describe) _____   _____

3. **Did you ever have a favorite or special pet?** .... Y N

   What kind? _____
   Why was the pet special? _____
   _____

4. **Has a pet ever been a source of comfort or support to you - even if you
   did not own the pet? (e.g. When you were sad or scared?)** .... Y N

   How old were you?
          a. Under age 6   **b.** 6-12 years   **c.** Teenager   **d.** Adult

   Describe the pet and what happened _____
   _____
   _____

5. **Has your pet ever been hurt?**... Y N

   What happened? (describe) _____
   _____
   _____

       a. Accidental? (hit by car, attacked by another animal, fell, ate something, etc.)
       b. Deliberate? (kicked, punched, thrown, not fed, etc.)

6. **Have you ever felt afraid for your pet or worried about bad things happening to your pet? (describe)**........ Y N
   _____
   _____

   Are you worried now? .... Y N

7. **Have you ever lost a pet you really cared about? (e.g. Was given away,
   ran away, died or was somehow killed?)** .... Y N

       What kind of pet? _____

If your pet died, was the death:

a. Natural   **b.** Accidental   **c.** Deliberate   **d.** Cruel or violent
(old age, illness, euthanized)   (hit by car)   (strangled, drowned)   (eg. pet was tortured)

What happened?

_____

_____

_____

Was the death or loss used to punish you or make you do something? .... Y N

How difficult was the loss for you?
     a. Not difficult   **b.** Somewhat difficult   **c.** Very difficult

How much does it bother you now?
     a. Not at all   **b.** Somewhat   **c.** A lot

How did people react / what did they tell you after you lost your pet?
     a. Supportive   **b.** Said it was your fault   **c.** Punished you   **d.** Other_____

How old were you?
     a. Under age 6   **b.** 6-12 years   **c.** Teenager   **d.** Adult

8. **Have <u>you</u> ever hurt an animal or pet?** .... Y N

How many?   **How many?**

a. Dog(s) _____
b. Cat(s) _____   **f.** Turtles, snakes, lizards, insects etc.
c. Bird(s) _____   **g.** Rabbits, hamsters, mice, guinea pigs, gerbils _____
d. Fish _____   **h.** Wild animals (describe) _____ _____
e. Horse(s) _____   **i.** Other (describe) _____ _____

What did you do ?

a. Drowned   **g.** Burned
b. Hit, beat, kicked   **h.** Starved or neglected
c. Stoned   **i.** Trapped
d. Shot (BB gun, bow & arrow)   **j.** Had sex with it
e. Strangled   **k.** Other (describe) _____
f. Stabbed

Was it
     a. accidental?   **b.** deliberate?   **c.** coerced?

How old were you? **(circle all that apply)**
     a. Under age 6   **b.** 6-12 years   **c.** Teenager   **d.** Adult

Were you hunting the animal for food or sport? .... Y N

Were you alone when you did this? .... Y N

Did anyone know you did this? .... Y N

What happened afterwards?_____

_____

9. **Have you ever been frightened —really scared or hurt by an animal or pet?**...................Y N

What happened? _____

_____

Are you still afraid of this kind of animal or other animals? ....Y N
(Describe)_____

_____

Demographics

Date: _____   Current grade or highest grade completed: _____
Date of birth: _____
Age: _____ _____   Gender: Male _____   Female _____
     (years) (months)

Ethnic Group:

        Caucasian _____   Asian _____
        African-American _____   Hispanic _____
        Native-American _____   Appalachian _____
                               Other _____

Maternal level education (highest grade completed) _____

Income _____

Interviewer: Did these questions add new information? .... Y N

Was the information useful? .... Y N

    How? _____

Was the client:

a. Responsive   b. defensive/resistant   c. withholding   d. upset/tearful

e. other _____

The Childhood Trust
CN-PAW
Department of Psychiatry ML 0539
University of Cincinnati
Cincinnati, OH 45267
(513) 558-9007
(513) 558-4107 fax

Barbara.Boat@UC.edu

Boat Inventory on Animal-Related Experiences

"These questions are about some of your experiences with animals and include things you may have heard about, seen, or done yourself. Although some of the questions are of a personal nature, please answer them if you can."

Ownership

1. Have you or your family ever had any pets? . . . . Y N
    If yes, what kind(s)? (read types below and circle all that apply)

	How many?			How many?
a. Dog(s)	_____			
b. Cat(s)	_____	f. Turtles, snakes, lizards, insects, etc.		_____
c. Bird(s)	_____	g. Rabbits, hamsters, mice, guinea pigs, gerbils		_____
d. Fish	_____	h. Wild animals (describe) _____		
e. Horse(s)	_____			

    How old were you when you or your family owned any animals or pets? (circle all that apply)
        a. Under age 6   b. 6-12 years   c. Teenager   d. Adult

2. Do you have a pet or pets now? . . . . Y N
    If yes, what kind(s)? (read types and circle all that apply)

	How many?			How many?
a. Dog(s)	_____			
b. Cat(s)	_____	f. Turtles, snakes, lizards, insects, etc.		_____
c. Bird(s)	_____	g. Rabbits, hamsters, mice, guinea pigs, gerbils		_____
d. Fish	_____	h. Wild animals (describe) _____		
e. Horse(s)	_____			

3. Of your animals, do you - or <u>did</u> you - have a favorite? . . . . Y N
        Which one? _____
        Why? _____

Support

"Sometimes pets or other animals are special sources of support in times of stress."

4. Has there ever been difficult or stressful times when a pet or animal was a source
    of comfort for you - even if you did not own the animal? . . . . Y N

    How old were you? (circle all that apply)
        a. Under age 6   b. 6-12 years   c. Teenager   d. Adult

    What kind of pet or animal gave you support? _____

    How did the pet or animal give you support?
    _____
    _____

5. Are there times when it has been easier to talk to animals than to people? . . . . Y N
    If yes, how often does or did this happen? (please circle)
        a. Just a little   b. Somewhat   c. A lot

6. Did you ever have a favorite stuffed toy animal? . . . . Y N
        Still have it? . . . . Y N

Loss

"Sometimes people lose animals that are special."

7. Have you ever lost an animal you really cared about? (For example, the animal was given away, ran away, died or was somehow killed?) . . . . Y N

    If yes, what kind of animal? _____

    If your pet died, was the death:

a. Natural	b. Accidental	c. Deliberate	d. Cruel or violent
(old age, illness, euthanized)	(hit by car)	(strangled, drowned)	(eg. pet was tortured)

What happened? _____
_____
_____

Was the death or loss used to punish you or make you do something? . . . . Y N

    How difficult was the loss for you?
      a. Not difficult   b. Somewhat difficult c. Very difficult

    How much does it bother you now?
      a. Not at all   b. Somewhat   c. A lot

    How did people react / what did they tell you after you lost your pet?
      a. Supportive   b. Said it was your fault   c. Punished you   d. Other_____

    How old were you?
      a. Under age 6   b. 6-12 years   c. Teenager   d. Adult

Was any person responsible for you losing the animal? . . . . Y N

    If yes, how do you feel now about what that person did? (please circle)
      a. Upset at first, but no longer   b. Still somewhat upset   c. Still <u>very</u> angry

8. Have you ever worried about bad things happening to an animal you really cared about? . . . . Y N
    What do or did you worry about? _____
_____
_____

Cruelty or Killing

"Sometimes people do mean things to animals, deliberately hurting, torturing or killing them in a cruel way."

9. Have you <u>heard</u> about people deliberately hurting, torturing or killing an animal? . . . . Y N
    What did you hear? _____
_____

10. Did you ever <u>see</u> anyone deliberately hurt, torture or kill a pet or animal in a cruel way? . . . . Y N

    If yes, who? (please circle)
a. Friend or Acquaintance
b. Family Member or Relative
c. Stranger
d. Other (who?) _____

What kind of animal(s)? (read types below and circle all that apply)

	How many?			How many?
a. Dog(s)	_____			
b. Cat(s)	_____	f. Turtles, snakes, lizards, insects etc.		_____
c. Bird(s)	_____	g. Rabbits, hamsters, mice, guinea pigs, gerbils		_____
d. Fish	_____	h. Wild animal(s) (describe) _____		_____
e. Horse(s)	_____			

How did they hurt, torture or kill the animal(s)? (read options and circle all that apply)

a. Drowned
b. Hit, beat, kicked
c. Stoned
d. Shot (BB gun, bow & arrow)
e. Strangled
f. Stabbed

g. Burned
h. Starved or neglected
i. Trapped
j. Had sex with it
k. Other (describe) _____

What happened afterwards? _____
_____
_____

How old were you when you saw this happen? (circle all that apply)
     a. Under age 6   b. 6-12 years   c. Teenager   d. Adult

11.   Have <u>you</u> ever deliberately hurt, tortured or killed a pet or animal in a cruel way? . . . . Y N

If yes, what kind? (circle all that apply)

How many?   **How many?**

a. Dog(s)   _____
b. Cat(s)   _____   f. Turtles, snakes, lizards, insects etc.
c. Bird(s)   _____   g. Rabbits, hamsters, mice, guinea pigs, gerbils   _____
d. Fish   _____   h. Wild animals (describe) _____
e. Horse(s)   _____

What did you do to hurt, torture or kill the pet or animal? (read options and circle all that apply)

a. Drowned
b. Hit, beat, kicked
c. Stoned
d. Shot (BB gun, bow & arrow)
e. Strangled
f. Stabbed

g. Burned
h. Starved or neglected
i. Trapped
j. Had sex with it
k. Other (describe) _____

What happened afterwards? _____
_____

How old were you? (circle all that apply)
     a. Under age 6   b. 6-12 years   c. Teenager   d. Adult

Were you alone when you did this? . . . . Y N

12.   Have you ever <u>seen</u> anyone give animals any drugs (alcohol, pot, etc.)? . . . . Y N
        Describe: _____
        _____

Have <u>you</u> ever given animals any drugs (alcohol, pot, etc.)? . . . . Y N
        Describe: _____
        _____

Have you ever <u>seen</u> animals being made to fight (cats, pit bulls, cocks, etc.)? . . . . Y N
        Describe: _____
        _____

Have <u>you</u> ever made animals fight? . . . . Y N
        Describe: _____
        _____
        _____

Coercion or Control

"Sometimes people make children or adults do mean things to animals, trying to control people with threats or actually hurting an animal, (e.g., If you tell, I'll kill your dog)."

13. Have you ever <u>seen</u> or <u>heard</u> about someone doing this? . . . . Y N
    What have you seen or heard? _____
    _____

14. Has anyone ever threatened you this way? . . . . Y N
    If yes. what happened?
    _____
    _____
    _____

    Who did this?   (circle)
        a. Friend or Acquaintance   c. Stranger
        b. Family Member or Relative   d. Other _____

    How old were you? (circle all that apply)
        a. Under age 6   b. 6-12 years   c. Teenager   d. Adult

Sexual Interactions

"Sometimes animals are used by people in sexual ways."

15. Have you ever <u>heard</u> about people being sexual with animals? . . . . Y N
    What did you hear? _____
    _____

16. Have you ever <u>seen</u> others do sex acts or sexual touching with animals? . . . . Y N
    If yes. what kind(s) of animals? _____
    Please describe what you saw: _____
    _____
    _____

    Where did you see this? _____

    Who did this?   (circle)
        a. Friend or Acquaintance   c. Stranger
        b. Family Member or Relative   d. Other _____

    How old were you? (circle all that apply)
        a. Under age 6   b. 6-12 years   c. Teenager   d. Adult

17. Have <u>you</u> ever done sex acts or sexual touching with animals? . . . . Y N
    If yes. what kind of animals? _____
    Please describe what you did or were made to do: _____
    _____

    Who made you do this? (if applicable)
        a. Friend or Acquaintance   c. Stranger
        b. Family Member or Relative   d. Other _____

    How old were you? (circle all that apply)
        a. Under age 6   b. 6-12 years   c. Teenager   d. Adult

Fears

"Some people are afraid of some animals."

18. Have you ever been really frightened by an animal (eg. chased or bitten)? . . . . Y N
    If yes, what kind of animal? _____

    What did the animal do? _____
    _____

    How old were you?
        a. Under 6   b. 6-12 years   c. Teenager   d. Adult

    Were you hurt? . . . . Y N
    If yes, how were you hurt or injured? _____
    _____

    Are you still afraid of the kind of animal that frightened you? . . . . Y N

"Roadkill"

"Seeing roadkill (dead animals by the side of the road) bothers some people."

19. Does seeing "roadkill" bother you? . . . . Y N

    If yes, how much? **(please circle)**
        a. Just a little   b. Somewhat   c. A lot

    What about the "roadkill" bothers you?
    _____
    _____

Movies, TV

"Seeing animals portrayed as hurt or mistreated bothers some people."

20. Does seeing movies or TV shows where animals are hurt or mistreated bother you? . . . . Y N

    If yes, how much? **(please circle)**
        a. Just a little   b. Somewhat   c. A lot

Barbara W. Boat, Ph.D.
Department of Psychiatry ML 0539
University of Cincinnati
Cincinnati, OH 45267
(513) 558-9007
(513) 558-4107 fax
Barbara.boat@uc.edu.

Risk Assessment Tool Three:
Lockwood's "Animals at Risk" Thematic Apperception Test

RANDALL LOCKWOOD, PH.D., THE VICE PRESIDENT OF RESEARCH AND EDUCATIONAL OUTREACH FOR THE HUMANE SOCIETY OF THE UNITED STATES (HSUS), IS A LEADING RESEARCHER IN THE FIELD OF CRUELTY TO ANIMALS AND ITS CONNECTION TO HUMAN VIOLENCE. As part of his work at HSUS, he has designed two instruments to assess risk to animals and others in the home. The first is the "Animals at Risk" Thematic Apperception Test. A projective test, the tool uses drawings as a prompt to elicit information about individual and family functioning. By design, the sketches in any projective test are minimal so that the person being tested will have to draw on personal experience to flesh out the story suggested by the prompt. Lockwood's instrument adds animals to scenarios typical in other thematic apperception tests to elicit information about pet care, discipline, loss, disposal and abandonment.

Like the Boat inventories, the Lockwood tool will help you assess the risk participants may pose the other program participants, both human and animal. This information can be used to select participants as well as to provide a suitable level of supervision for your program.

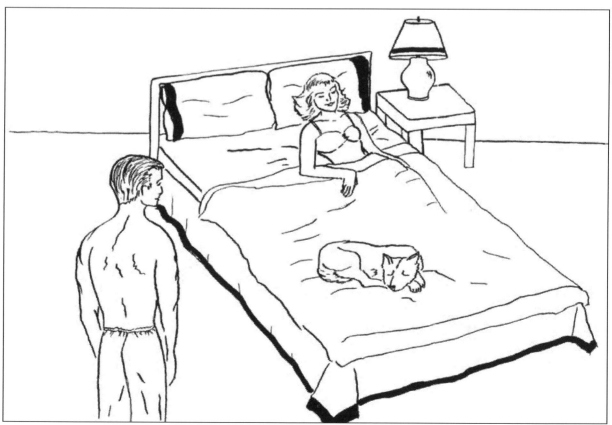

Risk Assessment Tool Four:
Loar's Family-Based Risk Assessment

L YNN LOAR, PH.D., LCSW IS A SOCIAL WORKER WITH EXPERTISE IN CHILD ABUSE AND NEGLECT AND THE ROLE THAT ANIMALS PLAY IN TROUBLED FAMILIES. She designed the Strategic Humane Interventions Program. She is also the president of the Pryor Foundation and a member of the Board of Directors of the Latham Foundation. Dr. Loar developed this family-based risk assessment to help program designers look at the interaction among risk factors of people and animals living together. Risk factors include the triggers and stressors common in family life. For example, noise, messiness, eating quirks, and other normal behaviors may serve as triggers for problematic or dangerous reactions in the familial and social contexts for some program participants. This tool is designed to assess risk to all living beings in the home based on interaction and the interplay between irritating behaviors of potential victims and limited tolerances of people in positions of power and responsibility.

Use this tool to determine the suitability of participants, the level of supervision needed for a safe, effective program, and problems your program can address.

Family-Based Risk Assessment

What is it?

The *Family-Based Risk Assessment Chart*, found on Page 149, is designed to help professionals determine how dangerous a potential offender is in a particular family situation involving children, dependent adults, frail elders, animals, and other members of the household. Because an offender does not function in a vacuum but responds to internal and external forces, this tool assesses the interaction of two factors:

1. the potential offender's personal triggers, and

2. the likelihood that these triggers will be set off by behavior in the household.

By comparing a potential offender's responses with what is going on in the household, we can assess the likelihood of violence in the home. For example, some people are easily provoked by noise while others might be indifferent to noise but be very aggravated by messiness or demands for assistance. A number of people find normal behaviors such as crying, barking, or whining highly stressful. High frequency, intensity and duration of stressful behaviors increase the probability of violence. Thus, the chronically noisy child or pet would be at greater risk in one home than another while exhibiting exactly the same behavior. Each family has its own unique combination of stressful circumstances that contribute to the degree of risk for violence. This is not to say that victims cause or are responsible for abuse, but simply that some normal behaviors are trying, and that some behaviors are more trying to some people than to others.

Larger social, economic and environmental factors affect risk as well. Psychosocial and economic impoverishment creates a context in which a potential abuser is less able to inhibit aggression. Sleep-deprived parents caring for a colicky and constantly crying infant who live in a nice home in a quiet neighborhood and can afford a babysitter pose less risk to their infant than do parents who live in a run-down apartment in a dangerous neighborhood and cannot afford in-home help.

This risk assessment considers which factors are most likely to act as triggers for a particular individual and the probability that other family members will activate these triggers. Realistically evaluating triggers and assessing how likely they are to be activated by others in the home allows us to suggest ways to prevent potentially dangerous situations from worsening and to take steps to protect potential victims from getting hurt.

What do I do?

You will assess the family's risk based on six common individual and family behaviors:

- Noisiness,

- Messiness,

- Disobedience,

- Eating difficulties,

- Toileting difficulties, and the

- Level of activity and need for supervision.

Using the definitions found on Pages 141-148 for these six factors, you will assess to what degree each behavior is a trigger for the potential offender, to what degree the behavior is evident in the household, and which household member is most likely to be at risk for each behavior. As you evaluate the family, you will assess these six factors for each animal, child, person with a disability, elder and adult partner in the home. After you have completed this assessment, you will consider two more risk factors: isolation and impoverishment.

Step one: Your first step is to assess the potential offender's likely response to these triggers.

To do this,

- Read the definitions on Pages 141-148, and
- Fill out the potential offender column – reactivity rating – of the assessment on Page 149, scoring the potential offender on a scale from 1 to 5 on his or her reactivity to each of six common behaviors.

    "1" indicates this individual finds the behavior minimally annoying.

    "5" indicates that it could be dangerously annoying.

- Add the ratings for each category to give the potential offender a Personal Reactivity Rating between 6 and 30.

Step two: Your second step is to assess the degree to which these triggers might be present in the household by looking at the likely behavior of children, dependent adults, frail elders, animals, and other members of the household.

To do this:

- Use the chart on Page 149.
- make a list of all human and animal members of the household. Include all children and pets (the text below focuses on dogs and cats because they are the most popular pets).
- Include other potential victims who reside in the home either permanently or temporarily, like an aging parent who lives in the guest room over the garage or another relative needing assistance while recuperating from an illness. Domestic violence of any sort can put even able-bodied adults in harm's way.
- Consider the frequency, intensity and duration of the behaviors of the potential victims, scoring them using a scale of 1 to 5.

    "1" indicates minimally provocative behavior.

    "5" indicates maximally provocative behavior.

- After you score each member of the household on each behavior, add the scores of the members of the household together. Then, multiply the cumulative score for each category by the potential offender's reactivity rating.
- Look at the resulting totals for high and low risk for individuals, for behaviors, for times of the day, such as meal times, and for a total indicating over-all risk of violence.

Family-based risk assessment definitions:

Six factors commonly increase the risk of violence or abuse in a household: noisiness, messiness, disobedience, eating difficulties, toileting difficulties, and the level of activity and need for supervision.

First, assess the potential perpetrator's response to these factors.

Then, assess family members for the likelihood that these factors will be evident in the household. As you evaluate the family, assess these factors for each animal, child, person with a disability, elder and adult partners. Consider your earlier assessment of the potential offender's triggers as you rank danger in each category.

Noisiness

■ animals

Unaltered cats howl when in heat, a sound many people find dismaying or even chilling. To some, it sounds like a child's cry. Some dogs bark only occasionally, when somebody comes to the door, for example, while others bark more often, at any movement outside the house; still others seem to bark almost constantly. While this may not matter to people who are comparatively indifferent to noise, the noise-sensitive person finds this very trying behavior. Noise complaints are among the most common and frequent that animal control agencies receive.

Score each animal for how noisy it is.

■ children

Children tend to be very noisy people: crying, whining, complaining, playing noisily, banging things, dropping things, and colliding with things. Some learn that they only get attention from their parents when they make a considerable amount of noise, the annoyed adults unwittingly reinforcing the behavior they abhor.

Score each child for noisiness.

■ people with disabilities, frail elders

Hearing loss afflicts a considerable percent of the aging population as well as a smaller segment of the general population. Aging friends or relatives may play the television very loudly, often to the point of causing pain to others around them. Those sensitive to noise may become uncomfortable at home because the aging parent, now living in the spare bedroom, blasts the television all day. They may notice their own tempers flaring more quickly and small irritants appearing larger. In addition, helpers may need to shout and repeat everything several times to be understood. This can add considerably to stress levels.

Score each disabled adult or frail elder for hearing loss and resultant noisiness.

■ adult partners

Adults make noise, especially when using a vacuum cleaner, washing machine or other household appliance. Talking on the phone, nagging or yelling at others may also activate triggers. Partners may have unrealistic – or at least unfulfilled – expectations of peace and quiet on demand. They may interpret noise as provocation worthy of retaliation, even if the noise is moderate and in response to normal boisterousness from young and energetic children or animals or hearing loss of older relatives.

Score the noise level of the adult partner and factor in the general level of noise in the home and environment.

Messiness, disregard for or destruction of property

- **animals**

Animals do not share human regard for possessions. Cats see drapes and couches as fine things to scratch their claws against – and scratching claws is necessary to keep nails trim. Smart cat owners understand that cats scratch of necessity and the best way to protect the drapes and the couch is to provide something the cat will prefer to scratch. Pet supply stores sell carpeted cat trees; they go up higher than the average couch and have a better nap than most drapes. Providing a more attractive alternative to the cat solves the problem; families without these alternatives are likely to find scratched furniture, curtains, and other household property.

Dogs, especially teething puppies, like to chew things. People who give their dogs rawhide to chew are nonetheless surprised that their dogs demolish leather shoes they leave lying around. From the dogs' perspective, leather is leather and their human cohabitant generously provides a variety of types and textures. The easy solution is to shut the closet door so the dog cannot get at the shoes and to give the dog non-leathery things to chew like nylon bones and densely stuffed Kongs.

With a few simple changes, families can avoid much destructive behavior by pets. However, many pet owners blame their animal for bad behavior. Having decided that the behavior was bad, they then feel justified in punishing it.

Score the animals' messy or destructive behavior, factoring in mitigations like cat trees and nylon bones and noting their absence as contributing to risk.

- **children**

Children are messy and clumsy. They drop and spill things. They also enjoy finger-painting, splashing in puddles, and other messy activities. They are too young to appreciate the value of an expensive vase on a small table and to steer clear of it while enthusiastically if imprecisely careening down the hallway on a tricycle. With good intentions but poor understanding of developmental stages, some parents decide to teach young children not to touch fragile and valuable objects instead of simply putting them safely out of reach. The young child's take on the situation is of being tantalized and constantly tempted. Intermittent if not frequent failure of impulse control is normative for children. A wiser parent would baby- and toddler-proof the home and generally keep treasured or valuable objects in safe and inaccessible places.

Score the messy or neat tendencies of the child and factor in the number of toys, and the number of parts they contain. A spilled set of Legos or a 1000-piece puzzle looks messier than a Gameboy left on the table.

- **people with disabilities, frail elders**

People with poor coordination or ambulation may also find navigation difficult. Weak or tremulous hands mean that things will inevitably if unintentionally get dropped and broken. Difficulty walking and the use of assistive devices mean more room is required than most floor plans provide for doorways, hallways, and bathrooms. Without wide openings, someone using a walker is likely to scratch the molding in doorways and other narrow passages.

Score the disabled adult or frail elder based on strength and coordination, and the presence or absence of canes, walkers, wheelchairs and other devises that tend to require more space than is available in the average home.

■ **adult partners**

Partners often differ in their needs for tidiness and orderliness. Even if they agree on standards of neatness and cleanliness, they are apt to disagree on the division of labor and the specific value of the other's personal and cherished property. Thus, one partner may keep personal items neat but neglect household chores, while another might clean the car but ignore spills in the kitchen. An adult partner is at greater risk of triggering the potential offender's rage when power is not shared in the relationship, when individual rights and preferences are generally not honored, and when the more powerful partner's expectations include maid and other services. Mess may then be misinterpreted as a deliberate provocation, and a violent reaction felt as justifiable retaliation. The potential offender often chooses to destroy the things lying around or to shatter a treasured object such as a family heirloom to show his or her power to hurt.

In the clinical literature on domestic violence, injuring or killing the family pet is discussed under the rubric of destruction of property. While true, the pet as a sentient being represents more than that. Violent adults may kick or throw a pet against the wall and refuse to let anybody help it. Thus, the family watches in horror as the pet suffers and dies a few days later. Family members identify and foresee their own fates in the pet's agony and death. Their pain goes beyond the sense of loss triggered when a treasured heirloom is thrown against a wall and breaks into pieces.

Another important point to consider is how the pet entered the family. Instead of chocolates or flowers, the remorseful gift accompanying the batterer's tearful apology may be a kitten and the words, "Honey, I don't know what came over me. I'll never do that again. To show you how much I love you and want us to be a family, I've brought you this kitten. We'll care for it together." The pet thus represents all the optimism and hope for the future that the human victim clings to.

Score this category on general demands for tidiness, the presence of valuable and treasured objects, the presence of and past history of pets living and dying in the home, the number of people in the home (four children inevitably create more disarray than two do), and the egalitarian or unequal division of labor in maintaining the home and its contents.

Disobedience, disrespect, non-compliance with rules, directions

■ **animals**

People say "sit" or "come" and expect the animal to comply. They tug vigorously on the leash expecting the animal to learn to walk without pulling. To humans the point of the talking or pulling is obvious. But to the animal, the message is indecipherable. For the animal to understand what is being asked and to learn to comply with the request, these behaviors must be taught in a variety of settings with clear and predictable directions and reinforcement. It is far easier to get a dog to come when called indoors, for example, than outdoors where competing smells, distractions and food sources abound. Some pet owners mistake inadequate training for disobedience.

Score this based on the animal's compliance and the owner's flexibility.

■ **children**

Children test limits to learn about themselves, other people, and the world around them. Limit testing is a normal – if trying – behavior, more intense at some stages (the "terrible twos" and the teens) than others. Adults sometimes have developmentally inappropriate expectations, expecting a young child to remember things or draw on life experience as though they were older. For example, a 3-year old has an attention span of roughly three minutes. So, if a parent tells that child 20 times in an hour not to go near a hot coffee pot, that child is actually fully compliant for his or her developmental stage. Few parents who tell their 3-year old something every three minutes also marvel at their child's flawless compliance. Rather, based on their own memory and attention span, they interpret the brevity of their child's retention as disobedience and respond angrily or punitively.

Score this based on the child's tenacity in testing limits and the adult's realistic or unrealistic appreciation of developmentally appropriate expectations.

■ people with disabilities, frail elders

People with disabilities or infirmity due to age may need assistance, even attendant care. Does this mean they should not get to make decisions for themselves? In some cases, when the impairment is cognitive, it does for safety's sake. But, what of the aging parent who moves in with an adult child after breaking a hip and does not do as told? Should the desire of an adult to make his or her own decisions be interpreted as disobedience? Does the adult child repeat the words remembered from his or her teenage years, "When you're under my roof, you'll do as I say"?

Such constraints naturally may elicit non-compliance. Loss of autonomy and the need for assistance are problematic enough without having to risk abuse when asserting oneself.

Score the empathy and flexibility of the caregiver as well as the vigorousness of the recipient's desire for autonomy. Take into account collusion between generations, as when a grandparent will seek to undermine a parent's authority with a child in the home.

■ adult partners

Some adults agree with their partner's right to make all the rules; others are overtly or covertly defiant. A partner may be at risk by breaking the rules, whether intentionally or not.

Score the rigidity of the rules, the frequency or infrequency of tolerated exceptions, and the partner's ability to fulfill the potential offender's expectations for respect, obedience, and compliance with rules.

Eating difficulties or quirks

■ animals

Cats are notoriously picky eaters for reasons largely having to do with their dietary and digestive needs. However, the cat owner who sees yet another can of food go uneaten after sitting untouched for hours can easily misinterpret the cat's refusal to eat as defiance. This behavior is a common source of frustration for owners who, believing the cat is deliberately ignoring the food, fail to understand the cat's delicate dietary and digestive needs.

Dogs get into trouble for the opposite reason: they eat everything. Scavengers and omnivores by nature, they delight in food old and new, moldy and fresh, the not-yet-eaten and the already excreted. The dog owner who opens the oven, takes out a chicken and then momentarily abandons it to answer the door, is likely to find a happy dog and an empty platter back in the kitchen. Unless the owner has invested substantial time teaching the dog impulse control around food using increasingly large and tempting challenges, the empty platter represents predictable behavior, not a bad dog. The empty platter indicates that more training is needed, that food should be put in inaccessible places, and that the problem of the consumed chicken was caused by the person's failure to exercise hypervigilance around coveted food.

Score the availability of generous enough amounts of fresh and appropriate food so the animal is not unduly hungry, the animal's drive and determination to hunt for extras, and the vigilance of the pet owner in putting things away.

■ children

Children control so little in life that they readily seek to control what they eat. They may develop quirks to feel in charge, eating the same food for lunch every day for three months, only to say they hate it the first day of the fourth month. They may eat carrots or apples if they are sliced a certain way, but not another, or they may refuse to eat foods that "touch" (e.g., peas roll that into mashed potatoes on a plate). Some parents understand their child's need for control and the advantages of choosing battles wisely; others take this behavior as an affront or a challenge and turn mealtimes into battlegrounds and power struggles.

Score the child's need for self-determination; the level of risk increases with the parent's need to control what the child eats and to attribute motives like disrespect to quirks.

■ people with disabilities, frail elders

Some adults find eating difficult. They may have trouble chewing or swallowing; they may have ill-fitting or uncomfortable dentures, or their hands may tremble making it hard to cut food or manage utensils. What used to be a pleasurable half hour for the family to eat and socialize may become, through age or disability, a labor-intensive hour, generating frustration, spills and despair.

Other adults need to be fed. When people feed children, they know their children will soon eat independently, outgrowing the need for mealtime assistance. When people feed adults, however, they foresee – realistically – that demands will continue indefinitely and may even increase. People who offered to help a relative for a short while may feel trapped when that relative's health deteriorates rather than improves and the need to provide assistance increases.

Score the level of assistance needed. Assess whether help is needed to cut or feed food, prepare special meals, or clean up messiness from feeding difficulties. Base this score on the level of repugnance or disgust the caregiver experiences and reaction to increased dependency.

■ adult partners

The adult partner may be at risk in this category not because of eating quirks but because of his or her role in food preparation. A controlling partner may make exacting demands on the timing, quality, and service of meals.

Score the potential offender's level of expectations and willingness to adjust expectations downward when other demands press.

Toileting or housebreaking accidents; incontinence; hygiene and grooming

■ animals

Cats tend to be fastidious, only avoiding litter boxes when the cat is ill or bothered by something or when the box dirty. People may misconstrue the cat's illness or their own failure to clean the litter box as the cat's misbehavior.

Dogs surpass humans in some physical capabilities such as hearing and sense of smell. But they are similar to humans in needing to relieve themselves a few times during the day. Yet owners will take a dog out in the morning to relieve itself, go to work for the day, and return ten hours later angry about a wet spot on the carpet – even though they themselves have gone to the bathroom two or three times during the day at work. This problem is simply a question of owners overestimating the dog's physical capacity.

Other toileting accidents may be due to improper or inconsistent training, failure to notice the dog's behaviors indicating a need to go out, insufficient time outdoors, or illness, particularly urinary tract infections. Some submissive and frightened dogs also urinate as one of their submissive behaviors. Scaring this dog will only increase the urinating indoors.

Score the owner's realistic or unrealistic expectations and willingness to provide clean litter boxes, sufficient training and frequent enough opportunities to go out.

■ children

Most parents look forward eagerly to the day their child will outgrow the need for diapers. This day usually arrives when the child is between 2 ½ and 3, although some children, particularly boys, wet the bed until they are older. Added pressure to toilet train children at an early age is put on parents by child care programs that only accept toilet trained children. Some children, due to illness, disability, emotional distress, or physical or sexual abuse are incontinent longer, particularly at night.

Parents are not always charitable with a child who wets the bed and may take it as an affront to their capacity as parents. This is especially likely if the parent was also a bed wetter and was humiliated or punished for the same behavior. Instead of engendering compassion, the memory increases the risk that the humiliated parent will repeat the abusive behavior with the bed-wetting child. Doubts about one's ability to control oneself can be projected on others, particularly when memories of self-regulatory failure are vivid and hurtful.

Score the parent's history of enuresis and emotional trauma sustained in childhood and the age of the child and current frequency of toileting accidents.

■ people with disabilities, frail elders

Some people with disabilities need toileting assistance throughout their lives, perhaps because of incontinence or needing help transferring from a wheelchair to a toilet seat. Some people become incontinent as they age. Incontinence is the single biggest trigger for elder abuse and the most common reason cited by family members for institutionalizing and older relative. This dependency takes a great toll on the caregiver and increases risk for the person with the disability. Even if an attendant provides the help, attendant care is poorly paid and poorly supervised, increasing the risk of both physical and sexual abuse by caregivers.

Score the level of assistance needed with toileting, frequency of needing to relieve oneself, screening and supervision of staff (if applicable), and other control issues around bodily functions, appearance, and access.

■ adult partners and teenage children in the home

Adult partners and teenagers are probably not incontinent, but they may, through hygiene or grooming, trigger control issues. They may dress or wear makeup in ways that seem sexy or provocative.

Score the level of control attempted by one adult over another's appearance, grooming and hygiene.

Need for supervision due to level of activity or maturity

- **animals**

People tend to fall in love impulsively with a cute and bouncy puppy without realizing the puppy's level of energy and need for supervision and exercise. Puppies chew and explore constantly, requiring as much baby-proofing as a toddler. Older dogs are more mellow, happy to go for a run and to take a nap. Shelter staff may recommend that busy people select an older dog, but this advice usually goes unheeded.

Score the animal's and human's levels of energy and the time the human allocates to exercise and recreate with the animal.

- **children**

Because young children have enormous amounts of energy and little sense of safety, they must be supervised at all times. Always on the go, children require a high degree of attention. Parents, meaning well, think getting a puppy for their young child would be nice – the child and puppy can grow up together and their comparable energy will allow them to play enjoyably together. These parents ignore shelter warnings that young children and animals may double, not halve, the need for attention.

Score the caregiver's willingness and level of energy to keep up with the child all his or her waking hours.

- **people with disabilities, frail elders**

People who have limited mobility or energy place demands on caregivers to get things for them and help in a variety of ways. They may also have bells to ring to summon help—and may ring them often. Particularly stressed are the people simultaneously supervising young and energetic children, a new puppy, and a bedridden in-law in the spare bedroom, bell ever at the ready to summon a glass of juice or the newspaper.

Score the multiple demands placed on the helper, factoring in tolerance for high and low levels of energy, patience with younger versus older charges and the understandable desire to have a moment to oneself.

- **adult partners**

Demands of infants, people who are ill, frail or disabled take precedence over the demands of teenagers and able-bodied adults. An insecure partner may be provoked when others come first, seem "more important" and more worthy of care and attention.

Score the number of competing demands and the potential offender's relative ability or inability to yield center stage to the needs of others.

Consider two additional factors as you score family-based risk in each category:

1. **Isolation**

Isolation is the biggest generic risk factor for abuse and neglect. Abuse and neglect take place at home in private when nobody outside the family is watching. Reducing isolation is the single most useful intervention.

Assess risk by calculating time the family is alone, and the availability and involvement of friends, relatives, and neighbors from work, school, church or other organizations.

2.   Impoverishment

While poverty does not cause abuse, economic hardship reduces ways to minimize risk. An overwhelmed parent with disposable income can place the dog in a kennel for a few days, hire a housekeeper and a babysitter, or bring in a nurse's aide for a disabled or elderly relative. Though stressed, and now the employer of a small staff, this person can carve out a few moments to regroup and delegate a number of tasks, especially those he or she finds most onerous or off-putting. Without money to hire help, people get pushed beyond their limits when forced to handle multiple and seemingly endless demands.

Assess existing level of demands, use of support services, ability to pay for additional help, and the availability of reduced fee and volunteer services in the community.

FAMILY RISK CHART

POTENTIAL OFFENDER

Triggers:	Reactivity Rating	Animal A	Animal B	Child A	Child B	Child C	Adult Partner	Other Adult	SCORE
Noise	___	___	___	___	___	___	___	___	___
Messiness	___	___	___	___	___	___	___	___	___
Disobedience	___	___	___	___	___	___	___	___	___
Eating Problems	___	___	___	___	___	___	___	___	___
Toileting Problems	___	___	___	___	___	___	___	___	___
Requirements for supervision	___	___	___	___	___	___	___	___	___

POTENTIAL VICTIMS

Total Risk Score ___

Add the scores of all potential victims together, then multiply that number by the potential offender's Reactivity Rating for each trigger to obtain scores.

Degree of Isolation: _____

Economic considerations: _____

Comments: _____

Risk Assessment Tool Five:
Assessing dangerousness toward animals

ALONG WITH THE THEMATIC APPERCEPTION TEST INCLUDING ANIMALS, HSUS' DR. RANDALL LOCKWOOD CREATED THE "FACTORS IN THE ASSESSMENT OF DANGEROUSNESS IN PERPETRATORS OF ANIMAL CRUELTY," A DETAILED TOOL FOR GAUGING SEVERITY OF BEHAVIOR INVOLVING CRUELTY TO ANIMALS. It indicates the significance and seriousness of a particular act and allows for responsible prediction of likely risk in the near future. Lockwood cautions that five factors are cause for serious concern and ten or more indicate likelihood that the offender has been or will be involved in serious acts of violence against people. You can use this tool to gain a realistic sense of the level of supervision they would need to guarantee in order to offer access to animals to the offender as part of treatment.

Factors in the Assessment of Dangerousness
in Perpetrators of Animal Cruelty

Randall Lockwood, Ph.D.
Vice President, Research and Educational Outreach
The Humane Society of the United States
2100 L Street NW, Washington DC, 20037

We are frequently called upon to assist cruelty investigators, law-enforcement officers, court officials or mental health professionals in evaluating the significance of an individual's involvement in a particular act of animal cruelty as an indicator of dangerousness or possible risk for involvement of future acts of violence against others. The relatively low level of attention given to even the most serious acts of animal abuse has made it difficult to systematically or quantitatively assess the various factors that should be considered in evaluating the potential significance of various violent acts against animals. However, the following factors are suggested as relevant criteria in such evaluations. They are based on several sources including:

1. Retrospective studies of acts of cruelty against animals reported by violent offenders;
2. Studies and reports of acts of animal cruelty committed prior to or in association with child abuse and/or domestic violence;
3. Extrapolation from criteria used in threat assessment by the National Center for the Analysis of Violent Crime;
4. Extrapolation from numerous studies on general characteristics of habitual violent offenders.

There is, as yet, no absolute scale that determines when a particular collection of factors reaches <u>critical</u> levels. It is suggested, conservatively, that more than five of these aggravating factors should be cause for serious concern, and that more than ten can indicate a high potential that the offender has been or will be involved in serious acts of violence against people.

1. Victim vulnerability

Acts of violence against victims that are particularly small, harmless or non-threatening by virtue of species, size, age, injury or disability are indicative of perpetrators particularly willing to gain a sense of power and control through violence against those least likely to retaliate, and thus should be considered at higher risk of aggression to children, the elderly, the disabled and other vulnerable victims.

2. **Number of victims**

   The selection of multiple victims killed or injured in the same instance suggests a greater potential for uncontrolled violence.

3. **Number of instances within a limited time frame**

   Several separate instances (e.g. attacks on animals at two or more locations) within a 24 hour period reflects a predatory style of attack that is suggestive of organized and premeditated violence against others.

4. **Severity of injury inflicted** (on continuum from minor injury to death of victim)

5. **Repetition of injuries on individual victim(s)**

   In general, perpetrators who have inflicted multiple blows, stab wounds, etc. on one or more victims should be considered a higher risk.

6. **Multiple forms of injury to individual victim(s)**

   Perpetrators who inflict two or more forms of injury (e.g. burn and bludgeon) should be considered a higher risk.

7. **Intimacy of infliction of injury**

   Abuse that involves direct physical contact or restraint and obvious opportunity to witness the victims' response (e.g. beating, strangling, crushing, hanging, stabbing) may be a more serious indicator than actions that are more remote (e.g. shooting, poisoning, vehicular injury).

8. **Victim(s) is bound or otherwise physically incapacitated**

   Abuse that includes binding, tying, securing with duct tape, confining in a box or bag or otherwise rendering the animal incapable of escape (e.g. crippling) is suggestive of a higher degree of intentional, premeditated violence.

9. **Use of fire**

   A large body of criminological and psychological literature points out the connection between animal cruelty and arson as significant predictors of violent and even homicidal behavior. The combination of these factors, i.e. the intentional burning of a live animal should be considered particularly significant as an indicator of the potential for other violent acts.

10. **Duration of abuse**

    Acts of prolonged maltreatment (e.g. torture) rather than sudden or instantaneous death are more indicative of potential for repeated violence against others.

11. **Degree of pre-planning or premeditation**

    Acts that were premeditated rather than reactive or opportunistic and which involved assembling tools or instruments of injury are more suggestive of high risk. Very long term planning (e.g. several days or weeks) suggests possibility of psychopathic thought processes as contributing factor.

12. **Act involved overcoming obstacles to initiate or complete the abuse**

    Abuse that involves risk or effort (e.g. climbing barrier, breaking and entering, etc.) or pursuit of a victim that escapes initial attack, is indicative of highly motivated violent behavior and thus should be considered an indicator of greater risk for future violence.

13. **Act was committed with high risk of detection or observation**

    Animal cruelty that is perpetrated in public or with high probability of detection should be considered indicative of low concern for consequences of the perpetrator's acts, and thus an indicator of risk for other violence.

14.   Other illegal acts were committed at the scene of the animal cruelty

Personal and property crimes occurring in conjunction with the commission of animal cruelty, (e.g. vandalism, theft, threats to assault on owner or witness) should be considered indicative of higher risk for other violent and/or criminal acts.

15.   Individual was the instigator of an act involving multiple perpetrators

Although the perpetration of many acts of violence may be more likely in a group setting, particular attention should be paid to instigators of such group violence against animals.

16.   Animal cruelty was used to threaten, intimidate or coerce a human victim

Killing or injuring animals to exercise control or threats over others, especially those emotionally attached to those animals, should already be considered a form of emotional abuse and a behavior that, by definition, already involves violence against people.

17.   Act of animal cruelty was indicative of hypersensitivity to real or perceived threats or slights.

Violent perpetrators often misread cues and intentions of others as indicative of threats, taunts, etc. Acts of violence against animals conducted with this motivation can be considered indicative of a high-risk response to social problems.

18.   Absence of economic motive

While an economic motive (e.g. killing and stealing animal for food) does not excuse animal cruelty, the presence of an economic motive, in the absence of other aggravating factors, may suggest a mitigating factor that could decrease the assessment of risk for future violence. Conversely, the lack of such a motive suggests the act was rewarding to the perpetrator by itself.

19.   Past history of positive interactions with victim

Instances of animal abuse in which the perpetrator has previously interacted positively or affectionately with the victim (e.g. acts against one's own pet) suggest an instability in relationships that can be predictive of other types of cyclic violence such as domestic abuse.

20.   Animal victim was subjected to mutilation or postmortem dismemberment

Mutilation is usually associated with disorganized motives of power and control which are often associated with interpersonal violence.

21.   Animal victim was sexually assaulted or mutilated in genital areas or perpetrator indicated sexual arousal as a consequence of the abuse

The eroticization of violence should always be considered a potential warning sign for more generalized violence. A past history of sexual arousal through violent dominance of animals has been characteristic of many serial rapists and sexual homicide perpetrators.

22.   Act of cruelty was accompanied by indicators of sexual symbolism associated with the victim

Written or spoken comments indicating that the perpetrator viewed the animal as representative of a substitute human victim (e.g. "that pussy had to die", "the bitch deserved it") should constitute a serious warning sign of the potential for escalation of violence to a human target.

23.   Perpetrator projected human characteristics onto victim

If other evidence suggests perpetrator viewed the animal victim as a specific human individual or class of individuals, this may indicate that the violence could be a rehearsal for related acts against human victims.

24. **Perpetrator documented the act of animal abuse through photographs, video or audio recording, or diary entries**

The memorialization or documentation of cruelty indicates that acts of violence are a continuing source of pleasure for the perpetrator, a serious indicator that such violence is strongly rewarding and very likely to be repeated and/or escalated.

25. **Perpetrator returned at least once to scene of the abuse, to relive the experience**

As above, the continuation of the emotional arousal experienced during the perpetration of cruelty is an indicator of significant likelihood of reenactment, repetition or escalation of the violence to reach the same rewarding emotional state.

26. **Perpetrator left messages or threats in association with the act of cruelty**

Using violence against an animal as a form of threat or intimidation is often symptomatic of more generalized violence. The additional intimidation of written or verbal threats (e.g. notes left with an animal body or letters sent to someone who cared about the animal), are strongly indicative of potential for escalated violence.

27. **Animal victim was posed or otherwise displayed**

Positioning or displaying the body of a victim (e.g. on front steps, in mailbox), or wearing or displaying parts of the remains (e.g. skins, paws) can be indicative of the use of such violence to gain feelings of power, control and domination - or to alarm or intimidate others. This should be considered a serious warning sign of potential for escalated or repeated violence.

28. **Animal cruelty was accompanied by ritualistic or "satanic" actions**

Animal cruelty accompanied by "satanic" or other ritualistic trappings suggests an active effort to reject societal norms or attempts to seek power and control through magical thought processes, which may escalate to fascination with the application of such ritual to human victims.

29. **Act of abuse involved staging or reenactment of themes from media or fantasy sources**

The reenactment of cruelty to animals in ways the perpetrator has been exposed to through media or fantasy sources (including video games) can be indicative of weak reality testing and a greater likelihood of copying other media portrayals of violent acts against human victims.

30. **Perpetrator reportedly experienced altered consciousness during the violent act**

Acts that are accompanied by blackouts, blanking, de-realization or depersonalization should be considered indicative of thought disorders that could contribute to acts of violence against human victims.

31. **Perpetrator reportedly experienced strong positive affective changes during the violent act**

Violent or destructive acts that are reportedly accompanied by strong positive affect (laughter, descriptions of a "rush", exclamations of generalized or sexual excitement) indicate that such violence is being strongly reinforced and is likely to be repeated and/or escalate.

32. **Perpetrator lacks insight into cause or motivation of the animal abuse**

Repeat violent offenders often display little or no insight into the motivation of their violent acts.

33. **Perpetrator sees himself as the victim in this event and/or projects blame onto others including the animal victim**

Repeat offenders and those resistant to intervention are less likely to take responsibility for their actions and often offer self-serving, fanciful or bizarre justifications for their actions.

Checklist for Factors in the Assessment of Dangerousness in Perpetrators of Animal Cruelty

Randall Lockwood, Ph.D.
The Humane Society of the United States

- [ ] 1. High victim vulnerability
- [ ] 2. Two or more victims in the same instance
- [ ] 3. More than one instance or attack with 24 hours
- [ ] 4. Injury resulted in death of victim(s)
- [ ] 5. Multiple injuries inflicted on one or more victims
- [ ] 6. Multiple *types* of injuries inflicted on one or more victims
- [ ] 7. Act involved restraint of or direct contact with victim
- [ ] 8. Victim was bound or otherwise physically incapacitated
- [ ] 9. Use of fire
- [ ] 10. Abuse or injury took place over a relatively long time frame
- [ ] 11. Act was preplanned rather than reactive or opportunistic
- [ ] 12. Act involved overcoming obstacles to initiate or complete the abuse
- [ ] 13. Act was committed with high risk of detection or observation
- [ ] 14. Other illegal acts were committed at the scene of the animal cruelty
- [ ] 15. Individual was the instigator of an act involving multiple perpetrators
- [ ] 16. Animal cruelty was used to threaten, intimidate or coerce a human victim
- [ ] 17. Act of animal cruelty involved hypersensitivity to real or perceived threats or slights.
- [ ] 18. Absence of economic motive
- [ ] 19. Past history of positive interactions with victim
- [ ] 20. Animal victim was subjected to mutilation or postmortem dismemberment
- [ ] 21. Animal victim was sexually assaulted or mutilated in genital areas or perpetrator indicated sexual arousal as a consequence of the abuse
- [ ] 22. Act of cruelty was accompanied by sexual symbolism associated with the victim
- [ ] 23. Perpetrator projected human characteristics onto victim
- [ ] 24. Perpetrator documented the abuse through photographs, video or diary entries
- [ ] 25. Perpetrator returned at least once to scene of the abuse, to relive the experience
- [ ] 26. Perpetrator left messages or threats in association with the act of cruelty
- [ ] 27. Animal victim was posed or otherwise displayed
- [ ] 28. Animal cruelty was accompanied by ritualistic or "satanic" actions
- [ ] 29. Act of abuse involved staging or reenactment of themes from media or fantasy sources
- [ ] 30. Perpetrator reportedly experienced altered consciousness during the violent act
- [ ] 31. Perpetrator reportedly experienced strong positive affective changes during the violent act
- [ ] 32. Perpetrator lacks insight into cause or motivation of the animal abuse
- [ ] 33. Perpetrator sees himself as the victim and/or projects blame onto others

Last revision December 16, 2003

Risk Assessment Tool Six:
Assessing dangerousness and risk

Steve Eckert, LCSW, is the Executive Director of North Peninsula Family Alternatives, a family counseling program in San Mateo County, California. He was also the Clinical Director for the Community-Based Program for Sex Offenders which ran from 1990-1994 at San Quentin State Prison. While there, he developed these instruments to assess and gauge ongoing risk in teens and adults who had already been found by a juvenile or criminal court to have committed a sexual crime against a minor.

This suite of tools includes three instruments: the Offender Risk Assessment, the Youth Offender Assessment Form, and the Offender's Family Assessment Form. The *Risk Assessment* is filled out by the case manager, probation officer, or other person with access to the case file. The *Youth Offender Assessment Form* structures an interview with the youthful offender about self-image, relationships, sexual behaviors, fantasies and experiences, the molestation and the offender's view of it. *The Offender's Family Assessment Form* elicits information from family members about the offending youth's development, behavior, and offense in the context of family life.

The instruments are included here without modification. They include questions about torturing and killing animals as well as sexual activity with animals. If you use this tool, excerpt only those questions relevant to the population you are working with.

OFFENDER RISK ASSESSMENT

Check the appropriate factors to determine risk.

Low risk:

_____ First offense

_____ Offense situational/opportunistic

_____ Offense involved no bodily penetration

_____ Offender admits responsibility

_____ Offender feels remorse/shame/empathy toward victim

_____ Family of offender aware of offense and supportive of treatment

_____ Supportive, functional family with good boundaries

_____ No significant history of alcohol use/abuse

_____ No significant history of drug use/abuse

_____ Good social skills with peers

_____ Good social skills with adults

_____ Balanced self-image (recognizes strengths and weaknesses)

_____ No violence in offense or history

_____ No predatory behaviors

_____ Low deviance in sexual behavior and fantasy

_____ No previous arrest or conviction for non-sexual felony

_____ No unauthorized contact with victim since offense was reported

_____ Strong motivation for treatment

_____ No history of psychosis, clinical depression, suicide attempt or ideation

_____ No history of abuse or neglect in childhood

_____ No history of protracted separation from primary caregiver(s) in childhood

_____ Developmental milestones achieved within normal ranges

Moderate Risk:

_____ More than one sex offense

_____ Offense involves penetration (not sodomy or use of a foreign object)

_____ Several arrests or convictions for non-sexual felonies

_____ Offender minimizes offense, responsibility

_____ Offender gives partial admission

_____ Offender shares blame with victim, projects responsibility

_____ Offender has little remorse, shame, empathy for victim

_____ Offender's family is dysfunctional

_____ Alcohol abuse, unrelated to offense

_____ Drug abuse, unrelated to offense

_____ Poor social skills

_____ Low or distorted self-image

_____ Implied or actual threat of violence associated with offense

_____ Client had unauthorized contact with victim since offense was reported

_____ Sexual deviance on a par with appropriate arousal

_____ Limited motivation for treatment

_____ History of depression and/or suicide, but no attempts

_____ History of child abuse

_____ History of cruelty to or killing animals

High Risk

_____ Significant history sex offenses

_____ Serious sex offense (sodomy, ritualistic, sadistic)

_____ Violent sexual fantasies

_____ Offender denies sexual fantasies

_____ Use of threats or force in offense

_____ Frequent use of force with others

_____ No remorse, shame, empathy for victim

_____ Offender blames victim

_____ Severe family dysfunction

_____ Chronic history of alcohol abuse, including in relation to offense

_____ Chronic history of drug abuse, including in relation to offense

_____ Very low or grandiose self-image

_____ Numerous arrests, convictions, periods of incarceration

_____ Offender denies offense, responsibility

_____ Poor social skills

_____ Threats made to victim since offense was reported

_____ Sexual deviance is higher than appropriate arousal

_____ Paraphilias

_____ Offender refuses treatment

_____ History of depression, risk of suicide, prior attempt(s)

_____ Evidence of thought disorder

_____ Severe history of abuse in offender's childhood

_____ Victim is an infant, disabled, or especially vulnerable for some other reason

_____ Offender tortures or kills animals

YOUTH OFFENDER ASSESSMENT FORM

Client's Name _____ Interviewer(s) _____

SMCMH# _____ Date _____

This interview is to be conducted after a general family intake session.

1. **Self Image**

   How would you describe yourself (strengths, weakness/talents… etc.)? _____

   How do you think others view you? _____

   Same sex: _____

   Opposite sex: _____

   What *one word* best describes how you see yourself? _____

2. **Relationships**

   Whom do you feel closest to, or trust the most, in your family? _____

   Outside your family? _____

   Who are the kids you hang out with and play with the most (relationship)? _____

   _____ How old are they? _____

   What do you do/play with these kids? _____

   Do you confide in your parents? _____

   Whom do you confide in? (For example, if you needed to talk about something important, would you have

      someone handy? _____ How would you make contact with them?) _____

   How do you express your anger? _____

   Do you have any pets? _____ What do you do when your pet does something bad? _____

   Are you ever cruel to your pet or other animals? _____

   Have you ever played with fire? _____ Have you ever set any fires on purpose or by accident? _____

   Has there ever been a period of time when you were wetting the bed? _____

3. **Previous Sexual Experience** - (Introduction to sensitive area; give client option of answering questions later)

   How did you learn about sex? _____

   What was your first sexual experience? _____

   Can you think of anything that happened before that? _____

Teaching Empathy / 157

How often do you have wet dreams? _____

How do you react to an "unexpected" erection? _____

Masturbation:
When did you start to masturbate? _____

How often do you masturbate (per day, week, month... location/time of day...) _____

Do you ejaculate? _____

Fantasies:
What kind of pornography have you looked at? (Magazines, Videos, Internet)? _____

Which of these turn you on? (ask about swim suits magazines, lingerie ads, children's underwear ads) ___

_____

What activities do you find sexually exciting? _____

What fantasies do you use to masturbate? (Sexual pictures? Your sexual offense?) _____

Which sexual activities have you engaged in? Kissing _____   Sexual touching _____   Oral Sex _____

   Dry Humping _____   Intercourse (anal/vaginal) _____

Sexual Preference:
Do you have a boyfriend or girlfriend? _____

Have you ever been sexually attracted to (opposite sex of above)? _____

Have you ever been sexually attracted to younger children? _____   What age? _____

Have you ever had any sexual experience with animals? _____ Thought about it? _____

4. Disclosure

How was the disclosure about the sexual offense made, to whom, and how did you learn about it? _____

_____

5. Client's Responses

What was your reaction when the allegations were made? _____

How do you explain what occurred? _____

On a scale of 0 to 10, (0 not very serious, 10 *very* serious), where do you rate the seriousness of your

   behavior? _____

6. Description of Sexual Molest

I want you to describe the offense. (What did you do?) If not already detailed in question #4. _____

_____

When was the last time it happened? _____   When was the first time? _____

How many times do you estimate it occurred? _____

What about the behavior worried you? How did you try to stop it? _____

Did the offense include bribery (rewards) _____

Threats? _____ Violence? _____

Use of weapons? (describe these) _____

What part if any of the sexual activity was OK? Why? _____

What did you think about the offense before doing it? _____

7. **Selection of Victim** - (If you know names of victims use name in questions)

How did you know the victim? (What is the relationship between you and the victim?) _____

How old was the victim? _____ What is the age difference between you and the victim? _____

What is the size difference between you and the victim? _____

8. **Victim Approach**

What were you doing with the victim before the offense? _____

How did you introduce the sexual activity to the victim? (What did you say/do?) _____

How did the victim respond? (Was there resistance or encouragement?) _____

How did you continue? _____

Once the sexual activity was completed, what did you say to the victim about it, and about telling? _____

_____

9. **Contributing Factors** - (At the time of the offense)

Ask the client to describe what was going on in his/her life when the sexual abuse began. _____

_____

School functioning (attendance, learning disabilities, behavior, peer connections): _____

Peer relationships (sexual identity issues, identity, self-esteem, etc.): _____

Substance use: _____

Family functioning: _____

Rejections/Losses/Adjustments: _____

10. **Current Reactions**

How do you feel about the incident? (Anger, Guilt, Remorse, Shame, Feeling towards police, etc.?) _____

_____

How is the offense a problem to you? _____

How is the offense a problem to the victim? _____

11. Responsibility

Who's responsible for what happened? (On a scale of 1-10) _____

Who or what would have prevented it? Kept it from continuing? _____

12. Outcome

What do you think are appropriate consequences for you? _____

_____

For the victim? _____

13. Future

Do you worry about the sexual offense happening again? _____

How do you control the impulse? _____

What kind of help do you need to keep the sexual offense from happening again? _____

14. Therapy

How do you feel about being in group therapy with other two kids who created a similar offense? _____

_____

What do you imagine about other two kids who have committed sexual offenses? What kind of kids will

they be? _____

15. Parental Knowledge of Actual Offense Behaviors

On a scale of 1-10, how truthful were you with your parents about the offense? _____

What did you tell them happened, or what did you fail to tell them happened? _____

_____

How do you think they will react if they learn you did more than you originally told them? _____

How did you think it would be best to tell them what really happened? _____

16. Closure

Do you have any questions about this interview? _____

Is there anything I haven't asked you that you feel I need to know? _____

_____

Thank the client for their cooperation and prepare them for anything that the therapist may want to bring up in the family session. You may want to bring the client back for a second individual interview, to give him/her another chance to "discuss more" about the offense (if he/she had trouble disclosing the first time)

OFFENDER'S FAMILY ASSESSMENT FORM

(Revised 9/20/03)

Client's Name _____ Interviewer(s) _____

SMCMH# _____ Date _____

1. Describe your child's (personality, interests, hobbies, character.) Is your child similar or different from any particular family member? _____
_____

2. On a scale of 1-10, how mature is your child compared to other kids his/her age? _____

3. How does your child express anger? How do other family members express anger? _____
_____

4. Has your child ever been cruel to animals? Played with or set fires? Had a period of time where he/she wet the bed? _____

5. How do people show their affection for each other in the family? _____
_____

6. In what ways have you discussed sexuality with your kids? How did your child learn about sexuality? _____
_____

7. What did your child do, or what is your child accused of doing? _____
_____

8. How did each family member find out about the sexual offense, and how did they react? _____
_____
_____

9. What are each family member's explanations for what occurred? _____
_____
_____

10. What consequences were imposed at home for the sexual offenses? _____
_____
_____

11. What is the history of sexual abuse or physical abuse in the family? _____
_____

12. What does each family member think should happen to and/or help your child? _____
_____

13. Does any family member feel there are important relevant circumstances that must be known in order to help the child? (Has the child experienced any past loss, trauma, or helplessness?) _____
_____

The six tools in this chapter provide a range of assessment instruments you can use in your program. Select the tools that are most useful and relevant as you assess the animals and people you are considering as participants in your program. The information you gain will help you answer three questions.

- Have I selected the most suitable animals for the program?

- Do I understand the potential risk of participants in the program?

- Do I have adequate supervision, and have I properly ensured the safety of all participants?

- If the answer to all three questions is "yes," you have used the tools appropriately to ensure safety and move the goals of your program forward.

This set of assessments happens at the front end of your program as part of your program design and implementation. Another set of assessments is equally important: the tools you use to measure how individual participants are progressing through the program.

Chapter Eight

Tools for assessing individual progress

Overview

SO FAR, YOU HAVE DEFINED THE CONTENT AND STRUCTURE OF YOUR PROGRAM AND ENSURED THE SAFETY OF ALL BY ASSESSING RISK. Once your program is running, you face a new challenge: assessing the progress of each participant. Why is it important to invest time and effort in such assessments?

To be successful, programs must be designed with clear goals in mind, specific skills that participants will attempt to master. Measuring participants' skills before and after their participation in the program will provide feedback on how well those goals have been met by each participant. This is different from noting positive things that happen during a session, a scared child finally petting an animal or a parent spontaneously praising a child, for example. Rather, individual gains are outcome measures, benefits the participants carry forward after the conclusion of the intervention.

Assessing individual gains provides participants with a measure of their progress, provides you with a measure of the program's progress, and enables you to adjust the program along the way and at the end. Such assessments avoid the pitfall of relying on anecdotal information gathered without structure. They provide real evidence of areas of success and areas requiring change, and offer information useful in planning for the future.

Three tools for assessing individual progress are provided in this chapter.

Measuring Individual Gains - provides a template based on a series of questions. Using this template, you can design your own instrument for measuring individual gains tailored to each participant.

Progress Evaluation and Treatment Goals - offers detailed steps to measure accomplishment and prevent relapse.

Pre- and Post- Project Testing - provides a series of pre- and post-questions used to establish a baseline and assess individual and family progress against that baseline.

Review these tools; select and modify those that will best help you measure individual progress so you can provide concrete feedback to participants and focus and adjust your efforts during and after the program.

Individual Progress Assessment Tool One: Instrument to Measure Individual Gains

GRETCHEN STONE, Ph.D., OTR, FAOTA, HAS CREATED A TEMPLATE FOR PROGRAM DESIGNERS ("MEASURING THE EFFICACY OF HUMANE EDUCATION: METHODOLOGICAL CHALLENGES AND POSSIBILITIES," *Latham Letter,* WINTER, 2002, PP. 14-16). Rather than establish a standardized assessment, this tool allows program designers to design their own assessment instrument based on the program's goals. Dr. Stone's template offers a series of core questions.

1.   What is the problem? (Research question)

2.   Why is this a problem? (Statement of the problem)

3.   What underlying factors contribute to this problem?

4.   What is the desired outcome?

5.   What observable behaviors typify the desired outcome? (Dependent variable)

6.   How can this behavior be measured? (Unit of measurement)

7.   What is the nature of the intervention? (Independent variable)

8.   How can I assure the stability of the intervention? (What controls are offered?)

9.   To what extent can I generalize these findings to the population at large? (Reliability and validity).

These questions help you focus on specific problematic behaviors, define goals and objectives clearly, and assess the impact and limitations of their intervention objectively. Let's look at how these questions can be applied.

1. What is the problem? (Research question)

John, age eight, is inattentive in class, increasingly combative with peers and argumentative with adults. He has been seen kicking and yelling at a dog.

2. Why is this a problem? (Statement of the problem)

John is learning little in class, has few friends and has alienated the adults in his life. He is beginning to pose a danger to children and animals.

3. What underlying factors contribute to this problem?

John's parents argue frequently, and his father hits his mother once or twice a month. Both parents use alcohol excessively. John stopped inviting friends home more than a year ago out of fear and embarrassment.

4. What is the desired outcome?

a.   John will measurably increase his ability to focus and pay attention in school.

b.   John will learn and apply social skills; he will improve his relationships with his teacher and classmates.

c.   John's aggression and arguing will decrease.

5. ***What observable behaviors typify the desired outcome?*** (Dependent variable)

   a. John will increase his ability to stay on task in his classroom.

   b. John will take turns with other children.

   c. John will cease hitting and kicking children and dogs; he will cease shouting and swearing at his teacher.

6. ***How can this behavior be measured?*** (Unit of measurement)

   a. John's time on task will be measured by the teacher using the classroom clock.

   b. During physical education, John will take turns with the other children, both by taking his turn on time and by ceding center stage when it is another's turn. He will take the ball when it is his turn to throw it, throw it appropriately, and give it to the next child readily when his turn is over. The teacher will track his participation.

   c. John will use words instead of feet and fists when he does not get his way. The teacher will keep track of the frequency and duration of outbursts and compare with their frequency and duration in the month before the intervention.

7. ***What is the nature of the intervention?*** (Independent variable)

   The intervention is a six-week clicker training class in which participants learn to shape the behavior of human and non-human animals using an acoustic event marker and treats.

8. ***How can I assure the stability of the intervention?***
   (What controls are offered?)

   The six-week program has a curriculum that is followed consistently. The same facilitators and format are used each week. The facilitators have no contact with the participants outside the program. No other interventions will be introduced during the child's participation in the program. Changes in classroom work and activity will be kept to a minimum.

9. ***To what extent can I generalize these findings to the population at large?***
   (Reliability and validity)

   To the extent that this child demonstrates behaviors typical of others his age who have also been exposed to domestic turbulence and alcoholism, his progress is likely to be similar to others of comparable age, maturity and circumstances.

Individual Progress Assessment Tool Two: Setting Treatment Goals and Preventing Relapse

IN WORK WITH PEOPLE WHO HAVE COMMITTED SERIOUS OFFENSES, VERY SPECIFIC TREATMENT GOALS ARE ESSENTIAL NOT ONLY TO MEASURE THE INDIVIDUAL'S PROGRESS BUT ALSO TO MAKE RECOMMENDATIONS TO PARENTS, THERAPISTS, PROBATION OFFICERS, PAROLE AGENTS, AND THE COURTS ABOUT RISK AND RECIDIVISM. To help set and measure such goals, Steve Eckert, LCSW, has created *Progress Evaluation / Treatment Goals* and a relapse prevention chart to measure accomplishments. Additional relapse prevention materials designed by Terence T. Gorski follow on pp. 168-169.

These tools provides information helpful to offenders who must anticipate future challenges and plan clearly, specifically, and practically how they will handle moments of weakness and risky situations that inevitably crop up and catch people off guard. A relapse prevention chart should be customized for each offender to provide detailed guidance for each person's idiosyncratic vulnerabilities. A sample generic relapse prevention chart follows the *Progress Evaluation/Treatment Goals.*

JUVENILE SEXUAL RESPONSIBILITY PROGRAM
PROGRESS EVALUATION/TREATMENT GOALS

Name: _____ Date: _____

Date entered program: _____ Therapist: _____

Attendance since last evaluation: Times present _____ Times absent _____ Times tardy _____

Progress scores are based on this scale:

N/A	0	1	2	3	4
not addressed	no progress	minimal progress	moderate progress	significant progress	fully achieved

Bases of Evaluation: **Score**

1. Completely describe the offense. _____

2. Accept responsibility for offense without denial, minimization, or justification. _____

3. Identify all methods of coercion used in offense. _____

4. Identify all feelings before, during and after assault. _____

5. Discuss in detail your own victimization issues. _____

6. Show sincere empathy for victim(s). Understand the effects of victimization. _____

7. Understand and apply the Relapse Prevention Method to offense behavior. _____

8. Understand and apply the Relapse Prevention Method to other problematic behaviors. _____

9. Show the ability to recognize and express a full range of feelings in an appropriate manner. _____

10. Increase assertiveness skills: reduce passive and aggressive behaviors. _____

11. Increase social skills and ability to trust in personal relationships. _____

12. Increase self esteem. _____

13. Show ability to control own behavior/avoid excessive control needs. _____

14. Show knowledge and ability to freely discuss sexuality. _____

15. Understand difference between sex and affection/responsible sexual behavior. _____

16. Group skills: show trust, support, respect, and openness to positive influences of group. _____

17. Attends family and individual therapy with progress. _____

18. Show positive management of stress and anger. _____

19. Discuss and begin positive short and long term plans for the future. _____

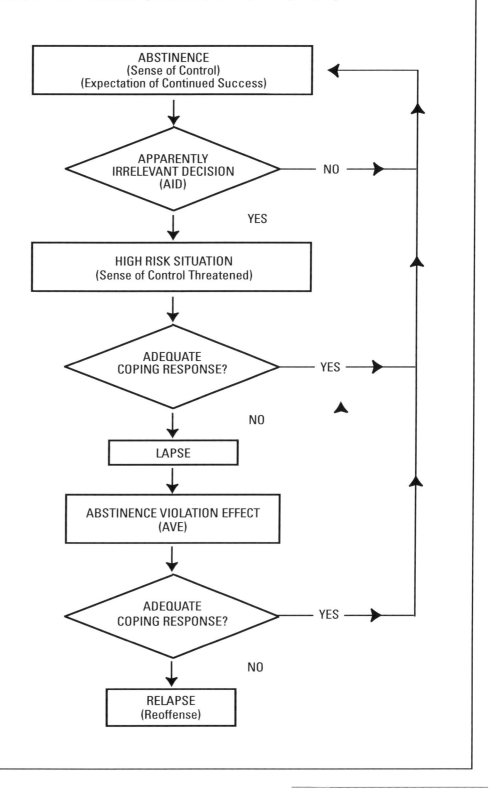

RELAPSE PREVENTION CHART
COGNITIVE-BEHAVIORAL MODEL OF REOFFENSE

ABSTINENCE
(Sense of Control)
(Expectation of Continued Success)

APPARENTLY
IRRELEVANT DECISION
(AID)

NO

YES

HIGH RISK SITUATION
(Sense of Control Threatened)

ADEQUATE
COPING RESPONSE?

YES

NO

LAPSE

ABSTINENCE VIOLATION EFFECT
(AVE)

ADEQUATE
COPING RESPONSE?

YES

NO

RELAPSE
(Reoffense)

THE DEVELOPMENT MODEL OF RECOVERY: THE RELAPSE/RECOVERY GRID

Developed By Terence T. Gorski Copyright, T. Gorski, 1987 (Revised May 1987)

I. Transition	II. Stabilization	III. Early Recovery	IV. Middle Recovery	V. Late Recovery	VI. Maintenance.
1. Develop motivating problems.	1. Recognition of the need for help.	1. Full conscious recognition of addictive disease.	1. Resolving the demoralization crisis.	1. Recognizing the effects of childhood problems on sobriety.	1. Maintain a recovery program.
2. Failure of normal problem-solving.	2. Recovery from immediate after-effects.	2. Full acceptance and integration of the addiction.	2. Repairing addiction-caused social damage.	2. Learning about family-of-origin issues.	2. Effective day-to-day coping.
3. Failure of controlled use strategies.	3. Interrupting pathological preoccupation.	3. Learning nonchemical coping skills.	3. Establishing a self-regulated recovery program.	3. Conscious examination of childhood.	3. Continued growth and development.
4. Acceptance of need for abstinence.	4. Learning nonchemical stress management methods.	4. Short-term social stabilization.	4. Establishing lifestyle balance.	4. Application to adult living.	4. Effective coping with life transitions.
	5. Developing hope and motivation.	5. Developing a sobriety-centered value system.	5. Management of change.	5. Change in lifestyle.	

(Return of the Recovery Process)

Coping With Stuck Points In Recovery

1. Denial and evasion:
(The relapse-prone style)
a. **E**vade/deny the stuck point.
b. **S**tress.
c. **C**ompulsive behavior.
d. **A**void others.
e. **P**roblems.
f. **E**vade/deny new problems.
MEMORY PEG = ESCAPE

2. Recogniton and problem solving:
(The recovery-prone style)
a. **R**ecognizing a problem exists.
b. **A**ccept that it is okay to have problems.
c. **D**etach to gain perspective.
d. **A**sk for help.
e. **R**espond with action when prepared.
MEMORY PEG = RADAR

(Start of Relapse Process)

High-Risk Factors	Trigger Events	Internal Dysfunction	External Dysfunction	Loss of Control	Lapse/Relapse
1. High-stress personality.	1. High-stress thoughts.	1. Difficulty in thinking clearly.	1. Avoidance and defensive behavior.	1. Poor judgment.	1. Initial use of alcohol or other drugs.
2. High-risk lifestyle.	2. Painful emotions.	2. Difficulty in managing feelings and emotions.	2. Crisis building.	2. Inability to take action.	2. Severe shame, guilt, and remorse.
3. Social conflict or change.	3. Painful memories.	3. Difficulty in remembering things.	3. Immobilization.	3. Inability to resist destructive impulses.	3. Loss of control over use.
4. Poor health maintenance.	4. Stressful situations.	4. Difficulty in sleeping restfully.	4. Confusion and overreaction.	4. Conscious recognition of the severity of loss of control.	4. Development of health and life problems.
5. Other illness.	5. Stressful interactions with other people.	5. Difficulty in managing stress.	5. Depression.	5. Option reduction.	
6. Inadequate recovery program.		6. Difficulty with physical coordination.		6. Emotional or physical collapse.	
		7. Shame, guilt, hopelessness.			
		8. Return of denial.			

For Further Information Contact: The CENAPS Corporation, PO Box 184, Hazel Crest, IL 60429, 312-335-3606

RELAPSE WARNING SIGNS — COMPOSITE LIST

(Copyright, Terence T. Gorski 1988, Reprinted with Permission)
Reprinted From Staying Sober Workbook

1. Internal Dysfunction.	2. Return of Denial.	3. Avoidance & Defensiveness.	4. Crisis Building.	5. Immobilization.
Difficulty in — □ Thinking Clearly. □ Managing feelings & Emotions. □ Remembering things. □ Managing stress. □ Sleeping restfully. □ Physical coordination. □ Shame, guilt and hopelessness.	□ Concern of well-being. □ Denial of the concern.	□ Believing "I'll never use again." □ Over-involved with others. □ Defensiveness. □ Compulsive behavior. □ Impulsive behavior. □ Tendencies toward loneliness.	□ Tunnel vision. □ Minor depression. □ Loss of constructive planning. □ Plans begin to fail.	□ Daydreaming & wishful thinking. □ Feelings that nothing can be solved. □ Immature wish to be happy.

6. Confusion & Overreaction.	7. Depression.	8. Behavioral Loss of Control.	9. Recognition of Loss of Control.	10. Option Reduction.
□ Periods of confusion. □ Irritation with friends. □ Easily angered.	□ Irregular eating habits. □ Lack of desire to take action. □ Irregular sleeping habits. □ Loss of daily structure. □ Periods of deep depression.	□ Irregular attendance at AA & treatment meetings. □ Development of an "I don't care attitude." □ Open rejection of help. □ Dissatisfaction with life. □ Feeling powerless & helpless.	□ Self-pity. □ Thought of controlled use. □ Conscious lying. □ Complete loss of self-confidence.	□ Unreasonable resentments. □ Discontinues all treatment & AA. □ Overwhelming loneliness, frustration, anger and tension. □ Loss of behavioral control.

11. Return to addictive use or physical/emotional collapse.	→	□ Contolled Use.	→	□ Shame & Guilt.	→	□ Loss of Control.	→	□ Life & health problems.	→	□ Renewed recovery or death.

Further information is available from The CENAPS Corporation, P.O. Box 184, Hazel Crest, IL 60429, 312-335-3606

Further information is available from The CENAPS Corporation, P.O. Box 184, Hazel Crest, IL 60429, 312-335-3606 (1988) and The Staying Sober Workbook — A Serious Solution For The Problem of Relapse (1988), Independence Press, Independence, MO 64055, 1-800-821-7550.

References: Gorski TT and Miller M, Staying Sober — A Guide For Relapse Prevention (1986) and The Staying Sober Workbook — A Serious Solution For The Problem of Relapse (1988), Independence Press, Independence, MO 64055, 1-800-821-7550.

Individual Progress Assessment Tool Three: Creating a Pre- and Post-Test for a Pilot Project

IN 2000, LYNN LOAR AND MARCIA MAYEDA IMPLEMENTED A PILOT ANIMAL-ASSISTED THERAPY PROGRAM IN SAN JOSE, CALIFORNIA FOR FAMILIES WHO HAD EXPERIENCED SEVERE FAMILY VIOLENCE (LOAR, 2000; MAYEDA, 2000). Three families participated: three mothers and five children ranging in ages from 7 to 14 made up the group. In addition to experiencing domestic violence, most had also had bad experiences with large dogs and were fearful. All the children were having trouble in school and at home, and all the families had received traditional therapy for several years without making much progress.

The families came for eight one-hour sessions. Thirty minutes of each session were devoted to clicker training dogs and 30 minutes to playing the training game. Neither Loar nor Mayeda had any contact with the families outside the group, nor did they allow conversation about past traumas in the session. The families were all referred by the same therapist who attended the sessions as an observer and remained available to them if needed.

Loar's and Mayeda's goals were to:

1. teach participants positive ways to elicit behaviors from others through clicker training and the training game;

2. improve participants' effectiveness and confidence as learners;

3. improve participants' effectiveness and confidence as teachers;

4. improve family members' abilities to appreciate one another's abilities and accomplishments;

5. help participants overcome their fear of dogs.

To measure individual progress, Loar and Mayeda created two sets of pre- and post-program questions. One set was used to collect information from parents. The other set was used to collect information from children.

Both sets of questions proved helpful to the facilitators. They yielded anecdotal information and encouraged parents and children to embellish their answers with stories showing how they applied their new skills to other settings including school, family gatherings, and birthday parties. The tests were not designed to gather statistical or quantifiable data but only to give the facilitators a sense of participants' accomplishments toward chosen goals.

Questions for Parent:

1. What has been your experience with animals?

2. How do you feel when you come across a dog?

3. What has been your child's experience with animals?

4. How does your child react around dogs?

5. Describe yourself as a student.

6. Describe yourself as a teacher, particularly teaching your child something.

7. Describe your child as a student and his/her learning style.

These questions were asked of prospective participants before the first session, and again after the final session. The questions gathered essential information about prospective participants' attitudes and experience with dogs, both as learners and teachers. The questions also revealed how well parents knew their children's attitudes and sense of efficacy.

The answers at the end of the program showed a significant shift from fear of to confidence around dogs and a more generalized concern for the welfare of animals. They also showed a shift from feelings of inadequacy as learners and teachers to feelings of confidence and capability in both roles. Moreover, discrepancies between the pre- and post-tests indicating the parent did not know the child's reality well were resolved, with parents and children seeing themselves and each other similarly and positively.

Questions for Child:

1. What has been your experience with animals?

2. How do you feel when you come across a dog?

3. How do your parents feel about animals?

4. Describe yourself as a student.

5. How do your parents teach you something new?

6. How do they learn new things?

In addition to progress noted over the course of the eight weeks and significant improvement recorded from pre- to post-test, several clients mentioned accomplishments in unrelated activities that they attributed to their participation in the animal-assisted therapy program.

Consider what these questions revealed about the individual progress of two program participants.

Nicole was a very bright 10-year-old girl underperforming in school because of ADHD (attention deficit hyperactivity disorder). In the pre-test questions, Nicole said she hated school, hated her teacher, and was constantly in trouble for disrupting her class. After five weeks in the program, she told the facilitators a story about an interaction with her teacher. She explained she went up to her teacher unbidden, and said that she was a problem in school but a whiz in the Monday afternoon group and could explain why her behavior was different in each setting. She told the teacher that if she could work for about ten minutes, take a breather for a minute or two and get a word of praise, she'd be able to get back to work without disturbing anybody. She had figured out the length of her attention span, the length of the break she needed, the reinforcer she desired that was practical and could be easily offered in a classroom without creating jealousy among peers, and showed awareness that her behavior was a problem for others. She also proposed a fair and equitable exchange, self-regulation in exchange for being allowed to pace things herself and being given momentary recognition for her efforts.

In another case, a 7-year-old boy, the youngest child in the group, had been in treatment with his mother for years after severe violence by his father who was, by then, serving a life sentence in a state prison. The child's behavior alternated between outbursts and withdrawal. He had no friends, would go nowhere other than school without his mother, refused to speak to anyone but her, and was frightened and miserable most of the time.

After the first three sessions, he said to Loar when it was his turn to be the trainer in the training game, "Stand next to me so I get the timing right." Not only had he figured out what skill he needed to learn to improve his technique, but he had also come up with a methodology.

About three weeks later, he and his mother were at his aunt's house watching the evening news. By coincidence Marcia Mayeda was being interviewed on that news program about an animal cruelty case her agency was investigating. Although she was in a "power suit" rather than the informal clothing she wore while bringing dogs to the program, was discussing a topic different from one the boy would associate her with, and was on television rather than in person, he recognized her immediately and said enthusiastically to his aunt, "That's Marcia. I know her and her dogs from the Monday program." He then told his aunt all about the program and his participation. It was his first spontaneous conversation with anybody except his mother in many years.

Two weeks later he was invited to and attended the birthday party of a classmate. He told his mother he would go without her, and would phone if he wanted to leave early. He did not phone her, and she came to collect him two and a half hours later when the party ended.

The boy's mother had always been devoted to her son and felt responsible for the trauma he had experienced. She had diligently followed all advice given by past therapists – and there had been several over the years. Following their instructions, she gave her son almost constant specific and non-judgmental feedback on what he was doing, both right and wrong. She attributed his considerable progress to the change in her behavior, giving positive feedback exclusively except in cases of safety or danger when immediate intervention was necessary. She had, on her own initiative, asked her son's teacher to follow suit. She wanted the teacher to praise all good behavior and ignore the rest, as any good clicker trainer would. The teacher, having noticed recent improvement in his behavior, agreed and reported that he made dramatic gains with this positive approach. She added that he would click himself back on task to stay focused.

These assessment tools provide a process and structure for assessing the progress of individuals in your program. With this information, participants can measure progress toward goals, plan for the future, and see their own improvement clearly. With the same information, you can begin to measure the success of your program against its stated goals and baseline information. The tools in the next chapter will help you take the next step: measuring the effectiveness of your program.

Chapter Nine

Tools for assessing the effectiveness of programs

Overview

YOU HAVE ASSESSED RISK TO ENSURE A SAFE PROGRAM; YOU HAVE ASSESSED INDIVIDUAL PROGRESS TO PROVIDE FEEDBACK AND DIRECTION AS YOU PLAN AHEAD. Your last assessment takes a look at the effectiveness of your program and answers one final question: "What difference did the program make?"

This assessment combines much of the work you have already done to look at progress from a different perspective, that of the program as a whole rather than of the individual participant. An effective assessment measures program goals against program feedback. It may combine all the pre- and post-tests to get a composite picture; it may compare those receiving the intervention with a control group; it may use videotapes of sessions and code behaviors. Additional guidance in developing a program evaluation can be found in Vanessa Malcarne's *Methods for Measurement: A Guide for Evaluating Humane Education Programs* published by the National Association for Humane and Environmental Education (NAHEE). The complete assessment tool can be found on the NAHEE web site, www.nahee.org.

This chapter uses the five components of effective treatment described earlier to set program goals and then to evaluate program effectiveness against those goals. It demonstrates how to use this tool to set goals for a therapeutic clicker training program and then suggests ways to collect information to measure the program's progress against these goals.

Methods for Measurement: A Guide for Evaluating Humane Education Programs

THIS SECTION DEMONSTRATES HOW THE TOOL USES THE FIVE COMPONENTS OF EFFECTIVE TREATMENT: MASTERY, EMPATHY, FUTURE ORIENTATION, LITERACY, AND BALANCED AND RESTORATIVE JUSTICE, TO SET CLEAR AND MEASURABLE GOALS AND OBJECTIVES.

Mastery

Goal:

Participants will learn operant conditioning with the use of an acoustic event marker (called *marker-based* or *clicker training*).

Objectives:

1. Participants will learn to break behaviors down into small increments and to mark each incremental gain with a click and a treat.

2. Participants will learn successive approximation, to mark small steps initially and develop them into larger and more precise behaviors.

3. Participants will develop accurate timing for the event marker and efficient and timely delivery of treats.

4. Participants will develop self-awareness and tolerance for frustration and uncertainty, become able to recognize which of their movements coincided with the click and to persevere toward their goal even when clicks are infrequent.

Empathy

Goal:

Participants will be able to recognize feelings of people and animals.

Objectives:

1. Participants will pace training at a speed comfortable for the learner.

2. Participants will click and treat more frequently if learner appears anxious or confused.

3. Participants will treat and use jackpots generously.

4. Participants will look at and pay attention to the learner and ignore distractions.

Future orientation

Goal:

Participants will demonstrate the ability to defer gratification.

Objectives:

1. Participants will undertake increasingly difficult tasks requiring longer periods to master.

2. Participants will work through periods of little progress to complete the task (instead of giving up when the going gets tough).

Literacy

Goal:

Participants will learn to use writing to externalize problems and structure subjective experience.

Objectives:

1. Participants will write each week. They may choose the format – a diary, journal, letter to a teacher, friend or relative. They may also choose the content – about an animal they trained, a person they worked with, or any other topic of interest.

2. Participants will follow grammatical and syntactical rules.

3. Participants will organize their narratives in paragraphs.

4. Participants will show a logical progression in their narratives from beginning to middle and then to conclusion.

Balanced and Restorative justice

Goal:

Participants will contribute to social justice in a way appropriate to their age, capabilities, and requirements for restitution.

Objectives:

1. Participants will demonstrate self-control and refrain from scaring or harming others. They will acknowledge accountability for their behavior and its impact on others.

2. Participants will demonstrate the mastery of useful skills in learning and teaching new behaviors.

3. Participants will contribute to the well being or betterment of another in a finite and tangible way.

Types of feedback

BOTH OBJECTIVE AND SUBJECTIVE FEEDBACK CAN BE USED TO COLLECT FEEDBACK ABOUT YOUR PROGRAM. Use the tool to obtain feedback that will provide you the information you need to assess your program's progress toward your goals and objectives.

Objective feedback

Objective feedback can be gathered by asking people who see the participant regularly in another context and who do not have a stake in the program what specific changes in behavior and outlook they have noticed. For this information to rely on more than vague memory and intuition, a few relevant questions should be asked just before the participants enter the program and repeated once the program is over. For example, a teacher or athletic coach might be asked before and after the child's participation in an animal-assisted therapy program to rate the child's attention span, ability to tolerate frustration, ability to break a task down into manageable components and ability to get along with others.

Subjective feedback

The feel of a program, to staff and volunteers as well as to participants, matters as well. It affects buy-in by all and retention of key staff members and volunteers. These questions are designed to elicit people's subjective impressions of the humane education or animal-assisted therapy program.

Questions for participants:

◆ What did you like best about this program?

◆ Please rate on a scale of 1-5 how safe you felt at this program, with 1 being very safe and 5 being very unsafe.

◆ How did you feel about the room we met in?

◆ How did you get along with the staff and volunteers?

◆ What did you want to learn from the program BEFORE you started?

◆ What have you learned from the program SINCE you started?

Questions for staff and volunteers to ask themselves:

◆ Are we respectful, caring and supportive of clients?

◆ Are we clear about our specific goals for our clients in general and for each client in particular?

◆ Is our space safe and comfortable?

◆ Do we provide skills that our clients can use in the future?

◆ Do we provide opportunities for peer and/or parent/child teaching?

◆ Do we have enough personnel to accomplish our goals?

Assessment is a critical part of creating, implementing, and evaluating animal-assisted therapy programs. From ensuring safety to providing information useful in modifying programs, assessment tools must be an integral part of your program. Information you gain by using these tools will help guide participants once the program is done, will help you decide what changes to make in the program, and can help others looking for data-based information about program design and implementation. As the field of animal-assisted therapy matures and we continue to collect and share more data, assessment tools will allow us to answer the fundamental question: how do we create animal-assisted therapy programs that are safe and effective?

Pulling it all together

THROUGHOUT THIS BOOK YOU HAVE READ ABOUT PROGRAMS DESIGNED TO HELP CHILDREN AND FAMILIES EXPOSED TO VIOLENCE. Rather than focus on failures or deficits, these programs focus on safe, simple and enjoyable interactions with animals. SHIP brings families together with shelter dogs; other programs center activities around horses, injured wildlife, or other animals. The outcome of these programs is twofold: improved possibilities for the animals as well as learning for the children and families that carries well beyond the classroom walls.

By training and caring for animals, the children and families who take part in these programs learn and integrate skills to manage both their own behaviors and their relationships with others. And because the programs focus on objective behaviors that the participants select and teach, children and families in these programs become the owners of the new behaviors. When the program is over, the skills of recognizing, rewarding and repeating positive behaviors and interactions reside in the family, not in the therapy program.

But creating programs that allow for the possibility of such change takes time and effort. Change takes more than the act of bringing an animal and a family together. Change requires a thoughtful and well planned program that attends to the principles of well designed animal-assisted therapy programs. At this point, you have all the information you need to construct such a program.

Stop for a minute and imagine the first graduation at the end of your program.

Your participants – no matter what population and need you serve – have been brought together with the right animals and staff in a setting conducive to learning and behavioral change. They have spent a manageable number of sessions working in an environment and structure designed to drive learning of the five core skills. Every week, they participated in activities that increased, step by step, their mastery, empathy, optimism, literacy, and social conscience. As they succeeded in small and large ways, they enjoyed recognition just as they gave recognition for the success of others. Immediate treats were followed with photographs, videotapes, and letters of recognition depicting changing behaviors.

And now, at the end, the participants have progressed: some in minimal ways and some in bigger ways. Each participant has a measurement of his or her individual progress, and you have information with which to compare the program's goals with the programmatic and individual outcomes.

This means that you are ready to start over, to review your program, and to improve it for the next time. You have resources to turn to and people to share your success with and seek advice from. You are part of a growing community dedicated to using animals in therapeutic programs designed to increase empathy in children and families exposed to violence. And you are part of the community dedicated to developing systematic, methodical, measured programs that can create and demonstrate real change through sound program design, assessment and measurement.

Overview

AS THE FIELD OF ANIMAL-ASSISTED THERAPY PROGRAMS HAS GROWN, IT HAS BECOME INCREASINGLY EASIER FOR PRACTITIONERS LIKE YOU TO START NEW PROGRAMS. Existing programs provide a wealth of resources ranging from program design documents to consent agreements. Program announcements, consent documents, volunteer agreements, program rationales, and assessments are all available for new programs to use. The following chapters provide models of a variety of resources.

Appendix 1: Programmatic Resources contains program documents used by SHIP as well as directions for clicker training.

Appendix 2: Resources contains a list of organizations that provide services of interest to those creating humane education and animal-assisted therapy programs. This list includes the name of each organization as well as address, phone and fax numbers, and web link.

The intent of these resources is to make it easier for you to get started. If you have already made progress in your design, the SHIP documents may be of use. If you are looking for more information about a specific area, the list of organizations is a quick way to find like-minded people with experience who may be able to help you. Use these tools for research, as models, or as program documents as you work through the logistics of your program.

Programmatic Resources

Overview

THIS APPENDIX PROVIDES THE VARIOUS PROGRAM DESCRIPTIONS, DOCUMENTS, AND PERMISSION SLIPS USED BY SHIP. Reproduce these materials and use them in your own programs, tailor them for your use, or use them as models of the types of written documents you will need to develop. *Teaching with a Clicker: How to Train People and Animals with a Clicker and Treats* is copyrighted in English, Chinese and Spanish. *Teaching with a Clicker: How to Teach Your Dog Good Manners and Tricks* is copyrighted in English. Spanish and Chinese versions will be available at www.Pryorfoundation.com. These brochures may be reproduced but not altered. The various consent forms and statements of purpose may be modified to fit the needs of individual programs. To facilitate adaptation, the certificates and program announcements are provided with blanks where program names, dates and locations should be entered.

SHIP's Program Rationale and Design

THE STRATEGIC HUMANE INTERVENTIONS PROGRAM (SHIP) WAS AWARDED A GRANT THROUGH THE GOVERNOR'S OFFICE OF CRIMINAL JUSTICE PLANNING (OCJP) EFFECTIVE OCTOBER 1, 2001, ENABLING IT TO OFFER INNOVATIVE ANIMAL-ASSISTED THERAPY TO CHILD VICTIMS OF ABUSE, NEGLECT, DOMESTIC OR COMMUNITY VIOLENCE, AND THEIR FAMILIES. SHIP offers services in both Sonoma and San Francisco Counties, the former as a program of the Humane Society of Sonoma County which is the fiscal agent for the grant, and the latter in collaboration with the San Francisco Department of Animal Care and Control.

Unique to this program is the involvement of parents and caregivers. By teaching both the parents/caregivers and children the ability to empathize with animals and the skills to teach useful behaviors exclusively using positive reinforcement, the families come away with the ability to influence one another's behavior positively, without resorting to coercive much less abusive behaviors.

Three to four families meet for a six-week program emphasizing gentleness and behavior shaping in animals and people (behavioral learning). Because the skills to influence behavior are learned initially through work with animals, focus is on new successes rather than past failures. Motivation is high because participants enjoy the companionship and the accomplishments of the animals.

Aftercare activities are individually designed and typically include field trips to the San Francisco Department of Animal Care and Control and the Humane Society of Sonoma County; mentoring programs at the animal shelter that focus on job skills and community service for human participants and increasing adoptability for the sheltered animals, and integration of acquired skills into academic work through collaboration with classroom instructors.

The participating families in San Francisco are under enormous economic stress, and have been for their children's entire lives. Indeed, hardship stretches back for generations in most families. As a result, it is a daunting task to get the parents to focus on their child's learning and teaching styles as the child teaches a dog to sit still or come when called. Such attention is the key to reducing the risk of child abuse and neglect and to improving parent-child relationships. It teaches the parent to break behaviors down into small, manageable and developmentally appropriate pieces and to pace things at a rate that facilitates the child's learning.

In addition, the harsh economic reality of the participants' circumstances makes it unlikely they will ever be able to afford a home in San Francisco that would permit them to have a pet. Thus, the program also creates a way for parents to share the joy of animal companionship with their children and provide happy respite from the grim life in impoverished and often dangerous neighborhoods. It also introduces them to job opportunities in animal welfare, a field most were unaware of, and provides the skills that would prepare them for responsible and meaningful employment.

The involvement of the San Francisco Department of Animal Care and Control creates mentoring and internship opportunities for families. The skills they acquire in the six-week program readily transfer to volunteer jobs at the shelter, dog walkers, adoption facilitators, cat socializers as examples. The staff is eager to mentor at-risk children and parents and give them opportunities to acquire the skills needed for volunteer and paid jobs in shelters, kennels, dog-walking services and other humane work. They would also provide flexible schedules for participants who, upon graduating from high school, want to work in animal protection and welfare and pursue a community college degree. Associate Degrees (AA) in veterinary technology, law enforcement, business administration or any human service field combined with experience working with animals would make candidates highly qualified in a field that is perennially short of skilled applicants.

Program Announcement

THE AIM OF THIS BROCHURE IS TO INTRODUCE THE PROGRAM TO PROSPECTIVE PARTICIPANTS AS AN ENJOYABLE WAY TO LEARN HOW TO TRAIN DOGS. It gives the program's name, date, time and location of meetings, minimum age required for participation and the request that a parent accompany the child. It identifies the San Francisco Department of Animal Care and Control as the agency responsible for the dogs and gives the name and phone number of a person to contact for enrollment and additional information. The photos were taken from www.dognoses.com, a delightful source of canine rhinological photographs (it is literally a web page of photographs of the noses of dogs).

Pages 184 and 185 show the program announcement with identifying information, and then a form with the identifying information deleted so that it may be adapted for use in other programs.

Writing Projects

THE WRITING PROJECTS SHIP USES ARE DESIGNED TO FOCUS ON THE DETAILS OF EFFECTIVE COMMUNICATION, OF TRANSLATING THE KEEN OBSERVATION THAT COMES WITH CLICKER TRAINING INTO EQUALLY CLEAR WRITTEN EXPRESSION, AND TO BRIDGE LANGUAGE AND CULTURAL GAPS. They involve attention to detail, managing time and effort to work on a complicated project in small pieces, eliciting the advice of others, and empathic writing, choosing idioms and phrases that will resonate with the project's intended audience.

Teaching With a Clicker: How to Train People and Animals with a Clicker and Treats by Hilary Louie, age 10, and Evelyn Pang, age 10, Pages 186-187. For the Chinese version, see Pages 188-189. For the Spanish version translated by Priscilla Galvez, age ll, Lina Tam-Li, age 13 and Maria Garcia, Priscilla's mother, see Pages 190-191.

Teaching With a Clicker: How to Teach your Dog Good Manners and Tricks by Hilary Louie, age 10, and Evelyn Pang, age 10, Pages 192-193.

A dog resume, reproduced from Page 194, can be completed and put on each dog's kennel.

Reinforcers are supplied on Pages 195-200.

Thank you notes can be seen on Pages 198-200.

 ## Consents

A CONSENT FORM IS DESIGNED TO EXPLAIN TO HIGH-RISK CLIENTS WHAT MATERIAL WILL BE REPORTED AND WHY. It includes mention of animal abuse and reports to the local humane society. By signing it, each client agrees that he or she understands what material will be reported to an outside authority and what material will be kept confidential. Such notices are essential parts of informed consent, and may reduce risk of suit. However, they are not likely to prevail in court if a client chooses to sue a therapist for reporting a crime involving cruelty to an animal to their local municipal animal control agency. It would be advisable to have the agency's attorney review any such document before it is put in use. See Pages 201-206 for reproducible consent forms.

 ## Volunteer Agreements

THIS SECTION PROVIDES THE VARIOUS DOCUMENTS STAFF AND VOLUNTEERS ARE ASKED TO SIGN REGARDING THEIR PARTICIPATION AND RESPONSIBILITIES. Each organization should make sure its attorney and insurance carrier has reviewed documents being used in the humane education or animal-assisted therapy program. See Pages 207-212 for reproducible agreements.

 ## SHIP's Curriculum

CLICKER TRAINING DOGS: TEACHING THE BASICS WITH A CLICKER AND TREATS. See Pages 213-216 for the curriculum.

> The following SHIP resources have been field tested and provide you with a starting point for the numerous documents required by any animal-assisted therapy program.
>
> These documents can be reproduced or tailored for your use in your program.
>
> If you are looking for additional resources, consider consulting some of the organizations listed in the next chapter.

HOW TO HAVE FUN WITH

DOGS!!!

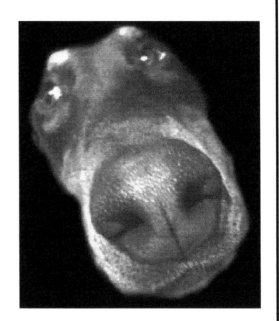

The SHIP Project

for
CHILDREN 8 AND OLDER
And a grown-up who
cares for them

- LEARN HOW TO TRAIN DOGS!
- FIND OUT ABOUT JOB OPPORTUNITIES WORKING WITH DOGS!

Learn *Clicker Training*, the hottest new way to train animals, with dogs from the San Francisco Department of Animal Care and Control.

When: Thursday evenings, 7:00-8:00 p.m.

Dates: May 16, 23, 30 & June 13, 20, 27

Where: Community Room, 201 Turk Street Apartments
Chinatown Community Development Center

How: Sign up with Susan Phillips at the
201 Turk Street Apartments, Office or
call (415) 674-1284

HOW TO HAVE FUN WITH

DOGS!!!

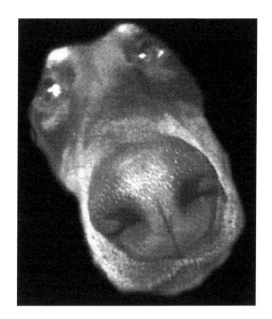

The SHIP Project

for
CHILDREN 8 AND OLDER
And a grown-up who
cares for them

- LEARN HOW TO TRAIN DOGS!
- FIND OUT ABOUT JOB OPPORTUNITIES WORKING WITH DOGS!

Learn *Clicker Training*, the hottest new way to train animals, with dogs from

When:

Dates:

Where:

How:

Teaching with a Clicker:

How to Train People and Animals with a Clicker and Treats

By
**Hilary Louie, age 10 and
Evelyn Pang, age 10**

TRAINING A DOG

The dog has to wiggle it's tummy c than is a very hard thing to do, but this dog has experience.

Adapted for children from Karen Pryor's "Getting Started with the Clicker" with Ms. Pryor's permission

© Copyright 2003

Do and Don't list:

Do:

— Click on time
— Click for every good behavior
— Give a treat for every click
— Click often for beginners
— Look at the learner
— Pay attention at all times
— Ignore distractions
— Give a handful of treats (called a "jackpot") if they're close or if they get it right
— Help by clicking a lot if the learner gets frustrated
— Pick something easy for beginners and something harder for intermediate and advanced learners
— Make sure it's safe

Don't:

— Look away from the learner
— Forget to click
— Forget to treat
— Walk away, get impatient or show disrespect in other ways
— Get distracted
— Click for no reason
— Click late
— Frustrate the learner through inattention

TRAINING DIFFERENT ANIMALS

Fish Tank

What is Clicker Training?

Is your dog like mine was? Does he or she jump and bark when friends come to the door? Does he or she run away or pull on the leash?

Would you like your dog to learn good behaviors and even tricks?

Clicker training is a game you play with dogs and other animals – even people – to teach good behaviors.

All you need is a clicker, some treats, and this brochure. You'll learn how to make learning fun. And you'll learn ways to say "yes" to your learner by clicking and giving treats for good behaviors while ignoring bad ones. If you learn what's in this brochure, you'll be able to train your pet yourself.

To have fun with clicker training, read on!

How to click:

You need a clicker, something that makes a short sound, and some treats.

Make the short sound when you think the behavior is close to what you want. Give a treat right after you click.

The trainer must give a treat with every click. The learner thinks "If I don't get a treat when I hear the click, I won't do it again." The trainer has to respect the rule that the treat must follow the click. The treat has to be something the learner really likes.

The trainer must always look at the learner and pay attention to the learner. If the trainer looks away, the learner will be frustrated and not want to do it again.

If you make it fun, easy and interesting, the learner will want to do it.

Click once and give extra treats when the learner is close to the movement (don't click more than once – let the extra treats show that you like the behavior a lot).

Use jackpots (a large handful of treats).

BUT, don't hurt the dog (or other learner). Don't pull the dog's leash. Never use force. Find a way the learner will like to do the behavior.

What to click for:

Pick something easy at first. Click for an easy task, and then go to a harder one. When you start, click for a step in the right direction. Remember, the learner's a beginner! Click step-by-step.

Click for something the learner is already doing. The click tells the learner, "You're close to the movement." Click for accidental moves toward the goal.

Click for what you want – no yelling, no complaining. Ignore mistakes.

Don't give orders. If the learner doesn't listen to you, he or she is not bad. He or she just doesn't understand what you want him or her to do. Make it easier. Go step by step, with very small steps. Then make the steps bigger.

Pay attention. Don't get distracted. When the learner is trying, be nice, give more time and extra treats. Don't be bossy. You will seem mean and the learner will think he or she is bad. Rely on the power of learning.

Click good or useful behaviors whenever you see them. When your dog or other learner does something cute or useful, click and treat. It may be surprising for the learner at first. The behavior will get better and better if you click and treat often.

When to click (timing):

Click when the behavior happens, not after.

Click a lot and click often. Otherwise the learner might get confused and not want to do it again.

If there's no progress, make your timing better. You're probably clicking late. If you click late, you're not paying attention.

Don't wait too long to click. Don't wait for the whole picture to click. Click for something close to the movement.

When the learner gets it, then wait a bit longer and click. The learner starts to know the behavior you want. The learner does the behavior longer. This is called *shaping the behavior*. Shaping the behavior means making it better.

How to succeed with the clicker:

Keep practice sessions short. Short sessions help the dog (or other learner) concentrate. They learn more with a few short tries. Breaks help. The learner remembers easily with short sessions and breaks.

Try training another behavior if you can't get what you are after. If you get mad – stop. Don't force yourself. Don't yell at the learner. Take a break and do it later.

Remember, make it fun!

If you want to learn more about clicker training, go to www.clickertraining.com

TRAINING DIFFERENT ANIMALS

"的嗒" 器教育法：

怎樣使用 "的嗒" 器和小獎賞來訓練人和動物

作者
雷曉瑩（十歲）和 龐紅敏（十歲）

TRAINING A DOG

TRAINING DIFFERENT ANIMALS

Fish Tank

由願芽女士允許
從卡溫佩芽的 "使用的嗒器的開始" 改編為兒童版

可以做和不可以做的事：

可以做的事：

- ▲ 按 "的嗒" 器的時間要準確
- ▲ 為每次好的動作行為按 "的嗒" 器
- ▲ 每次按 "的嗒" 器之後也給小獎賞（食物、糖果）
- ▲ 給初學者多按 "的嗒" 器
- ▲ 看著學習生
- ▲ 要常常注意和留心
- ▲ 不要受影響
- ▲ 如果他（他）們接近或做得對的時候，給多一些的獎賞（大獎）
- ▲ 如果學習生感覺挫敗，你可以多一點按 "的嗒" 器
- ▲ 選擇容易的教導初學生，選擇一些困難的教中級和高級學習生
- ▲ 要確定是絕對的安全

不可以做的事：

- ▲ 不可以不看著學習生
- ▲ 不可以忘記按 "的嗒" 器
- ▲ 不可以忘記給小獎賞
- ▲ 不可以走開，不耐煩或表現得不尊敬
- ▲ 不可以受打擾
- ▲ 不可以無原無故的按 "的嗒" 器
- ▲ 不可以遲了按 "的嗒" 器
- ▲ 不可以因為不專心令學習生感到挫敗

什麼是 "的嗒" 器訓練？

你的狗是不是和我的狗一樣？當有朋友來到門前，他會不會跳起吠？他會不會追跑或站立扯門鏈？

你想不想讓你的狗學好你的行為，甚至學一些小特技？

"的嗒" 器訓練是一種透過遊戲，讓你與狗和其他狗（甚至人），從當中學習好的行為。你只需要一個 "的嗒" 器和一些小獎賞（食物、糖果）和造小冊子。你將會學到怎樣使學習成為有趣味的行為。你亦將會應用 "的嗒" 器和這小冊子的獎勵好的行為，在同時亦不需要理會獎後的行為生出 "對"。籍此以不同的方式向你的學習者生做 "對"。如果你學到這小冊子的內容，你將會能夠訓練你的寵物。

如你想知道多一些關於這有趣的 "的嗒" 器訓練，請繼續看下去！

怎樣用 "的嗒" 器：

你需要一個 "的嗒" 器（可以用任何會發出短促的物件），和一些小獎賞（食物、糖果）。

當你見到那些動作行為近你想要的，便按一下短促，然後再給小獎賞！

訓練的人必須在每次按短促獎後再給小獎賞。因為學習生會想 "的嗒" 的聲音告訴學習生，我是不會再做的。所以，訓練的人必須確實這道理。那就是按短促獎後必須給小獎賞。那只得小獎賞必定要是學習生喜歡的東西。

訓練的人必須常常看看和注意著學習生。如果訓練的人看著其他的地方，學習生會感覺到那非常混亂和不清楚再繼續做。

如果你令這訓練變得容易和有趣味，按一下短促，然後再給額外的小獎賞（不要按多過一下的短促），讓額外小獎賞來代表你很喜歡學習生能做出好的動作行為。

當學習生做一些你想要的動作行為時，記著按 "的嗒"。

應用大獎（把多一些的小獎賞洽出）。

但是，不要傷害你的狗（或其他學習生），不要拉扯狗鏈，看找一個學習生喜歡的方式，做出好的動作行為。

因什麼事才按 "的嗒" 器：

首先是選擇一些容易做的動作行為，然後才選擇難的。在開始時，如踏步踏到了，便按一下 "的嗒" 器。記著，學習生是一個初學者，要慢慢的學習！

當學習生重復做一些動作，你可以按 "的嗒" 器。這 "的嗒" 的聲音告訴學習生 "你做的動作很接近"，如學習生做了一些意外的動作而又接近目標的話，亦可按 "的嗒" 器。

為想要的動作按一下 "的嗒" 器，千萬不要大聲叫喊，不要抱怨亦不需理會錯誤。

不要給命令，如果學習生不聽你的指示，這並不代表他（他）不好，只是學習生不明白你想他（他）做些什麼，盡量簡單些，慢慢的首先讚學習生容易的，然後再學習困難的。

要注意，不要受其他的事情分散你的注意力。當你的學習生當試的時候，你要表現友善，給多一些時間和小獎賞，千萬不要諸多管制，不然的話，你的學習生會感到自己非常差勁；同樣，你亦會看見很難相處的樣子。記著按 "的嗒" 器和給小獎賞，要依靠學習的力量。

當你見到正確的或有用的動作時，記著按 "的嗒" 器。當 "的嗒" 器出現有趣或有用的時候，按一下 "的嗒" 器和給小獎賞。這第一次的獎賞對學習生次數可能是很驚奇，但如果訓練者常常按 "的嗒" 器和給小獎賞，他（他）們做的動作行為就會越來越好的。

什麼時候按 "的嗒" 器：

當你看到那動作行為發生時，要立刻按 "的嗒" 而不是在發生之後。

要多按 "的嗒" 器，不然，學習生可能會覺得混亂及不清楚和不想再繼續做。

如果沒有進步，你便要在時間上作出好一點的安排，如你按漏了按 "的嗒" 器，那代表你沒有注意學習生。

不要等太久才按 "的嗒" 器，不要等所有動作完結後才按，要在你看到與你想要的動作行為差不多時，立即按 "的嗒" 器。

當學習生知道怎樣做的時候，你可以等選一點才按，學習生開始知道你想開始做那些動作行為時，學習生會做那些動作長一點，這可以幫助改善學習生所做的動作行為。

怎樣能成功地應用 "的嗒" 器：

保持訓練班的時間短一些，因為短時間的練習班能幫助狗（或其他學習生）集中精神，在短的情況下他（他）們會學習多，短的休息也有幫助。短時間的練習班和短的休息能幫助學習生更容易記得。

如你不能得到你想要的動作行為，試試練另一個動作。如果你生氣一請暫停止，不要叫罵學習生，不要強迫他自己，休息一會再繼續。

記著，令學習有趣一些！

如果你想學多更多關於 "的嗒" 器的訓練，請瀏覽 www.clickertraining.com的網頁！

Enseñando con un Clicker:

Cómo Entrenar a Gente y a Animales con un Clicker y Comida

Traducido y adaptado por

Priscilla Galvez, 11 años, Lina Tam-Li, 13 años y Maria García, madre de Priscilla

Adaptación para Niños del libro de Karen Pryor "Getting Started with the Clicker" Con permiso de Ms. Pryor

La lista de lo que debes y no debes de hacer.

Lo que debes de hacer.

1. Usa el clicker a tiempo.
2. Usa el clicker por cada buen comportamiento.
3. Dale una recompensa por cada click.
4. Usa el clicker seguido para los nuevos estudiantes.
5. Mira al estudiante.
6. Pón atención todo el tiempo.
7. Ignora las distraciones.
8. Dale comida cada vez que usas el clicker.
9. Si se acerca al comportamiento o si hace el comportamiento correctamente, dale bastante comida. Esto es como ganar la lotería.
10. Si el estudiante se frustra, ayúdalo usando el clicker bastantes veces.
11. Escoje algo fácil para los nuevos estudiantes y escoje algo más difícil para los estudiantes con más experiencia.
12. Tienes que estar seguro/a que es seguro.

Lo que no debes de hacer.

1. No dejes de ver al estudiante.
2. No te olvides de oprimir el clicker.
3. No te olvides de darle al estudiante la comida.
4. No te alejes del estudiante.
5. No te pongas impaciente.
6. No le faltes el respeto al estudiante en otras maneras.
7. No te distraigas.
8. No uses el clicker solo por usarlo.
9. No oprimas el clicker tarde.
10. No frustres al estudiante porque no le pusiste atención.

¿Qué es "enseñando con el clicker"?

¿Es tú perro como era el mío antes? ¿Brinca y ladra cuando vienen tus amigos o amigas a la puerta? ¿Se va corriendo de ti o te jala cuando tiene puesta la correa?

¿Te gustaría que tu perro aprenda buenos comportamientos y también trucos?

Enseñando con el clicker es un juego. Un juego que juegas con los perros o otros animales – hasta con la gente. Es un juego que enseña buenos comportamientos. Lo único que necesitas es un clicker, un poco de comida, y la información en este folleto. Vas a aprender cómo el estudiante se puede divertir y aprender al mismo tiempo. También vas a aprender cómo decirle que "Sí" al estudiante usando el clicker y la comida.

Marca con el clicker los buenos comportamientos y ignora los malos. Si aprendes la información en este folleto, vas a poder enseñarle a tu animal o otro estudiante a hacer lo que tú quieras.

¡Para divertirte con el clicker, sigue leyendo!

COMO DEBES USAR EL CLICKER.

Necesitas un clicker, algo que hace un ruido cortito, y un poco de comida.

Usa el clicker cuando tú pienses que el comportamiento se acerca a lo que tú quieres. Dale comida después de cada vez que usas el clicker.

El/La maestro/a necesita darle comida cada vez que usa el clicker. Sino el estudiante va a pensar "Si no me dan comida cuando yo oigo el clicker, no voy a hacer el comportamiento otra vez." El/La maestro/a tiene que seguir la regla que dice que tienes que darle comida después de cada vez que usa el clicker. La comida tiene que ser algo que al estudiante le guste mucho.

El/La maestro/a no debe de dejar de poner atención ni dejar de ver al estudiante. Si el/la maestro/a deja de ver al estudiante, el estudiante se va a frustrar. El estudiante no va a querer hacer el comportamiento otra vez.

Si el juego es fácil, divertido e interesante, el estudiante va a querer hacerlo.

Para enseñarle al estudiante que te gusta mucho el

comportamiento, usa el clicker una vez, y dale más comida.

Si le das bastante comida cuando te gusta un comportamiento, es como si el estudiante ganó la lotería.

PERO, no le pegas al perro o otro estudiante. No le jales la correa. Nunca uses fuerza. Trata de buscar cómo al estudiante le va a gustar hacer el comportamiento.

Para cuales cosas usas el clicker.

Primero escoje un comportamiento que sea fácil. Después escoje uno que sea más difícil. Recuerda que el estudiante está comenzando a aprender. Por eso tienes que usar el clicker paso a paso.

Usa el clicker por algo que el perro o otro estudiante ya sabe hacer, como sentarse. Usa este comportamiento para comenzar a enseñarle el juego del clicker. El sonido del clicker le va a decir al estudiante, "Te estás acercando al comportamiento." Usa el clicker por cada comportamiento que el estudiante hace por accidente pero que se acerca a la meta.

Usa el clicker para los comportamientos que tú quieres. No le grites al estudiante, ni te quejes de él. También ignora sus errores.

No le des órdenes. Si el estudiante no te escucha, no es porque se está comportando mal. Es porque el estudiante no entiende lo que tú quieres que él haga. Si esto te pasa, haz que el comportamiento que tú quieres sea más fácil. Ve paso a paso. Usa pasos muy pequeños, y después pasos más grandes.

Pón atención. No tengas tu mente en las nubes. Sé amable cuando el estudiante está tratando de hacer lo que tú quieres. Dale más tiempo y más comida. No lo mandes. Sino el estudiante va a pensar que tú eres malo/a, y que él se está comportando mal. Confía en que el estudiante puede aprender.

Usa el clicker cada vez que un comportamiento sea bueno o útil. Después dale la comida. Puede ser que el estudiante se sorprenda. Usa el clicker seguido y el comportamiento se va a mejorar más y más.

Cuando debes usar el clicker.

Usa el clicker en cuanto pase el comportamiento, no después.

Usa el clicker seguido y bastantes veces. Sino el estudiante se va a confundir, y no va a querer hacer el comportamiento otra vez.

Si no progresa, tal vez estás usando el clicker demasiado tarde. Si estás usando el clicker demasiado tarde, no estás poniendo atención.

No esperes que pase mucho tiempo para usar el clicker. Ni esperes que haga todo el comportamiento completo. Usa el clicker para algo que se acerca al comportamiento.

Cuando el estudiante entienda el comportamiento que tú quieres que haga, espera un poco antes de usar el clicker. El estudiante va a comenzar a hacer el comportamiento por más tiempo. Esto se llama *formando el comportamiento*. Formando el comportamiento significa mejorarlo.

Como triunfar con el clicker.

Haz que las clases sean cortas. Las clases cortas ayudan a que el perro o otro estudiante se concentre. El estudiante aprende más en unos cuantos intentos cortos. Los descansos ayudan. El estudiante va a recordar las cosas más fácil cuando las clases son cortas y hay descansos.

Si no consigues lo que tú quieres, trata de enseñarle otro comportamiento. Si te enojas, deja de hacer lo que estas haciendo. No le grites al estudiante. No le fuerces. Toma un descanso y trátalo después.

¡Recuerda, diviértete!

¡Si tú quieres aprender más de como usar el clicker, ve a www.clickertraining.com!

Teaching with a Clicker:

How to Teach Your Dog Good Manners and Tricks

By
**Hilary Louie, age 10 and
Evelyn Pang, age 10**

Adapted for children from Karen Pryor's
"Clicker Training for Dogs"
with Ms. Pryor's permission

Impulse control – Teaching the dog good manners around food

Food in hand

1. Put a treat in your fist. The dog will sniff, lick and slobber on your hand because he or she can smell the food.

2. When the dog stops sniffing, licking, and slobbering – even for a second – click and treat.

3. Do this a few more times. If the dog doesn't sniff, lick, or slobber for a bit longer, click and treat. Practice until the dog doesn't sniff, lick or slobber on your hand at all. He or she just looks at it – or even at you.

Food on the ground

1. Put a treat on the ground and cover it with your hand or your foot. The dog will sniff, lick and slobber on your hand or foot because he or she can smell the food.

2. When the dog stops sniffing, licking and slobbering – even for a second – click and treat.

3. Practice until the dog doesn't sniff, lick or slobber at all. He or she doesn't run to the treat. Practice until the dog waits patiently.

Telling the Dog to Wait for Food

1. Teach the behavior without words.

2. Say "off" when the dog backs away from the food in your hand or on the floor. Do that a few more times and the dog will remember the sound and the movement.

3. Say "off" before the dog moves toward the food. If the dog waits, the dog knows the word. Try putting away the clicker and telling the dog "off." If the dog doesn't wait when you say "off," the dog doesn't know the word "off" yet. Do numbers 1 and 2 again.

If you want to know more about clicker training, go to www.clickertraining.com!

Teaching Good Manners and Tricks with a Clicker and Treats

Does your dog pull on the leash when he or she is not supposed to? Does your dog eat food off the floor when he or she is not supposed to? Does he or she run around the house?

Would you like your dog to learn good behaviors and even tricks?

Teaching your dog good behaviors and tricks can be really easy with the clicker. All you need is a clicker, some treats, and this brochure. You'll learn how to train your dog using the simple steps in this brochure. Once you know that teaching your dog tricks is easy, you can make up your own tricks.

If you want to find out how much fun it can be to teach your dog new tricks and behaviors, read on!

You will need these supplies: a clicker (something that makes a short sound), treats (something the dog likes a lot), a dog.

SIT

Teaching the Dog to Sit

1. Show the dog the treat by putting it in front of his or her nose.

2. Bring the treat up and back a few inches from the dog's nose to the top of the dog's head. Keep it close to the dog's head. If you lift the treat too high, the dog will jump.

3. The dog's nose will follow the treat. The dog's nose will go up and the tail will go down. The dog might sit all the way, or just a little. If the dog sits a little bit, click and treat. If the dog sits all the way, give the dog more treats.

4. Do that a few times so the dog can remember it.

5. Then, make it a little harder. Have the dog sit longer. Then click and give him or her a treat.

Telling the Dog to Sit

1. Teach the behavior without words.

2. Say "sit" when the dog begins to sit. Do that a few more times and the dog will remember the sound and the movement.

3. Say "sit" before the dog sits. If the dog sits, the dog knows the word. Try putting away the clicker and telling the dog to sit. If the dog doesn't sit when you say "sit," the dog doesn't know the word "sit" yet. Do numbers 1 and 2 again.

DOWN

Teaching the Dog to Lie Down

1. Tell the dog to sit.

2. Get a treat and put it in front of the dog's nose. Lower the treat to the ground. The dog's nose will follow the treat down. Move the treat straight down. If you move it away from the dog's body, the dog will get up to follow it.

3. If the dog goes lower, click and treat. You may have to do this a few times for the dog's body to go all the way down.

Telling the Dog to Lie Down

1. Teach the behavior without words.

2. Say "down" while the dog begins to go down. Do that a few more times and the dog will remember the sound and the movement.

3. Say "down" when the dog is sitting. If the dog goes down, the dog knows the word. Try putting away the clicker and telling the dog "down." If the dog doesn't go down when you say "down," the dog doesn't know the word "down" yet. Do numbers 1 and 2 again.

Hand Targeting

Hand targeting is when the dog touches your hand with his or her nose when you tell the dog to. You teach hand targeting because you can help your dog to walk near you, to go where you want, and to teach tricks like spinning around, rolling over, and crawling under chairs and tables.

Teaching the Dog to Target Your Hand

1. Put your hand out near the dog's nose. The dog may sniff your hand. If the dog does touch your hand with his or her nose, click and treat exactly when the dog's nose touches your hand. The dog may only move toward your hand at first. Click and treat that.

   If the dog ignores your hand, rub a little cheese or other treat on your hand so the dog can smell it and try again. If the dog taps or licks your hand, click and treat. You may have to do this a few times for the dog to understand. Then try without rubbing the treat on your hand.

2. Put your hand farther back so the dog has to move more to touch it with his or her nose. If the dog targets your hand, click and treat. If the dog does not target your hand, try again but make it a bit easier for the dog by putting your hand closer.

3. Then, move your hand under or over something so the dog learns to follow your hand.

   Repeat until the dog understands and follows your hand.

Telling the Dog to Target Your Hand

1. Teach the behavior without words.

2. Say "touch" while the dog begins to touch your hand. Do that a few more times and the dog will remember the sound and the movement.

3. Say "touch" just before the dog touches your hand. If the dog touches your hand, the dog knows the word. Try putting away the clicker and telling the dog "touch." If the dog doesn't touch your hand when you say "touch," the dog doesn't know the word "touch" yet. Do numbers 1 and 2 again.

Using hand targeting to teach coming when called

1. Make sure the dog knows the word "touch." While you are teaching that trick, say "touch" at first. Then, say "come" for the same trick. Click and treat when the dog targets your hand.

2. Try stretching your arm out so the dog has to go farther to target. As you practice, go farther and farther away for the hand target, and say "come" when you put out your hand each time.

Using hand targeting to teach walking on a leash without pulling

Use a clicker and treats to get started. Put your hand out and say "touch" while you are walking. The dog stays near you to keep touching your hand. Click and treat for a step near you a few times, then for 3 steps. If the dog does that, go longer. Make it more advanced. If the dog doesn't stay near you, go back and click every step. Try again to make it more advanced. Keep doing that and the dog will get used to it and walk close to you.

TRAINING GAME!!

CANDY BAG   CLICKER   CANDY

Lifting his foot

My name is _____ .

I am _____ months/years old.

I am _____ (breed, heritage).

Here's what I can do:

_____

_____

_____

Here's how I learned these skills:

_____

_____

_____

This is my learning style:

_____

_____

_____

The Clicker Promise

I, _____, promise to use my clicker as a signal to people or animals when I **like** a behavior that they are doing!

I promise to click on time.

I promise to click often if I am teaching a new behavior.

I promise to give a treat for every click.

I promise to ignore mistakes and never give orders, yell, scold or criticize when I am using the clicker.

_____

signed

_____

date

Dog Protection Promise

I, _____, know that candy is not good for dogs and that chocolate can make dogs very sick. Therefore, I promise to do my best to keep dogs safe by:

1. immediately putting my candy in my fanny pack or pocket, and immediately picking up any that drops accidentally;

2. being watchful for any candy accidentally dropped or left lying around, and taking responsibility for putting the candy in a safe place where the dogs cannot get it;

3. doing my best at all times to keep dogs and others safe from avoidable harm.

_____
signature

_____
name printed

_____
date of birth

_____
today's date

CERTIFICATE OF ATTENDANCE

SHIP

A thank you note from two children enjoying SHIP

Lynn is a very nice person. Lynn helped us alot. Lynn has a great smile. Lynn has friends named Dinora, Hilary and Evelyn.

R = Hilary

B = Evelyn

Sincerly,

Evelyn Pang

Evelyn Pang

Hilary Louie

Hilary Louie

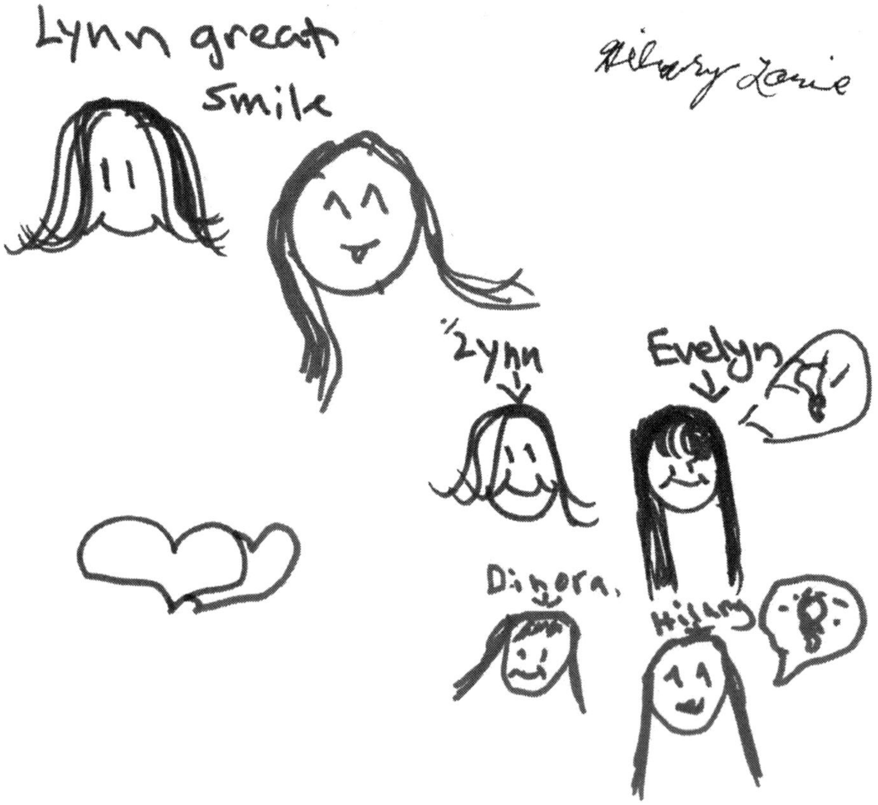

*Gift Subscription
to the
Latham Letter
for*

Hilary Louie

*Received in recognition of
work in the field of
Humane Education.*

Hugh Tebault , President

November 12, 2003

Letter of Commendation by Hugh Tebault, III, President of the Latham Foundation, to a SHIP participant

THE LATHAM FOUNDATION incorporated 1918
PROMOTING RESPECT FOR ALL LIFE THROUGH EDUCATION

November 12, 2003

Dear Evelyn:

Thank you for your excellent work to promote understanding of "clicker" training. It was an honor to meet you at the awards dinner on October 29th.

It is our practice to give a gift subscription of the Latham Letter to all our authors, and I am very pleased to do this for you.

Please fill out and return the short form that is enclosed and return it to Ms. Loar.

My wife and I enjoyed meeting you and Hilary and your families, and we look forward to reading your forthcoming opera.

Sincerely,

Hugh H. Tebault III
President

Attachment: Gift Form

Latham Plaza Building, 1826 Clement Avenue • Alameda, California 94501 • Phone 510-521-0920 • Fax 510-521-9861
E-mail: info@latham.org • http://www.latham.org

Consent for Participation in the
SHIP (Strategic Humane Interventions Program) Project

_____

The SHIP project shows people how to teach dogs – and people – new skills in an enjoyable way. Participants learn how to use positive reinforcement to make learning and teaching fun and rewarding. After just a couple of weeks, participants will be able to teach a dog to sit, shake hands, wait until being invited to go through a doorway or eat a treat and any number of other skills. Participants will also get to practice their teaching skills with human learners who also earn rewards and praise for their progress. People of any age can enjoy the time with dogs and the opportunity to learn and teach in an upbeat and rewarding setting.

To provide the best possible experiences for participants, the SHIP project videotapes sessions. These tapes are viewed only by SHIP facilitators to assess teaching techniques and the progress of participants. We will track improvement in teaching techniques, timing, efficiency of movement, attention, and interaction among participants. Participants are welcome to review the tape of any session they have participated in.

I, _____, agree to participate in the SHIP project and to have my participation videotaped. I also give permission for my children

_____

(name and age)

_____

(name and age)

to participate and have their participation videotaped.

_____   _____

signature of parent/guardian   date

Consent to Publish (Child's)

_____

I give permission to Lynn Loar and Libby Colman to include my writing and/or drawings in their book and accompanying CD to be published by the Latham Foundation within the year. I will be given a copy of the book when it is published.

I also give permission for the Latham Foundation, www.Latham.org, the Pryor Foundation, www.Pryorfoundation.com, and Sunshine Books, www.clickertraining.com, to post my work on these web pages.

I give permission to Lynn Loar, Karen Pryor, Barbara Boat and Libby Colman to use my work (e.g., on transparencies) in presentations to professional audiences.

_____

name (printed)

_____

signature

_____

date of birth

_____

today's date

Consent to Publish (Parent's)

_____

   I give permission to Lynn Loar and Libby Colman to include my child's writing and/or drawings in their book and accompanying CD to be published by the Latham Foundation within the year. My child will be given a copy of the book when it is published.

   I also give permission for the Latham Foundation, www.Latham.org, the Pryor Foundation, www.Pryorfoundation.com, and Sunshine Books, www.clickertraining.com, to post my child's work on these web pages.

   I give permission to Lynn Loar, Karen Pryor, Barbara Boat and Libby Colman to use my child's work (e.g., on transparencies) in presentations to professional audiences.

_____

name of child (printed)

_____

name of parent (printed)

_____

signature of parent

_____

child's date of birth

_____

today's date

ENDORSED
F I L E D
San Francisco County Superior Court

OCT 1 6 2002

GORDON PARK-LI, Clerk
BY: _____S. DAVID_____
Deputy Clerk

SUPERIOR COURT OF THE STATE OF CALIFORNIA

CITY AND COUNTY OF SAN FRANCISCO

JUVENILE DIVISION

IN THE MATTER OF:	)	COURT ORDER RE:
	)	VIDEOTAPING AND
	)	PHOTOGRAPHY
THE STRATEGIC HUMANE INTERVENTIONS	)	
PROGRAM	)	[As Amended on October 10, 2002]
_____	)	

A request has been presented to the Supervising Judge of the Juvenile Court seeking

permission to videotape and photograph participants of The Strategic Humane Interventions Program

("The Program") who are under the jurisdiction of the San Francisco Juvenile Court ("Participants").

The Program will provide animal-assisted therapy for abused and neglected children and their

parents/guardians/foster parents by teaching gentleness and self-control through supervised

interaction with and training of dogs.

Permission is hereby granted for the videotaping and photography of such Participants by

The Program under the following conditions:

1. The Program will videotape sessions to track progress and occasionally to show

Participants an excellent moment caught on tape to reinforce a particular skill. In addition, Polaroid

photos will be given to Participants to memorialize their enjoyment and successes with the dogs.

2. Confidentiality of Participants will be maintained consistent with standard practices.

3. Only the referring agencies and their staff will know the surnames of the Participants,

and they will be responsible for clinical record keeping. The Program will learn first names only,

1 | and no history beyond what is necessary for safety.

2 | 4.   The Program will code the names to protect the identity of the Participants.

3 | 5.   Videotapes will only be viewed by The Program and referring agency professionals in
4 | order to gauge progress and improve the intervention.

5 | 6.   Photographs will be given to the Participants and the agencies and not retained by
6 | The Program.

7 | 7.   Should The Program desire to use a specific segment of a videotape for presentations
8 | to professional audiences, a specific release will be prepared.

9 | 8.   Gretchen Stone, Ph.D, OTR, FAOTA, Associate Professor, Division of Occupational
10 | Therapy, Shenandoah University, Winchester, Virginia, and her students are authorized to review the
11 | videotapes and photographs taken of the Participants for the purpose of measuring Participants'
12 | gains accurately and objectively. Confidentiality of Participants will be maintained.

13 |

14 | DATED: October 10, 2002

15 |

16 |

17 | DONNA J. HITCHENS
Supervising Judge
Unified Family Court

2

Sample Consent Form

The staff of Agency X is committed to your health and safety, and to provide the most effective services possible.

Therefore, we videotape sessions so that we can review material and learn what works best for each person. These tapes are for our use during your therapy only and will not be shared with others without your express permission. You may review the tapes too if you wish.

What is discussed in therapy is confidential except:

1. if you request that we provide information to someone

    (for example, your doctor or insurance company);

2. if a child, dependent adult or frail elder has been abused or neglected;

3. if you or someone else pose a serious danger to yourself or another;

4. if an animal has been abused or neglected.

Out of our concern for your family's safety and our legal responsibilities, in these dangerous situations we will request assistance from child protective services, adult protective services, law enforcement and the humane society as appropriate. We report risk in order to bring additional resources to a dangerous situation and make it safer for you and your family.

By signing below, I indicate that I have been informed of and understand the reporting policies of the agency.

(Signature) _____

(Date) _____

VOCA (Victims of Crimes Act) Volunteer
Letter of Agreement

Dear Volunteers,

As you have all heard by now, we have been awarded a grant through the Governor's Office of Criminal Justice Planning with funding from the Victims of Crimes Act (VOCA). This enables our organization to continue with our animal assisted therapy for child victims of abuse and neglect. But, not unexpectedly, the gift comes with certain conditions. And we are diligently attempting to meet all the conditions so we don't jeopardize our funding.

As volunteers, you are essential to our program. We would not have been eligible for this grant without our volunteers. We, therefore, hope you will understand and be patient with us as we ask that you assist in complying with the conditions that the VOCA grant has placed on our organization.

In order to be in compliance with their conditions, each of you must:
* have a formal application, including three references, on file
* agree to a criminal records check, including fingerprinting and processing through Department of Justice
* review, sign and retain a copy of our confidentiality policy
* attend monthly meetings with therapist
* complete the sign in/sign out sheet every week, including all time spent preparing snacks, purchasing treats, driving to and from, etc.
* complete 40 hours of training if you cannot document at least 2 years of experience or training in working with child abuse victims

Most of these conditions are satisfied with a one-time only compliance. We are here to answer any of your questions and assist you in any way we can. Once again, we'd like you to know how much we appreciate your kindness and generosity.

Please call LaVerne at 542-0882, ext. 207, with any of your questions.

Sincerely,

LaVerne E. Ruddle

Child Abuse and Neglect Reporting Law

(P.C. 11166) Reporter Responsibility and Sample Employee Form

Definitions: The following situations are reportable conditions:
- Physical abuse
- Sexual abuse
- Child exploitation, child pornography and child prostitution
- Neglect
- Extreme corporal punishment resulting in injury
- Willful cruelty or unjustifiable punishment

Who Reports: The following individuals are legally mandated reporters:
- Child care custodians
- Health practioners
- Commercial film or photographic print processors in specified instances
- Child Protective Agencies

When to Report: A telephone report must be made immediately when the reporter observes a child in his/her professional capacity or within the scope of his/her employment and has knowledge of, or has reasonable suspicion that the child has been abused. A written report, on a standard form, must be sent within 36 hours after the telephone report has been made.

To Whom Do You Report: You have a choice of reporting to the Police or Sheriff's Department or the Probation Department or Child Welfare Agency. Each County has preferred reporting procedure. Commercial film of photographic processors report only to law enforcement.

Individual Responsibility: Any individual who is named in the reporting law must report abuse. If the individual confers with a superior and a decision is made that the superior file the report, one report is sufficient. However if the superior disagrees, the individual with the original suspicion must report.

Anonymous Reporting: Mandated reporters are required to give their names. Non-mandated reporters may report anonymously. Child protective agencies are required to keep the mandated reporter's name confidential, unless a court orders the information disclosed.

Immunity: Any legally mandated reporter has immunity when making a report. In the event a civil suit is filed against the reporter, reimbursement for fees incurred in the suit will occur up to $50,000. No individual can be dismissed, disciplined or harassed for making a report of suspected child abuse.

Liability: Legally mandated reporters can be criminally liable for failing to report suspected abuse. The penalty for this misdemeanor is up to six months in county jail, a fine of not more that $1,000 or both. Mandated reporters can also be civilly liable for failure to report.

Notification Regarding Abuse: You are not legally required to notify the parents that you are making a report; however, it is often beneficial to let the parents know you are reporting for benefit of a future relationship.

I understand that I am a legally mandated reporter. I have clarified any information listed above which I did not understand, and am now aware of my reporting responsibilities, and am willing to comply. I have also requested an explanation of reporting policies within this agency and understand them as well.

_____   _____
Employee's Name   Witness (Supervisor)

Date: _____

HUMANE SOCIETY OF SONOMA COUNTY
5345 Highway 12 West
P.O. Box 1296
Santa Rosa, CA 95402-1296
(707) 542-0882

DATE _____

FORGET-ME-NOT FARM VOLUNTEER APPLICATION

Last _____ First _____ Middle _____

Street _____ City _____ Zip _____

Home Phone _____ Work Phone _____ Cell Phone _____

Home E-Mail _____ Work E-Mail _____

May we contact you at work by phone? _____ Yes _____ No

May we contact you at work by E-Mail? _____ Yes _____ No

Days available to volunteer: M T W TH F   Times available_____

How many hours can you commit?   Can you commit to volunteer for at least 6 months?

_____   _____   _____   _____
Week   Month   Yes   No

EDUCATION

_____
HIGH SCHOOL NAME AND LOCATION

_____
UNDERGRADUATE COLLEGE/UNIVERSITY AND LOCATION

| YEARS COMPLETED
1 2 3 4 | MAJOR COURSE OF STUDY: | TYPE OF DEGREE |

_____
GRADUATE/PROFESSIONAL SCHOOL AND LOCATION

| YEARS COMPLETED
1 2 3 4 | MAJOR COURSE OF STUDY: | TYPE OF DEGREE |

FOREIGN LANGUAGES

LANGUAGE	SPEAK FLUENT FAIR	READ FLUENT FAIR	WRITE FLUENT FAIR
_____	_____	_____	_____
_____	_____	_____	_____

SPECIAL SKILLS, TRAINING, APPRENTICESHIPS

_____

_____

_____

_____

REFERENCES
Please provide three professional references who are not related to you and who know your qualifications.

NAME	OCCUPATION	YEARS KNOWN	ADDRESS, CITY, STATE, ZIP	PHONE NO.
1.				
2.				
3.				

What is your current occupation and who is your current employer? If currently not employed, what is your usual occupation by trade or study?

_____

_____

Do you have any previous volunteer or work experience with animals? Please describe, if any.

Do you have any previous volunteer or work experience with children? Please describe, if any.

Do you have any skills that you would be willing to share with the Humane Society?

Would you be willing to be fingerprinted?

IN CASE OF EMERGENCY, NOTIFY:

Name   Relationship   Phone #

Humane Society of Sonoma County, Strategic Humane Intervention Program
Confidentiality Policy and Agreement

It is the policy of the Humane Society of Sonoma County, Strategic Humane Intervention Program that all client identity, information and records be maintained in the strictest confidence.

To assure privacy and confidentiality, the Humane Society of Sonoma County, Strategic Humane Intervention Program, has instituted a system to protect client records deemed confidential by law.

- All staff, volunteers, contractors and contracting agencies are required to secure client records and maintain the confidentiality of the information in the records as required by federal and state law. This should include handling and transmission of data and information that contains client identifiers.
- Client records will be maintained in secure locked files to prevent disclosure of confidential information to unauthorized personnel.
- Any additional needed precautions will be taken to limit access to client records.
- The confidentiality policy will be reviewed at all volunteer and staff meetings.
- The confidentiality policy will be reviewed individually with all staff, volunteers and contractors.
- In addition, all staff, volunteers and contractors will be required to sign and retain a copy of the policy after review.
- The confidentiality policy will also be explained to our clients and a copy will be provided to them.

I have read the above Confidentiality Policy of the Humane Society of Sonoma County, Strategic Humane Intervention Program. In addition, it has been reviewed with me individually and I will retain a copy for myself after signing.

_____

Signature

_____   _____
Printed Name   Date

By signature, I give Humane Society of Sonoma County permission to verify any and all statements made in this application. I understand that this application does not ensure acceptance as an Humane Society of Sonoma County, Strategic Humane Intervention Program volunteer, nor should it be construed as a contract of any kind.

_____   _____
Signature of Applicant   Date

HSSC NOTES

Date of Fingerprinting _____

Copy of Driver's License _____

3 References Checked _____

Confidentiality Policy Reviewed and Copy Given to Applicant _____

Humane Society of Sonoma County
Strategic Humane Intervention Program
Confidentiality Policy and Agreement

It is the policy of the Humane Society of Sonoma County, Strategic Humane Intervention Program that all client identity, information and records be maintained in the strictest confidence.

To assure privacy and confidentiality, the Humane Society of Sonoma County, Strategic Humane Intervention Program, has instituted a system to protect client records deemed confidential by law.

- All staff, volunteers, contractors and contracting agencies are required to secure client records and maintain the confidentiality of the information in the records as required by federal and state law. This should include handling and transmission of data and information that contains client identifiers.
- Client records will be maintained in secure locked files to prevent disclosure of confidential information to unauthorized personnel.
- Any additional needed precautions will be taken to limit access to client records.
- The confidentiality policy will be reviewed at all volunteer and staff trainings.
- The confidentiality policy will be reviewed individually with all staff, volunteers and contractors.
- In addition, all staff, volunteers and contractors will be required to sign and retain a copy of the policy after review.
- The confidentiality policy will also be explained to our clients and a copy will be provided to them.

I have read the above Confidentiality Policy of the Humane Society of Sonoma County, Strategic Humane Intervention Program. In addition, it has been reviewed with me individually and I will retain a copy for myself after signing.

_____

Signature

_____

Printed Name

_____

Date

SHIP's Curriculum
Clicker Training Dogs:
Teaching the Basics With a Clicker and Treats

Teaching the dog to pay attention to the click:

Click once and give the dog a treat. Repeat until you notice that the dog startles to the sound. The dog may even look at the hand holding the clicker instead of the hand holding the treats.

Teaching the dog to sit:

Hold a treat in your fist near the dog's nose and bring it up and back along the dog's muzzle toward the ears, keeping the treat close to the dog's head. The dog will track the treat with his nose. As his nose goes up, his hindquarters will drop, approximating a sit. Some dogs will sit readily; others will just go part of the way down at first. Click and treat for part or all of the desired behavior, and drop the treat on the ground so the dog will have to get up to eat it. Then, use another treat to lure the dog into another sit. After a few repetitions, the dog should sit readily. You can begin fading the lure and adding the cue at that point.

Teaching the dog to lie down:

Have the dog sit. Place the treat in your fist just below the dog's nose and lure the dog down. Click and treat for incremental descent. After a few repetitions, the dog should go down to the floor. At that point, begin fading the lure and adding the cue.

Hand Targeting – introducing good manners:

Place your open hand (the one that had been holding the treats) a few inches in front of the dog's nose. The dog will probably sniff your hand. Click and treat as the dog's nose touches your hand, or as the dog approaches your hand if that is the first increment offered. Once the dog is readily tapping your hand with his or her nose, begin making it more challenging by moving your hand a little farther back, to the right, left, a bit higher and then lower. Develop this so the dog will target your hand from a greater distance and at any angle. Not only will you polish a useful behavior but you will also learn a great deal about the incremental stages of your dog's learning style.

Hand targeting is useful in any number of ways, including:

1. *Exhibiting good manners when people approach*

Most people will extend a hand to a dog, and now the dog knows what to do. A shy or skittish dog will gain confidence by knowing how to greet a new human and what behavior is expected and worthy of reward in such circumstances.

2. *Coming when called*

By extending the distance between the dog and the hand, the behavior of targeting can turn into coming when asked or cued with a hand signal. Combining coming with the now minimal gesture or cue for sit gets a dog who approaches, sits in front of and looks up at the owner. It also teaches the owner to form behavior chains backwards.

3. *Walking without pulling on a leash*

By targeting the hand holding the leash every few steps, the dog learns to walk near the person on a loose leash. Ask the dog to target your hand at every step, then every few steps, then at random intervals. Keep treats in your side pocket (the side you want the dog on); that will make you attractive to your dog.

4. *Walking past scary or smelly things; walking past cats, dogs, squirrels and other temptations, walking into the veterinarian's office*

Hand targeting focuses the dog's attention on the person's hand, which is at the forefront of attention and line of sight. It subordinates other visual stimuli and makes it easier for the dog to walk past frightening or tempting things, animals or people.

Impulse Control around food:

First ask the dog to sit. It is easier to teach self-control to a dog who is sitting.

1. *Treat in Hand*

Hold a treat in your fist near the dog's mouth. The dog will probably lick your hand and try to get the treat. Click and treat when the dog backs off however fleetingly, even if it is just to take a breath in order to begin slobbering on your hand again. If your timing is precise, the dog will realize in a few clicks that backing off causes the hand to open. Add the release word (most people use "OK") as you give the dog the treat. When the dog sits and waits for the treat to be offered, begin adding the cue.

2. *Treat in Bowl*

Have the dog sit. Take the dog's full bowl from the counter and begin lowering it. If the dog gets up, return the bowl to the counter and begin again. If the dog remains seated while the bowl moves, click and treat. The dog knows that the bowl moving downward is a good thing. Once the dog realizes that sitting and waiting causes the bowl to go down, he or she will recognize the cue and politely wait for the release word.

3. *Treat On Floor*

Have the dog sit. Let the dog see you putting a treat on the floor and blocking the dog's access to it with your shoe. Click and treat when the dog backs off however fleetingly, even if it is just to take a breath in order to begin slobbering on your shoe again. If your timing is precise, the dog will realize in a few clicks that backing off causes the shoe to move. Add the release word as you let the dog have the treat. When the dog sits and waits for the treat to be offered, begin adding the cue. Mastery of this behavior protects the dog from ingesting bits of a broken plate along with the dropped dinner. It is also the beginning of the behavior of ignoring edibles outdoors, but it requires much more training to get a dog to forego temptation outside – and much more vigilance by the trainer who has to scan the area constantly for treats dropped by passersby.

Goals and objectives for court-ordered and other supervised visits:

SHIP designed the following goals and objectives for court-ordered and other supervised visits:

Goals:

Reduce conflict and physical coercion, and increase rapport and empathy in parent/guardian-child relationships and direct new skills toward employability in jobs that reinforce behavioral and empathic skills learned in the program.

Objectives:

Participants will learn to read behavioral cues of human and non-human learners.

Participants will learn the basics of marker-based shaping, i.e., coercion-free operant conditioning with a marker signal to identify desired behaviors and reinforcements.

Participants will develop awareness of own and others' learning and teaching styles and abilities.

Participants will be more able to use positive and non-coercive techniques in interpersonal relationships, especially childrearing and behavior management.

Models of program elements for single- parent, low-conflict two-parent program and for high-conflict two-parent program

Model 1 offers services to single-parent and low-conflict two-parent families. Model 2 offers services to high-conflict two-parent families. Each parent agrees to attend six sessions and take a pre- and two post-tests. Model 2, in which the child comes with one parent once a week for six weeks and with the other parent a different day each week for six weeks, allows both parents to learn to interact positively with their children, enjoying the same services and learning the same language without having direct contact with each other. The child is not in the awkward position of telling one parent about the activities enjoyed while in the other parent's care.

Schedule of Activities:

<u>Model 1: Single Parent Families or Low-Conflict Two Parent Families</u>

pre-test

6 one-hour sessions of animal-assisted therapy, marker-based shaping; session six includes a graduation ceremony

follow-up letter to each participant listing accomplishments and cover letter which can be submitted to CPS, family court, other involved agencies

post-test

field trip to animal shelter

career counseling/job opportunities consultation at animal shelter with interested participants

design of internship for interested participants

4-6 week internship

letter of reference from animal shelter

post-test #2

<u>Model 2: High-Conflict Families or Families with Court-Ordered Visits with A Parent</u>

pre-test

12 1-hour sessions (two sessions a week for six weeks) of animal-assisted therapy, marker-based shaping; six weekly sessions with custodial parent/grandparent/other guardian and child; six weekly sessions with court-ordered parent, CASA/GAL and child;

last session in each six-week series includes a graduation ceremony

follow-up letter to each participant listing accomplishments and cover letter which can be submitted to CPS, family court, other involved agencies

post-test #1

field trip to animal shelter

career counseling/job opportunities consultation with interested participants

design of internship for interested participants

4-6 week internship

letter of reference from animal shelter

post-test #2

Organizational Resources

LISTED BELOW ARE SOME OF THE ORGANIZATIONS PROVIDING RESOURCES FOR THERAPISTS, HUMANE EDUCATORS AND OTHER PERSONS INTERESTED IN PROMOTING COMPASSION AND NON-VIOLENT BEHAVIOR. The groups represent a range of diverse views among clinicians, educators, animal welfare and animal advocacy groups. Their inclusion on this list does not necessarily signify endorsement by the Latham Foundation or the authors.

American Humane Association (AHA)
63 Inverness Drive East
Englewood, CO 80112-5117
(303) 792-9900
(303) 792-5333 fax
www.americanhumane.org

American Professional Society
   on the Abuse of Children (APSAC)
PO Box 26901, CHO 3B3406
Oklahoma City, OK 73190
(405) 271-8202
(405) 271-2931 fax
www.apsac.org

American Society for the Prevention
   of Cruelty to Animals (ASPCA)
424 E. 92 St.
New York, NY 10128
(212) 876-7700
www.aspca.org

American Veterinary Medical Association (AVMA)
930 N. Meacham Rd.
Schaumburg, IL 60196
(800) 248-AVMA
(708) 330-2862 fax
www.avma.org

Animal Legal Defense Fund (ALDF)
127 4th Street
Petaluma, CA 94952-3005
(707) 769-7771
(707) 769-0785 fax
www.aldf.org

Association of Professional Humane Educators
   (APHE, formerly WHEEA)
c/o The Latham Foundation
1826 Clement Ave.
Alameda, CA 94501
www.aphe.humanelink.org

Canine Companions for Independence (CCI)
2965 Dutton Avenue
Santa Rosa, CA 95407
(707) 528-0830
(707) 577-1711 fax
www.caninecompanions.org

Cat Fancy Magazine
P. O. Box 6050
Mission Viejo, CA 92690
(949) 855-8822
(949) 855-3045 fax
www.catfancy.com

Center for Animals & Public Policy
Tufts University
School of Veterinary Medicine
200 Westboro Road
North Grafton, MA 01536
(508) 839-7991
(508) 839-3337 fax
www.tufts.edu/vet/cfa

Childhelp USA
15757 N 78th Street
Scottsdale, AZ 85260
(800) 4-A-CHILD (422-4453)
(480) 922-8212
(480) 922-7061 fax
www/childhelpusa.org/

Child Trauma Academy (Bruce Perry)
www.ChildTrauma.org/
www.ChildTraumaAcademy.com/

Child Welfare League of America
440 First Street, NW, Third Floor
Washington, DC 20001-2085
(202) 638-2952
(202) 638-4004 fax
www.cwla.org

Children's Defense Fund
25 E Street, NW
Washington, DC 20001
(202) 628-8787
(202) 662-3510
www.childrensdefense.org

Delta Society
Century Building, Suite 303
321 Burnett Ave. South
Renton, WA 98055-2569
(425) 226-7357
(425) 235-1076 fax
www.deltasociety.org

Dog Fancy Magazine
#3 Burroughs
Irvine, CA 92618
(949) 855-8822
(949) 855-3045 fax
www.dogfancy.com/

Doris Day Animal League
227 Massachusetts Ave., NE, Ste. 100
Washington, DC 20002
(202) 546-1761
(202) 546-2193 fax
www.ddal.org

Humane Society of the United States (HSUS)
First Strike Campaign
2100 L Street, NW
Washington, DC 20037
(202) 452-1100
(202) 778-6132 fax
www.hsus.org

Institute for Animals and Society
Animal Rights Network, Inc.
3500 Boston Street, Suite 325
Baltimore, MD 21224
(410) 675-4566
(410) 675-0066 fax
www.animalsandsociety.org

International Society for Traumatic Stress Studies
60 Revere Drive, Suite 500
Northbrook, IL 60062
(847) 480-9028
(847) 480-9282
www.istss.org

Latham Foundation for the Promotion
    of Humane Education
Latham Plaza Building
1826 Clement Avenue
Alameda, CA 94501
(510) 521-0920
(510) 521-9861 fax
www.latham.org

National Center for Equine Facilitated Therapy
5001 Woodside Road
Woodside, CA 94062
(650) 851-2271
(650) 851-3480 fax
www.nceft.org

National Center for PTSD
U.S. Department of Veterans Affairs
PILOTS database provides a comprehensive
    index to literature on PTSD courtesy
    of Dartmouth College
www.dartmouth.edu/dms/ptsd/

National Clearinghouse on Child Abuse and Neglect
(NCCAN)
P.O. Box 1182
Washington, DC 20013
(800) 394-3366
(703) 385-7565
(703) 385-3206 fax
www.calib.com/nccanch/

Prevent Child Abuse, America
(formerly the National Committee for the Prevention
  of Child Abuse)
200 S. Michigan Ave., 17th floor
Chicago, IL 60604
(312) 663-3520
(312) 939-8962 fax
www.preventchildabuse.org

National Organization for Victim Assistance (NOVA)
1757 Park Rd., NW
Washington, DC 20010
(800) 879-6682
(202) 462-2255 fax
www.nova.org

National Association for Humane and Environmental
  Education (N.A.H.E.E.)
P. O. Box 362
East Haddam, CT 06423-0362
(860) 434-8666
(860) 434-9579 fax
www.nahee.org

North American Riding for the Handicapped
  Association (NARHA)
P.O. Box 33150
Denver, CO 80233
(800) 369-7433
(303) 452-1212
(303) 252-4610 fax
www.narha.org

Office for Victims of Crime
Training and Technical Assistance Center
(800) 627-6872
Resource Center
(800) 627-6872
www.ojp.usdoj.gov/ovc/

Office of Juvenile Justice and Delinquency
  Prevention (OJJDP)
U.S. Department of Justice
Office of Justice Programs
Washington, DC 20531

    For publications:
    Juvenile Justice Clearinghouse
    Publication Reprint/Feedback
    P.O. Box 6000
    Rockville, MD 20849-6000
    (800) 638-8736
    (301) 519-5600 (fax)
    www.ncjrs.org

People for the Ethical Treatment of Animals
  (PETA)
501 Front Street
Norfolk, VA 23510
757-622-PETA
757-622-0457 fax
www.peta.org

Pryor Foundation
17 Commonwealth Rd.
Watertown, MA 02472
www.Pryorfoundation.com

Psychologists for the Ethical Treatment of
  Animals (PSYETA)
4330 Leland Street
Chevy Chase, MD 20815
(301) 656-6844
(301) 913-2804 fax
www.psyeta.org

Southern Poverty Law Center
Teaching Tolerance, Klanwatch
400 Washington Avenue
Montgomery, Alabama 36104
(334) 956-8200
www.splcenter.org

Sunshine Books (Karen Pryor)
49 River Street, Suite 3
Waltham, MA 02453-8345
(800) 47-CLICK
(781) 398-0754
(781) 398-0761 fax
www.clickertraining.com

Bilchik, Shay, *Guide for Implementing the Balanced and Restorative Justice Model,* Washington, DC: U.S. Department of Justice, Office of Juvenile Justice and Delinquency Prevention (OJJDP), 1998.

Boat, Barbara, "Assessing the Effectiveness of Our Humane Education Interventions with High-Risk Children," *The Latham Letter,* spring 2001, pp. 8-9.

Boat, Barbara, Loar, Lynn and Pryor, Karen, "The Training Game – More than meets the eye or the ear," *The Latham Letter,* summer, 2001, pp. 6-9.

Butterfield, Fox, *All God's Children: The Bosket Family and the American Tradition of Violence,* New York: Alfred A. Knopf, 1995.

Craig, Nancy and Loar, Lynn, "Confronting Abuse," *The Latham Letter,* summer, 1998, pp. 8-10.

Duel, Debra, *Violence Prevention & Intervention: A Directory of Animal-Related Programs,* Washington, DC: The Humane Society of the United States, 2000.

Garbarino, James, *Lost Boys: Why Our Sons Turn Violent and How We Can Save Them,* New York: The Free Press, 1999.

Glasersfeld, Ernst von, "An Introduction to Radical Constructivism," *The Invented Reality: How Do We Know What We Believe We Know? (Contributions to Constructivism),* Paul Watzlawick, ed., New York: W. W. Norton & Co., 1984, pp. 17-40.

Glasersfeld, Ernst von, *Radical Constructivism: A Way of Knowing and Learning,* London: The Falmer Press, 1995.

Goleman, Daniel, *Emotional Intelligence: Why It Can Matter More Than IQ,* New York: Bantam Books, 1995.

Gorski, Terence, *The Staying Sober Workbook – A Serious Solution for the Problem of Relapse,* Independence, MO: Independence Press, 1988.

Holt, John, *How Children Fail,* New York: Dell Publishing Company, 1964.

Holt, John, *How Children Learn,* New York: Dell Publishing Company, 1967.

Jenkins, Alan, *Invitations to Responsibility: The Therapeutic Engagement of Men Who Are Violent and Abusive,* Adelaide, Australia: Dulwich Centre Publications, 1990.

Loar, Lynn, "I Liked the Policeman Who Arrested that Dog!" *The Latham Letter,* spring, 1996, pp. 1, 4-8.

Loar, Lynn, "Making Visits Work," *Child Welfare,* 1998, pp. 41-58.

Loar, Lynn, "Shaping Behavior with Positive Reinforcement & Joy," "Clicker Training with At-risk families," *The Latham Letter,* Spring, 2000, pp. 6-7, 13.

Loar, Lynn, "To Click or Not to Click: The Role of the Marker Signal in Shaping Behavior," *APDT Newsletter,* Nov., Dec., 2000, pp. 1 and 6.

Malcarne, Vanessa, *A Guide for Evaluating Humane Education Programs,* NAHEE: www.nahee.org.

Mayeda, Marcia, "Clicker Training with At-risk Families Succeeds at the Humane Society of Santa Clara Valley," *The Latham Letter,* Fall, 2000, pp. 14-15.

McConnell, Patricia, *The Other End of the Leash: Why We Do What We Do Around Dogs,* New York: Ballantine Books, 2002.

Pithers, W.D. and Cummings, G.F., "Can Relapses Be Prevented? Initial Outcome Data from the Vermont Treatment Program for Sexual Aggressors," in D. R. Laws, ed., *Relapse Prevention with Sex Offenders,* NY: Guilford Press, 1989, pp. 313-324.

Pryor, Karen, *Clicker Training for Cats,* Waltham, MA: Sunshine Books, 2001.

Pryor, Karen, *Clicker Training for Dogs,* Waltham, MA: Sunshine Books, 1999.

Pryor, Karen, "The Creative Porpoise: Training for Novel Behavior," *Karen Pryor On Behavior,* North Bend, WA: Sunshine Books, 1995, pp. 33-49.

Pryor, Karen, *Don't Shoot the Dog!,* revised edition, New York: Bantam Press, 1999.

Pryor, Karen, "The Poisoned Cue," *Teaching Dogs,* Vol. 1, no. 1, Aug. & Sept., 2002, pp. 8f.

Pryor, Karen, "Reinforcement Training as Interspecies Communication," *Karen Pryor On Behavior,* North Bend, WA: Sunshine Books, 1995, pp. 223-233.

Pryor, Karen, "A Transformation Devoutly to be Wished: What we are beginning to discover from the clicker training revolution," *The Latham Letter,* spring 2000, pp. 8-12.

Raphael, Pamela, Colman, Libby and Loar, Lynn, *Teaching Compassion: A Guide for Humane Educators, Teachers, and Parents,* Alameda, CA: The Latham Foundation, 1999.

Rathmann, Carol, "Forget Me Not Farm: Teaching Gentleness with Gardens and Animals to Children from Violent Homes and Communities," in *Child Abuse, Domestic Violence, and Animal Abuse: Linking the Circles of Compassion for Prevention and Intervention,* Ascione, Frank R. and Arkow, Phil, eds., West Lafayette, IN: Purdue University Press, 1999, pp. 393-409.

Roseberry, Kelly and Rovin, Laurie, "Animal Assisted Therapy for Sexually Abused Adolescent Females: The Program at Crossroads," in *Child Abuse, Domestic Violence, and Animal Abuse: Linking the Circles of Compassion for Prevention and Intervention,* Ascione, Frank R. and Arkow, Phil, eds., West Lafayette, IN: Purdue University Press, 1999, pp. 433-442.

Ross, S., "Green Chimneys: We Give Troubled Children the Gift of Giving," in *Child Abuse, Domestic Violence, and Animal Abuse: Linking the Circles of Compassion for Prevention and Intervention,* Ascione, Frank R. and Arkow, Phil, eds., West Lafayette, IN: Purdue University Press, 1999, pp. 367-379.

Rugaas, Turid, *On Talking Terms With Dogs: Calming Signals,* Carlsborg, WA: Legacy by Mail, Inc., 1997.

Sternberg, Sue, *Great Dog Adoptions: A Guide for Shelters,* Alameda, CA: The Latham Foundation, 2002.

Stone, Gretchen van Mater, "Measuring the Efficacy of Humane Education: Methodological Challenges and Possibilities," *The Latham Letter,* Winter, 2002, pp. 14-16.

Straus, Murray, *Beating the Devil Out of Them: Corporal Punishment in American Families,* New York: Lexington Books, 1994.

White, Michael and Epston, David, *Narrative Means to Therapeutic Ends,* New York: W. W. Norton and Co., 1990.

Index

The Latham Foundation for the Promotion of Humane Education

Founded in 1918, Latham is:
A clearinghouse for information about:
 – Humane issues and activities
 – The human-companion animal bond (HCAB)
 – Animal-assisted therapy (AAT)
 – The connections between child and animal abuse and other forms of domestic violence
Producer and distributor of videos and publications on the above topics
Publisher of *The Latham Letter*
Creator and sponsor of the "Search for Excellence" Video Awards

As a private operating foundation, Latham does not make cash grants: rather, it works in many non-partisan roles including publisher, producer, facilitator, sponsor, and colleague.

1826 Clement Avenue • Alameda, CA 94501 • Phone 510-521-0920 • Fax 510-521-9861
www.Latham.org • info@Latham.org

25023233R00135

Made in the USA
San Bernardino, CA
15 October 2015